10/00

Happy Birthday,
Michael

Mom

Love, Soul & Freedom

Dancing with Rumi

LOVE, SOUL & FREEDOM

on the Mystic Path

DENISE BRETON
&
CHRISTOPHER LARGENT

*Featuring translations of Rumi
by Coleman Barks*

 HAZELDEN®

Hazelden
Center City, Minnesota 55012-0176

1-800-328-0094 (Toll Free U.S., Canada, and the Virgin Islands)
http://www.hazelden.org

Library of Congress Cataloging-in-Publication Data

Breton, Denise.
    Love, soul & freedom : dancing with Rumi on the mystic path /
Denise Breton & Christopher Largent ; featuring translations of Rumi
by Coleman Barks.
        p.   cm.
    Includes bibliographical references.
    ISBN 1-56838-207-3
    1. Mysticism.   2. Spiritual life.   3. Jalāl al-Dīn Rūmī, Maulana,
1207–1273.   I. Largent, Christopher.   II. Title.
BL625.B677   1998
291.4′22—dc21   97–48972
                                                            CIP

01 00 99 98 6 5 4 3 2 1

Book design by Will Powers
Typesetting by Stanton Publication Services, Inc.
Cover design by David Spohn

Editor's note
Hazelden offers a variety of information on chemical
dependency and related areas. Our publications do not
necessarily represent Hazelden's programs, nor do
they officially speak for any Twelve Step organization.

DEDICATED TO

Judy Delaney

&

to the memory of
Willis Harman

&

to mystics lurking everywhere
in the emerging culture

CONTENTS

At last, you've shaken your wings
and broken the cage apart and
flown off into the unseen.

You were the favorite pet falcon
kept by an old earth-woman.

Then you heard the king's drum,
and nothing could keep you
from the open sky-void.

You were a lovesick nightingale
put in with owls.

Then the Spring rose-garden fragrance came,
and you left. You,

with the sorest hangover from this
fermented bitterness, entered a new kind
of tavern, the company of eternal ecstatics,
who drink Nothing.

True as an arrow into the heart of the sun,
you that were soul-gazing became soul.

Like some heraldic shield-bird
opening its wings to a spearpoint,

like a rose strangely loitering
in the December wind,

like roof-rain escaping
down every drainpipe,

like the pain of speaking dissolving
in silence, not sleep,
you take refuge in the Friend.

Jelaluddin Rumi

Reworked from R. A. Nicholson's
Divani, XLVIII by Coleman Barks

A Note on Translations

For many centuries, the work of the famous Persian Sufi sage, mystic, and poet Jelaluddin Rumi (1207–1273 C.E.) was simply not available in English. Even today, of his two mammoth works—the six-volume, 25,632-verse *Mathnawi*, known as the *Qur'an* in Pahlavi (Persian), and the even more voluminous collection of his poems, the *Divan-i Shams-i Tabriz*—only the first is fully translated. This 1926 translation of the *Mathnawi* was done by Reynold A. Nicholson, who stayed as close as possible to the original Persian, though casting the translation in Victorian, Bible-ese English. Considering that medieval Persian is flowery and its poetry rigidly metered, Nicholson's translation is a bear to read. He did a monumental job, but the job wasn't finished as far as current readers are concerned.

Fortunately, thanks to poet and translator Coleman Barks, Rumi's work has been emerging in a poetic form that makes Rumi's ideas jump off the page. Many other translations have appeared as well. Kabir and Camille Helminski—whose Vermont publishing company, Threshold Books, specializes in Sufi literature—have published four of Coleman Barks's collections as well as several excellent collections on Rumi of their own, including *The Ruins of the Heart, Daylight,* and *Jewels of Remembrance* (Threshold Books, 139 Main Street, Room 701, Brattleboro, VT 05301; phone: 802-254-8300; e-mail: threshld@sover.net).

Other highly respected translators include A. J. Arberry, Annemarie Schimmel, E. H. Whinfield, William C. Chittick, James G. Cowan, Afzal Iqbal, Nevit Oguz Ergin, Eva de Vitray-Meyerovitch, Andrew Harvey, and, in collaboration with Coleman Barks, Robert Bly. We admire all these translators, whose intellectual and aesthetic sensitivities approach the superhuman.

Our own introduction to Rumi's poetry, though, came through the remarkable translations of Coleman Barks. His beautifully poetic and at the same time down-to-earth translations grabbed us and have never let go. We marvel at how he captures Rumi's brilliance. His renditions go beyond clear, lucid, or even beautiful, though they're always that: the poetry is vibrant—pure Sufi energy and inspiration. We heartily recommend the following collections of his, available directly from Maypop Books (196 Westview Drive, Athens, GA 30606; phone: 800-682-8637; e-mail: rudra@ccnet.com), Threshold Books, or bookstores:

Open Secret.
with John Moyne.
Threshold, 1984.
Odes, quatrains, and resettings
of the *Mathnawi.*

Unseen Rain.
with John Moyne.
Threshold, 1986.
Quatrains.

We Are Three.
Maypop, 1987.
Odes, quatrains, and sections
of the *Mathnawi.*

This Longing.
with John Moyne.
Threshold, 1988.
Sections of the *Mathnawi* and letters.

These Branching Moments.
with John Moyne.
Copper Beech, 1988.
Forty odes.

Like This.
Maypop, 1990.
Additional odes.

Delicious Laughter.
Maypop, 1990. Rambunctious teaching
stories from the *Mathnawi.*

One-Handed Basket Weaving.
Maypop, 1991.
Poems on the theme of work.

Feeling the Shoulder of the Lion.
Threshold, 1991.
Teaching stories.

Birdsong.
Maypop, 1993.
Fifty-three short poems.

The Hand of Poetry:
Five Mystic Poets of Persia.
with Inayat Khan.
Omega Publications, 1993.
Poems and commentary.

Say I Am You.
with John Moyne.
Maypop, 1994.
Poetry and stories of Rumi and Shams.

The Essential Rumi.
HarperCollins, 1996.
A compendium of poetry and stories
with short section-commentaries.

The Illuminated Rumi.
with Michael Green.
Broadway Books, 1997.
Poetry illustrated by Michael Green's
images, a work of art.

A Note on Our Use of Rumi's Poetry

Poetry in general, mystical poetry in particular, and Rumi's poetry most especially convey meaning on many levels. Using Rumi's poetry as we do in the context of the mystic path by no means suggests that this is the only or even the right interpretation of these poems, if indeed there is such a thing.

While we don't believe any poem can mean anything, we do believe that one poem can speak to many issues. That's what makes poetry so rich. It's constructed to say the most with the least, bypassing our analytic minds to speak directly to our whole- and meaning-oriented souls. The meaning we derive from poetry, therefore, is never final and depends on the questions we put to it. Where we are in inner development determines what we see—even what we're capable of seeing—in poetry. In a few years or decades, we may read the same poem and see something quite different.

Then there's the cultural context. Were we Sufis ourselves or steeped in the background that Rumi had, we would surely see other dimensions of meaning. One section of a poem on love, for instance, didn't click until we read it in light of Plato's *Symposium*, which suddenly made sense of the poem for us. How many other ancient and medieval resources shed light on his poetry?

Acknowledging our limits in knowledge, we must say we have been overwhelmed by the relevance of Rumi's ideas for the inner journeys that people are experiencing today. Yet how could it be otherwise? Technology has changed, but has the inner life? Rumi's wisdom is too valuable—too helpful for shedding light on the mystic path—not to use it in the service of connecting with our souls, even if we only scratch the surface of the wisdom that his poetry offers. Our purpose, therefore, is not to present a definitive interpretation of Rumi's poetry—even if it were possible, we are not the ones to do it—but rather to explore the mystic journey and to engage Rumi along the way as a friend and guide.

Having a structure for this book—seeking the unity of soul, love, and freedom through the mystic path—we've naturally approached each chapter with our own ideas of what to explore. Yet with every chapter, Rumi has, so to speak, had his own ideas of what wants to be said, and it's always a surprise.

We hope that, as for us, you the reader will experience this book as the beginning or perhaps as a continuation of a romance with Rumi. This much we know of him: as a lover, he's never boring, never short on surprises, always fun, and always leading you on, whatever the heck he really means.

Finally, for those a bit leery of poetry, you have a sympathetic ear. One of us in particular couldn't figure out why poets wouldn't just tell us what they mean instead of making us work so hard to figure it out. Indeed, early on in our marriage, we had a "discussion" of this point: isn't prose better? Over the years—it wasn't a short discussion—we've finally concluded that schooling failed us, killing enjoyment of the medium with the curse of having to give the "right answer" and the threat of failing if we didn't. How could poetry become a friend under such circumstances? It is perhaps poetic justice that one so annoyed at poetry twenty-plus years ago should fall in love with Rumi now. So even if poetry isn't your passion, give Rumi a try.

Acknowledgments

This project started in 1993 during a conversation with Judy Delaney, our editor at Hazelden at the time. She loved the poetry of Rumi that we used at the beginning of each chapter of *The Paradigm Conspiracy*, and we said, "You haven't seen a fraction of it." Her enthusiasm got us going and, through difficult times, kept us going. Finding the right framework, though, was a process. In the end, trade publisher Dan Odegard's uncanny ability to see through our early drafts set us free to write what was most in our hearts. Thanks to his urgings, this book marks a kind of turning point for us. Steve Lehman, our editor—with whom we feel a unity of mind and spirit that's a most treasured gift— gave us the professional and personal support that not only inspired us but also made us better writers. Steve is always grounding us, yet he's equally passionate about the heights—someone who'd forsake "a thousand half-loves . . . to take one whole heart home." What better companions on the mystic path could we have?

Once again, it's been a joy to work with the entire staff of Hazelden. In particular, Cathy Broberg and Will Powers of Stanton Publication Services have gone untold extra miles in making the text and layout both beautiful and transparent to the book's ideas, as has David Spohn in designing a magnificent cover, a fourteenth-century Uzbeki-stan carpet design. Gordon Thomas has, together with Steve, certainly gone the distance in helping the book find its market niche. To them and Dan we owe the *Love, Soul & Freedom* title, rather than the *Soul, Love & Freedom* original. Though the original reflects the order of the mystic path as we understand it, their inclination to have the title lead with *love* resonates both with how people first experience these three and with love as central to the mystic path, especially Rumi's sense of it. We consider ourselves most fortunate to collaborate with everyone at Hazelden in the shared endeavor to explore transforming ideas and take them to the public.

On the home front, our partner and colleague Mary Joy Breton was, as always, a source of unending help, encouragement, and support, while Mickey Robertaccio's enthusiasm for the subject, Linda Brackin's heartfelt insights, Kayla Evan's expertise, and Helen Woodhull's wise and generous feedback came just when we needed them.

We are deeply grateful to everyone at Threshold Books for their kindness in working with us and for their invaluable contributions to the Rumi renaissance. We also wish to thank Copper Beech Press and Omega Publications for their permission to reprint Coleman Barks's work.

When it comes to Coleman Barks, thank heavens for mystic ineffability, for we cannot put in words how his translations have touched us. Perhaps this book gives some indication. On top of that, he's been extraordinarily generous with his work and supportive of ours. We've found him to be as remarkable a person as he is a poet. Our own personal theory is that this man must have some weavings or currents of Rumi's soul in him, for we could swear that it's Rumi's voice we hear in the poetry and Rumi's spirit we feel when we read it. Whoever he is and however it came to be that "the Ocean splashes inside his chest" so clearly, this is one case where it's true that without him, this book would not exist.

Finally, there's Rumi. On finishing this manuscript, we sat down and read through *The Essential Rumi* and felt, with Thomas Aquinas, that all our words seem as straw. Yet we couldn't not write this book, and doing so has been one of the happiest times of our lives. Working with his poetry, we feel like ants in the granary:

> *I'm like an ant that's gotten into the granary,*
> *ludicrously happy, and trying to lug out*
> *a grain that's way too big.**

---

* Barks, *One-Handed Basket Weaving*, 110.

Love, Soul & Freedom

Introduction

The Quest for Invisibles:
Love, Soul, and Freedom

Love, soul, and freedom: these three weave the stories of our lives. The who, what, when, and where fill in the details and give variation to the plots, but the themes don't get more basic.

Love is what we all want in life and what we look for first. It's our passion for living, forming the sea in which our souls swim. Like the sea, love nurtures and sustains us, but it also offers us somewhere to go with our lives. Love creates the worlds that our souls explore. Who and what we love channel our energies, drawing us to this person or that, down one path or another. Led by our loves, we connect with the worlds around us. We create places where we belong, where our souls are nourished with meaning and purpose, as well as where we relax, play, and have fun. Through the intimacy of relationships, we come to know both others and ourselves in love's mirror. Love brings our souls into focus.

Soul is our guiding center, our touchstone for what feels right in life and what's ours to do. Soul is our reason for coming here as well as our reason for staying. Soul tells us about us—not as others want, expect, or imagine us to be, but as we are in our innermost being. When we go to the depths of sorrow, confusion, or despair, it's our souls that take us there and see us through. Or if we experience exhilarating joy, it's our souls that lift us up with a bigger-than-life knowing: "So that's what it all means!" Soul is our core, our essence, the ground of who we are, even if we're not at all sure who this soul of ours is or what he or she has in mind for us.

Freedom gives our souls and loves air to breathe. Like the air, freedom is a given, at least as far as our souls are concerned. It's not granted

by people, institutions, or governments, or else it'd be theirs to with-
hold. Freedom is air to us, because it gives us the space we need to follow our souls and pursue our loves. Without freedom, our souls
suffocate. With it, they take off; we create, experiment, fumble, and
learn. Freedom says that anything is possible and that it's our birthright
to explore possibilities wherever our souls and loves take us. Sometimes our souls take us down the path of losing everything—a terminal
disease, divorce, bankruptcy, or scandal—to show us how free we are
beyond externals. With "nothing left to lose," we abandon shoulds and
oughts and go for our dreams.

Love, soul, and freedom are natural companions, together creating
the fire in the mind, heart, chest, belly, or wherever that makes us happy
to get up in the morning. United, love, soul, and freedom are the Force
incarnate, guiding us and permeating our lives with meaning and purpose, even if their presence isn't evident until hindsight. Love, soul, and
freedom are inseparable, and on the deepest levels of our being, that's
how we experience them. When we're on vacation, for instance, we
get a taste of these three living happily together: we surround ourselves
with who and what we love, let down our hair, and do as we choose.

Bargaining with Love, Soul, and Freedom

It's the rest of the time that tests their union. Something about being in
families, schools, religions, businesses, and governments makes us
think these three are separate and that joining them comes at a price.
Before we know it, we find ourselves using one as a bargaining chip to
secure our stock of the other—our souls for love, our loves for freedom,
or our freedom for loves.

Mostly, though, it's love we bargain for. When we're growing up in
families and schools, we want acceptance and need it to survive. Plus
we're trained to seek it: smiles and *A*s mean approval, rewards, and acceptance; frowns and *F*s mean disapproval, punishments, and rejection. If parents or teachers find our souls unacceptable, we're stuck.
Our souls and the freedom to live them are all we have. If our souls
meet disapproval—"who you are is unacceptable; become what I tell
you to be"—we're in trouble.

So we trade. We set aside who we are to gain love. If we get the message that our souls don't measure up, we become someone else. We make ourselves into what others want us to be, if that's the condition for their acceptance. To find a place for our souls, we surrender our souls.

Not that we have much choice as children. Our souls may regard freedom as a given, but the social systems we're born into generally don't. Not only love but also freedom come at a price. The more we become what families, schools, religions, and peers demand, the more they leave us alone to do what we want. But by then, "what we want" doesn't mean much. We're free to express system-conforming images, not our souls. That is, we're free to be straight-A students, submissive believers, and obedient children, not dreamers, skeptics, or independent thinkers.

The same choices confront us as adults, when we're better equipped to make them. Yet even then, the stakes are high, and the decisions tough. Making money means we're accepted by society; some segment of it approved of us enough to let it flow our way. Not having money—and the consumerist perks that go with it—means we're less acceptable.

But how much does society's approval mean? On one hand, if we chuck approval and exercise our freedom to be who we are, chances are we'll have to live on air. Institutions pay us to do their bidding; we can be who we are on our own time. On the other hand, if we choose to bond with political, professional, or religious systems, the bond lures us into preset roles. Retired Admiral Gene LaRocque, director of the Center for Defense Information, summed up the terms for success: "A journalist once asked me how I became an admiral. I said, 'It's very simple. I did everything my bosses asked me to do.'"[1]

Bargaining soul and freedom for love becomes a way of life, and we abandon the hope of keeping them together.

Not a Good Deal

Yet no matter how great the pressures to bargain, we're not convinced that it's worth it. Not only will the memory of what it's like to have love, soul, and freedom united not leave us, but also bargaining them proves unsatisfying. The rewards, once obtained, aren't worth what we sacrificed to get them.

When we lose touch with life's essentials, hope and enthusiasm leave too. Our inner fire goes out. If we're not permitted to live who we are, what's left to live? What's freedom, if only our images possess it? What we sacrifice to connect with family, school, business, religious, and political systems leaves us short of the intangibles that make life worth living. Trade-offs on soul levels don't work.

How could they? When we sacrifice our souls to connect, who's left to be bonded? Who's left to enjoy the benefits that we sacrificed so much to get? There's no one home to connect or be connected.

What do we get from bargaining? Not what we wanted. Love bought with our souls isn't for us but for an image we devised. Our masks are the ones approved and accepted. They're the "success"; we're not. Our souls don't feel loved, which was the original reason for making the sacrifice. Quite the reverse, our souls feel rejected, which in fact they are.

Nor can using soul and freedom or even our loves as bargaining chips be good for society. When we trade them to join social systems, there's no one home in our schools, businesses, and governments to be creative or to make wise, humane decisions. Obeying rules and performing roles, we're reduced to programmed shells. How can our social systems thrive if we're unplugged from within?

Societies need us, not shadows of us. They need our vision, courage, and persistence, but the shells left after bargaining don't have these to give. When we're deprived of soul and freedom—and lose love in the process—we pass our loss on to our systems, and fragmented, soulless, enslaving patterns settle into our shared social bones.

Given the high costs of bargaining, is it necessary? If love, soul, and freedom thrive in unison, where do the trade-offs come from, and why do they persist as a cultural habit?

Reality or Our Paradigm?

Either the trade-offs are our response to reality, or they're our response to the way we see reality. That is, either love, soul, and freedom are actually in conflict, trapping us in no-win contests among them, or our concepts of them are confused, forcing us into deadly but unnecessary trade-offs.

If love, soul, and freedom don't go together—if mutual exclusion is their reality—then we're stuck. We can't escape bargaining. If connecting with any person, group, or system necessarily means abandoning our real loves, setting aside our souls, or surrendering our freedom, then there's no way around it.

This is a convenient view for keeping established orders in place. Systems don't change; we do. They don't accommodate us; we accommodate them. They set the price, and we pay—"that's just the way it is." With this view, what we call the control paradigm in *The Paradigm Conspiracy* goes unchallenged. Control mechanisms remain in force, and we obey them, grateful if we can come away with a degree or a paycheck.

But if this were the reality of love, soul, and freedom, why wouldn't bargaining systems work better than they do? Why wouldn't we adjust more easily to the terms? David Korten, author of *When Corporations Rule the World*, argues that the corporate culture of control is dying, because it's not sustainable. Too much is lost by bargaining. When employees trade love, soul, and freedom for maximizing profits, corporations lose their human center, and that's as deadly for corporations as it is for us.

The very failures of bargaining—the unhappiness and suffering that trade-offs create—suggest that the paradigm is the culprit. We're using bad software, and it's distorting our concepts of what's going on.

If our souls need both love and freedom to thrive—if that's our souls' reality—then it's no surprise that we and our systems grow self-destructive when we're deprived of them. We need all three together to be creative. When we're destructive, it's not because our nature is destructive but because the trade-off paradigm is destructive to us, making us trade away more than we can afford to lose. Not reality but a paradigm is playing fast and loose with us.

Nor do we receive reality in return. The "love" that demands loss of soul or freedom isn't love but a perversion of it—manipulation, domination, and abuse. If our souls need real love, this counterfeit won't satisfy us. We'll still be connectedness-hungry, no matter how many fake—not-us, not-love, not-free—unions we negotiate.

This is good news. If our paradigm is the problem, then there's hope. Trading soul and freedom for love is a necessity created by our software, not by reality. Fortunately, the planet's spiritual heritage offers more than one software program. Exploring paradigms that honor love, soul, and freedom united, we can explore realities different from those created by no-win trade-offs.

Sufi Wisdom

That's where Sufis in general and mystic, sage, and poet Jelaluddin Rumi (1207–1273 c.e.) in particular come in. We're neither Sufis nor experts in Sufism, but as far as we can tell, love, soul, and freedom lie at the heart of Sufi inspiration—and of Rumi's.

Sufis are a funny lot. No one really knows when Sufism started. Some Sufis trace their wisdom tradition back to the mystical perceptions of the most ancient seers. Can we really fix a date, they ask, when the perception of the unity of all being—the essence of Sufism—first dawned? Most Sufis, however, trace their origins to the seventh century just after Muhammad.

Nor is anyone sure what religion Sufis belong to, since they're dead-set against sectarianism. Rumi's poetry, for instance, borrows from the great mystical strains in Hinduism, Buddhism, Zen, Confucian and Taoist philosophies, Judaism, Christianity, Zoroastrianism, and indigenous spiritualities. His adopted city of Konya, now in Turkey, was smack dab on the trade route from the Orient and Africa to Europe, and ideas from all over the world crossed Rumi's path. However, since Sufis adhere to the Five Pillars of Islam, quote the *Qur'an* and Muhammad the most, and came to full bloom in Muslim cultures, they're classed with Islam.

And they are funny. Sufis can clothe the most sublime insights in the most ordinary images, from mice and gnats to sex and bathroom habits. Rumi is famous for this, as well as for being the greatest mystic poet of all time. Not all images click, since we're not familiar with the details of life in Persia eight centuries ago. But most images are familiar. With them, Rumi explores the heights of mystical inspiration with an everyday groundedness that's unique in mystical literature.

Whatever images Rumi uses, the effect is to bring love, soul, and freedom into a practical unity—not because we want them together but because in reality they are together, and we're made up of that reality. In fact, for Rumi, the unity of love, soul, and freedom is our life. Each needs the others to function as the genuine article in our lives. Clearly our souls suffer when we're deprived of love and freedom—and thrive when we keep them together—but love and freedom fare just as badly alone and just as powerfully united.

Love Needs Freedom and Soul to Be Love

Without freedom, for example, love isn't love but duty and obligation. That's why classical literature valued love between friends more than family love, since women and children were considered possessions, not free agents. Love between friends, however, is free—freely given, freely received. Once we get a taste of love that's not laden with obligations, our experience of love changes. Relationships aren't about gaining leverage but about letting love flow freely. As Rumi said, "Love has no calculating in it."[2]

That's powerful—and revolutionary. Rumi loved his two wives (the first died young and he remarried) and his children, but his love for his friend, the wandering dervish Shams of Tabriz, revolutionized his life. Rumi's love for Shams set him free to discover his own soul's expression, which found voice through his poetry. Love, soul, and freedom united.

But as they did, they turned Rumi's life upside down. Claiming his freedom to love from his soul, Rumi stopped behaving the way good sheikhs behaved and no longer cared about meeting conventional expectations. Connectedness was no longer about trade-offs—about "walking away" from who he was. He became radically free, answering only to his own soul and its free love for God. Rumi says (and unless we note otherwise, everything we quote is from Rumi):

> Again, I'm within my self.
> I walked away, but here I come sailing back,

feet in the air, upsidedown,
as a saint when he opens his eyes
from prayer: Now. The room,
the tablecloth, familiar faces.[3]

His new love transformed his relation both to himself and to the world. Rumi saw the Friend and Beloved everywhere. If love isn't to be traded for—if it's truly free—then it's all around us, like sunlight or oxygen:

There's a strange frenzy in my head,
of birds flying,
each particle circulating on its own.
Is the one I love *every*where?[4]

Needless to say, Rumi's break with tradition ruffled feathers. In the end, it cost Shams his life, for he was murdered by some of Rumi's jealous students, one of Rumi's own sons being among the conspirators. But Rumi couldn't go back. He couldn't surrender his freedom for how people thought he as a holy person and pillar of the community ought to behave. His "new love" didn't call for bargaining soul or freedom, and he wasn't going back to the bargain variety:

Don't think of good advice for me.
I've tasted the worst that can happen.
So they lock me up somewhere, bound and gagged,
they can't tie up this new love I have.[5]

Love without soul doesn't work either. Two masks, two shells can't love. They make habits of being in the same vicinity, and the habits may even heat up. Yet however caught in intense emotions we become, without our souls to ground the relation, both sides have a hollow ring.

True love engages the soul and, as it does, it opens us to ourselves. Our love for another calls our own souls forth, as we tap the reality in us that's there to connect with another. Rumi's love for Shams put him in touch with his own inner "Presence" and "Beloved," which he came to know as his "Friend." Love invites us to discover the same—to find within ourselves a rich and diverse kingdom, in fact, "hundreds of thousands of kingdoms":

> The work of love is to open that window
> in the chest and to look incessantly
> on the Beloved. You can do this.
>
> Listen. Make a way for yourself
> inside your self. Stop looking
> in the other way of looking.
>
> You already have the precious mixture
> that will make you well. Use it.
>
> Old enemies will become friends.
> Your beauty will be God's beauty.
>
> Your friendlessness will change to moisture
> and nourishment for your friends.
>
> It's not a kingdom like any you know,
> the kingdom of God that's within you,
> but hundreds of thousands of kingdoms.[6]

Freedom Needs Soul and Love to Be Freedom

How can these "hundreds of thousands of kingdoms" within find expression, though, if social systems have no tolerance for them? Yet without these inner kingdoms, how can we be free? When our soul centers get brushed aside, our freedom doesn't express who we are but who we're not. We act from shells and masks, approved images. That's not free, because there's not much soul—not much of us—in the acting. Whereas soul without freedom means we're trapped in roles, freedom without soul means we're not there anymore; the traps have taken over. They're doing the living; our souls are somewhere else:

> There's a kind of person whose expertise
> is display, subtly to hold and catch

the eye, builder of lovely traps,
not thinking what constant trap-building does.
You make your friends affectionate for a moment,
then leave. This has been your habit,
now your career, since you were born. Touch
the cloth you've woven of applause and compliments.
Stretch the warp and woof. Is it there?
Your life is more than half gone with you still working
these charming traps. Catch one person,
let another go, no reason for deciding anything,
like children feeling mean, in a game with no rules.
Night. The empty traps follow you back to your house.
You have locked yourself inside disappointment.
No actual hunter would trap himself.
You've seen a man chasing a wild pig. His life is fatigue,
and what he finally gets he can't eat.
Only One is worth chasing with your living.
He can't be trapped. You must throw away your love-traps
and walk into His.[7]

If freedom means living our souls, these "puppet shows of ourselves" are no substitute:

They say I tell the truth.
Then they ask me
to do a puppet show
of myself in the bazaar.

I'm not something to sell.
I have already been bought![8]

Without our souls, what's called freedom becomes license. It goes wild. Freedom without soul is addiction personified, like politicians addicted to raising money and selling their souls, the nation, and the earth as they go. Because they have power, it seems as if they're free, yet they're not. Controlled by opinion polls and corporate funders, they play at freedom—and make a mess of it:

> . . . Without purity of spirit,
> if you're still in the middle of lust and greed
> and other wantings, you're like children
> playing at sexual intercourse.
> They wrestle
> and rub together, but it's not sex!
>
> The same with the fightings of mankind.
> It's a children's quarrel with play-swords.
> No purpose, totally futile.
>
> Like kids on hobby horses, soldiers claim to be riding
> Boraq, Muhammed's night-horse, or Duldul, his mule.
>
> Your actions mean nothing, the sex and war that you do.
> You're holding part of your pants and prancing around,
> *Dun-da-dun, dun-da-dun.*[9]

Freedom without love is equally pointless. It's like traveling around but never finding meaning—never going "home":

> Late and starting to rain, it's time to go home.
> We've wandered long enough in empty buildings.
> I know it's tempting to stay and meet those new people.
> I know it's even more sensible
> to spend the night here with them,
> but I want to be home.[10]

Without love, freedom is actually dangerous, because it means acting unconnected to what's around us. Blind to the webs in which our actions occur, freedom without love says we're not responsible for what happens. We just do our thing, and a disconnected thing at that.

Unfortunately, there's a lot of freedom without love around. When, for instance, we asked our college students whether they'd dump toxic waste illegally to save a business, a third of the class said they would. That's freedom without love: acting oblivious to the connectedness of actions. But then we don't call that freedom. If it kills people, it's a felony.

Splitting love, soul, and freedom doesn't work. Neither we nor society prosper by dividing them.

A Mystic's Response: Go to the Unseen

Sufis are mystics, and when mystics see things falling apart, they don't try to patch them. They seek a deeper level of reality where things aren't split. They go to the invisible worlds, where connectedness isn't broken. From there, they forge a new understanding of unity—of how things hang together.

The strategy has its logic. What generally goes wrong are relationships—relationships that are by nature unseen. When the relationships among love, soul, and freedom break down, all our relationships flounder. Yet looking at things outwardly, we don't understand what's happening.

Knowing the invisible sorts it out. If we took fifty married couples of the same race, age, and style of dress and put the husbands on one side of a room and wives on the other, the couples could rematch themselves immediately without a mistake. If scientists tried to do the same using only physical observation (size, hair color, blood type, DNA), they'd be lucky to get any right.

Of course, we see evidence of relationships (hugs and kisses, children, contracts, paychecks), and we see evidence of their not working (divorces, wars, court cases, defective products), but the connections themselves remain unseen. Their quality surpasses outward forms. Nothing external can capture the bond between friends, colleagues, or spouses, nor can anything capture the pain of relationships lost or gone bad.

If the invisible quality of connectedness has gone awry, more of the outward can't put it right. Patching the visible doesn't work. We need to recapture the invisible quality, and we do this by cultivating the invisible in ourselves. We go to the inner place where nothing is split, where connectedness exists within an unbroken whole. That way, we call the invisible connectedness into our experience, and before we know it, what was split isn't anymore.

Historically, this method has given mystics a bad name: they've been considered inscrutable, since they're always pointing to a reality beyond words, impractical, since they don't jump in and fix things right off, and elitist, since most people don't have time to sit in a cave and have tea with the unseen.

Fortunately for Rumi and other mystics, this image is changing. Millions of people are now finding strength, insight, healing, and peace through meditation and contemplation—exactly what mystics have done for ages. We're spending time with the invisible in hospitals, homes, schools, and workplaces, because it's a natural method. We draw the invisible realm into our lives, and suddenly we see the everyday visible in a new light.

Indeed we're seeing many things in a new light, as invisibles receive an attention and respect they didn't have a few decades ago.

Much of this respect comes from physics, which for the last century has plunged into invisibles. We can't see the law of gravity. We see its effects but not the law itself, which describes relationships among physical bodies. Then there's the issue of hard-core visibles being not so hard core. Tables, bodies, rocks, and mountains are 99.9 percent space. Suddenly 99.9 percent of our visible world is something invisible: the empty space in atoms. But that's not the end of it. Quantum mechanics has discovered not only a host of invisible subatomic particles but also the concept of nonlocality: the idea that particles moving toward opposite ends of the universe are simultaneously linked by an unseen and unbroken connectivity. Something invisible is going on between particles that visible-only theories can't explain.

Physician Larry Dossey applies the nonlocality concept to consciousness and finds evidence of a "nonlocal mind" operating in prayer, healing, and telepathy—invisible processes that can have visible effects. According to a nonlocal concept of consciousness, our minds aren't confined to our brains but can send thoughts around the globe, and someone out there can pick them up.

Ecology is another concept that describes something invisible. We

see forests, lakes, insects, birds, and animals, but how they all work together is unseen—a network of relationships. Their totality as one
ecosystem is invisible, but it's no less real for that. We know when it
breaks down.

Or consider our bodies. Few doctors would now deny that mental
states affect physical health. Things as invisible as attitudes, emotions,
and personal philosophies can either cause heart disease or assist in
healing it. That's why psychiatrists and psychologists investigate the
unseen orders embedded in the soul—an invisible that's receiving re-
newed attention these days. Even traditional psychology, though, deals
heavily with invisibles: the unseen facets of our personalities and the
stories they tell about who we are.

Recovery from addiction also turns to invisibles. Alcoholism, drug
abuse, and other addictions are observable forms, but what's behind
them? What are the invisible dynamics that lead to addiction, and how
can we change them? In Twelve Step recovery programs, shifting the
dynamics involves coming to trust a Higher Power at work in change.
Since the invisible construct called an ego is part of the dynamics that
needs to shift, the idea is to ground the shift in something deeper—in a
Power that brings transformation and healing. The fact that this Power
is invisible isn't a problem.

Mystic Yearnings

The invisible is suddenly everywhere in our lives, and like good mystics, we're investigating it. Indeed, there may well be a mystic hidden
in everyone, manifested in yearnings for the invisible on the deepest
levels of meaning—levels that speak to who we are and how we feel
about being here.

First, we yearn for inner peace, for a sense of everything coming together in a meaningful way. Separateness and fragmentation wear us
out. It's exhausting to keep up a competing ego that's always on call to
either defend itself or protect its turf. We yearn for love—soul to soul
love, yes, but even more for love as a quality of reality, as a sense that
the universe is a generous, supportive place to be, a place that needs us
here and cares whether we stay or not. Romantic love doesn't work out

for everyone, but everyone can live in a universe of love, at least we yearn for it to be so. We dream of Shangri-la, "a place where there [is] peace and security, where living [is] not a struggle but a lasting delight."[11] The visible world says such yearnings are naive and impossible, yet we still feel them.

Second, yearning for such a universe, plenty of normal-looking people feel that they don't quite fit in here—that they're on the wrong planet—no matter how hard they try to adjust. Their true home, they feel, is elsewhere, and they yearn for home. In Steven Spielberg's film, E.T.'s stranded predicament struck a chord. People want to journey back to a place where they belong. For mystics like Rumi, that place lies within, and the longing for home is really a yearning to come home to who we are.

Third, rich and poor, young and old, worker and boss yearn for liberation: a time when they can call their lives their own. Today's economic slavery is still slavery, still devouring lives and families with bills, debts, demands, schedules; leaving them with no time, no rest, nothing being enough. The trap is half internal, half external, and we'd like to rid ourselves of both halves. The other-worldly peace of watching snow fall or the timeless feeling of lying in a field and looking at clouds makes us yearn for freedom as more than fleeting moments.

These are classic yearnings of a mystic, signs of the invisible love, soul, and freedom pulling us. We feel called in ways that don't come from the visible world. The invisible weaves itself through our thoughts, dreams, and passions, and its presence won't be brushed aside. If the invisible is coming after us, instead of running from it, Rumi suggests we turn and embrace it.

Seeking the Invisible Soul—Our Lost Camel

Embracing the quest for invisibles, though, shifts the order for seeking them. If we start with love, we're tempted to sacrifice who we are to get it. Our souls get lost in the bargain. Moreover, thanks to all the soul bargaining we've had to do, who we are isn't clear anymore. We don't feel grounded in our souls but scattered in pieces. If love comes our way, which piece is it for?

To have the love we want and need, we must first find our souls and
ground ourselves in them—and our souls know it. When we've bargained our souls for love, they're the ones to tug at us first. Our souls
know when love-deals aren't working, since they're the ones to pay
the price. The loss of our souls and our yearnings to get them back start
us on the mystic path.

Rumi's poetry is filled with metaphors for seeking the invisible soul,
and what's waiting there is a surprise. Rumi says that "a person's presence is more to learn from than a book."[12] We're living libraries of "wisdom and beauty" that "cannot be contained by any skin." The invisible
has stories to tell that we'd never guess from the visible—not only
about us but also about "every object and being in the universe":

> Every object and being in the universe is
> a jar overfilled with wisdom and beauty,
> a drop of the Tigris that cannot be contained
> by any skin. Every jarful spills and makes the earth
> more shining, as though covered in satin.[13]

Given years of bargaining, though, such treasures seem lost to us.
One of Rumi's stories uses the image of a lost camel and efforts to find
it. Some set about the search immediately, while others aren't so sure:
Why bother with invisible stuff? What do we get out of it? How do we
know we had a camel in the first place? Nonetheless, looking for soul
camels seems the thing to do, and there's a promise of a reward. So we
begin, sometimes in earnest, other times in imitation. Mystics aren't
picky. What gets us going on the soul quest doesn't matter:

> You've lost your camel, my friend,
> and everyone's giving you advice.
>
> You don't know where your camel is,
> but you do know these casual directions
> are wrong. Even someone who hasn't lost a camel,
> who's never even owned a camel, gets in on
> the excitement, "Yes, I've lost my camel too.
> A big reward for whoever finds it."

He says this
in order to be part-owner of your camel when you find it.
If you say to anyone's suggestion, "I don't think so,"
the imitator says the same thing immediately.
When good information comes, you know it right away,
but not the imitator.
                          That bit of information
is medicine to you. It gives color to your face
and strength to your body. Your eyes brighten.
Your feet get lively and agile. You say,
                                    "Thank You,
my Friend, this Truth you give feels like freedom to me.
Please go in front. Be the leader! You have the scent
of my camel better than I do."
                                    But the imitator doesn't feel
the intensity of those clues. He hears your wild outcries,
though, and gets some inkling of what it might be like to be close
to finding a lost camel.

He has, indeed, lost a camel,
but he doesn't know it!

Wanting and imitating someone else's wanting
has blinded him. But as he follows along in the searching,
calling out what the others call out,
                                    suddenly he sees
his own camel browsing there, the one
he didn't know he'd lost.

Only then, does he become a seeker.
He turns aside and goes by himself toward his camel.

The sincere one asks, "Why have you left my search?"

"Up until now I was a fake. I was flattering you,
because I wanted to be part of your glory.
Now that I've separated myself from you,
I am more truly connected to you.

I know what you're doing. Before,
I was stealing camel-descriptions from you.

When my spirit saw its own camel, that seeing
filled everything. Now all my insincerity
and copycat words have changed to virtues.
They brought me *here*! I was sowing my own seed,
though I thought I was working for nothing.

Like a thief I crept and entered a house,
and it was my own home!"

Be fiery, cold one, so heat can come.
Endure rough surfaces that smooth you.

The subject of all this is not *two camels*.
There's only one lost camel,
but language has difficulty saying that.[14]

Seeking Love's Universe

Seeking the invisible soul when we really didn't intend to suggests that invisibles draw us to themselves in ways we weren't imagining, but which got us there just the same. Going to the unseen isn't a way we "decide to go." We're brought to it by guides who are resourceful about getting around our obstacles—who "drink from an undammed stream":

You thought union was a way
you could decide to go.

But the world of the soul follows
things rejected and almost forgotten.

Your true guide drinks
from an undammed stream.[15]

Finding our camel, our soul—the "thing rejected and almost forgotten"—puts something alive and real back at the center of us, and from that centered aliveness we connect with others. Love follows, since now there's someone in us to love and be loved. Our true connectedness with people, other beings, as well as the universe begins to emerge.

Through our souls' eyes, we see the universe and who we are in it differently. We're not alone here, disconnected. In fact, we're not the sort of creatures that can be alone. We look as if we're separate and self-contained entities, but that's the visible side. The invisible says we're the whole incarnate—the "macrocosm" focused and made specific:

> In form you're the microcosm,
> but in reality you're the macrocosm.[16]

Rumi uses ideas that we now associate with holism or holography. The whole is encoded in each part, just as each dot of holographic film contains the total image or each DNA strand contains information about the entire body. Parts aren't parts; they're the whole manifested in specific ways. The diversity within the whole is mirrored in "one wheat-grain"—"many beings in one being":

> This moment this love comes to rest in me,
> many beings in one being.
> In one wheat-grain a thousand sheaf stacks.
> Inside the needle's eye, a turning night of stars.[17]

Woven into the whole as we are, love isn't something we have to bargain for. It's the essential nature of the universe and of who we are in it. As far as Rumi is concerned, the invisible connectedness we have with the whole is love. The kind of universe we yearn for may well turn out to be the way it is. Granted, the visible hides it well, especially if we're using a paradigm that construes the universe in survival-of-the-fittest terms. But just over the border in the invisible, reality has a different character. Visibly, we seem small and on our own, but invisibly, a "great love"—a connectedness with all that is—lives inside us:

> I am so small I can barely be seen.
> How can this great love be inside me?

Look at your eyes. They are small,
but they see enormous things.[18]

If anything, this unseen love is the greater reality, greater than its visible expressions. Whereas the visible has all sorts of boundaries and limits, the invisible has no such divisions. It's the "undiscovered country." Shams said:

> People say that human beings are microcosms and this outer universe a macrocosm, but for us the outer is a tiny wholeness and the inner life the vast reality.[19]

Greater though it may be, our unseen connectedness is by no means up in the clouds. Love is something we're good at making visible. Though invisibly we're connected to all that is, we choose which connections to make visible. Choosing on the basis of inner qualities—"the innermost nature"—creates relationships that are grounded in the visible but drawn from the invisible.

We don't marry someone for his or her body or possessions, for instance, but for his or her character and soul. Naturally, bodies come in handy, but invisible qualities make relationships work—make visible interactions passionate, meaningful, and fun. We build on "a real connection between people," "the inmost nature," and visible forms follow:

> What is a real connection between people? When the same
>   knowledge
> opens a door between them. When the same inner sight exists
> in you as in another, you are drawn to be companions.
> When a man feels in himself the inmost nature of a woman,
> he is drawn to her sexually. When a woman
> feels the masculine self of a man within her,
> she wants him physically in her.
>
> When you feel the qualities of Gabriel in you, you fly up quickly
> like a fledgling not thinking of the ground.
> When you feel asinine qualities in you, no matter how you try
> to do otherwise, you will head toward the stable. . . .
>
> Always search for your innermost nature in those you are with.[20]

Romantic relationships aren't the only ways we make love visible, though. Everything we do is an act of love. We're always drawing on the "great love" of connectedness that's inside us and bringing it out in new forms of expression:

> In a sky so restless and changing
> the moon wears a silver belt. Every detail,
> every feature of every thing, shows how
> that one is in love.[21]

Through the diversity of who and what we love, the intangible becomes concrete, the unseen experiential. The invisible isn't remote but present in the loves we pursue each moment. Our loves guide what we do with our connectedness—how we respond to the universe in a way that's uniquely ours:

> Traveling is as refreshing for some
> as staying at home is for others.
>
> Solitude in a mountain place
> fills with companionship
> for this one,
>   and dead weariness
> for that one.
>   This person loves
> being in charge of the workings
> of a community.
>   This one loves
> the ways that heated iron can be shaped
> with a hammer.
>   Each has been given
> a strong desire for certain work.
>
> A *love* for those motions,
> and all motion is love.
>
> The way sticks and pieces of dead grass and leaves
> shift about in the wind

and with the directions of rain and puddle-water
on the ground, those motions
are all a following
of the love they've been given.[22]

Reclaiming Freedom

Seeking the invisibles of soul and love, we create a space where freedom is once again a given. First, attuned to our souls, we don't trade them. Whatever we do, we do from our inner compass. That's free:

Take someone who doesn't keep score,
who's not looking to be richer, or afraid of losing,
who has not the slightest interest even
in his own personality: He's free.[23]

Second, linked invisibly with everyone and everything, we explore connectedness in whatever ways our souls direct. We taste the freedom of real love, the kind that doesn't exact a price but "becomes one spiritual thing . . . love mixing with spirit":

When your love reaches the core,
earth-heavals and bright irruptions spew in the air.

The universe becomes one spiritual thing, that simple,
love mixing with spirit.[24]

The challenge, of course, is to stay free when we're living in systems that pressure us to bargain. We have to protect our link to the invisible—our "jewel"—in the face of systems that judge us only in terms of what's visible. In a letter, Rumi writes:

The story is told of a warrior whose horse was wounded in battle. The king gave him one of his own horses, an Arabian that the king was particularly fond of. That horse was also wounded. The king showed displeasure.

The warrior dismounted and refused further service to the king. "I did not show displeasure when I risked my life that you might have a victory, but you are irritated that the animal you gave me is hurt! I will serve a King who appreciates my soul. I shall take my jewel to One who knows jewels."[25]

One Flow: The Holomovement

Moving between the visible and the invisible is the mystic's method, the trick being to find a balance. Too much focus on the invisible, and we lose our groundedness, our link to daily life. Too much focus on the visible, and we lose the invisible matrix of meaning that makes life worth living.

Yet the more mystics connect with the invisible, the less they perceive it as separate from the visible. The unseen isn't other than where we are. By definition it's not bound by time or space, which means we don't have to leave the visible to feel it. Where is the invisible, if not here? Mystics see the two together, converging in one flow of meaning:

It's sweet not to look at two worlds,
to melt in meaning as sugar melts in water.[26]

One of the best models for discussing the visible and invisible as one flow of meaning comes from the late David Bohm, a protégé of Einstein's and a pioneer in quantum mechanics. His holographic model of physics, designed to unify quantum mechanics and relativity theory, qualifies as a full-blooded mystical model.[27] Not only are his ideas Neoplatonic, but also his language borrows directly from the fifteenth-century churchman, philosopher, mathematician, and mystic Nicholas of Cusa.

The model starts from the premise of holism. In Bohm's terms, the "holomovement" includes all that is, visible and invisible, matter and mind, in one ordered totality of meaning. But the whole isn't static. Reality's invisible side is always "unfolding" its embedded order and meaning into the visible, which in turn is always being "enfolded" by the holomovement back into the invisible context, which is its source.

As a result, every aspect of the visible—from subatomic particles to living beings to galaxies—has the energy, quality, and meaning of the whole built into it. Invisible and visible aren't separate. There's one process of whole-meaning going on that can be looked at two ways all along the spectrum, from the most inclusive to the most specific, the most invisible to the most visible.

On this model, the holomovement is what really "exists," even though it's "hidden" like the wind or the ocean, which we can't see as a whole. "What does not exist" are the surface forms coming and going. They're shadowy appearances, having all the permanency of a passing breeze, not the bottom-line reality. Even so, we get fooled by appearances:

> What does not exist looks so handsome.
> What does exist, where is it?
> An ocean is hidden. All we see is foam,
> shapes of dust, spinning, tall as minarets, but I want wind.
> Dust can't rise up without wind, I know, but can't I understand this
> by some way other than induction.[28]

Living the Coincidence of Invisible and Visible

The mystical urge is to live in between visible and invisible—to see both moving together. But that's not easy. We're fooled because the visible side of things has a mesmeric hold on our attention. If something isn't visible, the old conditioning kicks in telling us not to believe it, that only visibles count. The visible functions like a hypnotist's pendulum, lulling us into a trance that sees no farther: if we can't see something, we can't trust that it's there.

Mystics turn off the pendulum regularly. Sometimes that means literally closing their eyes, but more often it means engaging in a consciousness and way of being that keeps the visible and invisible in balance. When mystics seem too other-worldly, it's because their inner scales tell them that their cultures have become too worldly, too en-tranced by visibles. Mystics throw their weight on the invisible side to offset their culture's one-sided focus.

As mystics see it, it's only natural to move closer to the invisible. "Too other-worldly" is a relative term. Life as an adult seems other-worldly to a child, and a child's world seems other-worldly beyond imaginings to an embryo:

> Little by little, wean yourself.
>
> This is the gist of what I have to say.
>
> From an embryo, whose nourishment comes in the blood,
> move to an infant drinking milk,
> to a child on solid food,
> to a searcher after wisdom,
> to a hunter of more invisible game.[29]

Rumi is an interesting mystic because he grew up in a Sufi society. Compared with modern culture, this was a spiritually oriented envi-ronment. Not all mystics have had this. To seek the spiritual, many had to step outside cultural institutions and go it alone, sometimes literally living outside town in the woods. That wasn't necessary for Rumi. He was held in the bosom of Sufi institutions and continued to play a role in them until his death. Instead of retreating to a cloister or cave, Rumi started the famous Sufi Order of Whirling Dervishes. He created not only a new community but one that grounds meditation in dance and music—the invisible and visible united. In fact, when Hamza, Rumi's fa-vorite flute player died, Rumi went to his house and told him to get up:

> And immediately Hamza sat up saying, "I'm here!" He reached for his flute, and for three days and nights sweet music came from that house. When Rumi left, life went from the corpse again, and he was buried.[30]

This is not the behavior of someone who has no time for the visible. Rumi took the visible seriously because, in his view, the visible is part of the holomovement too. Only our eyes give us the impression that the visible constitutes its own separate realm. Because mystics cultivate an eye for the invisible, they see things differently: everything has the mantle of the invisible over it, and nothing is separate from it anymore. Another story about music expresses this coincidence of visible and invisible in Rumi's mind:

> Rumi said, "A secret is hidden in the rhythms of music. If I revealed it, it would upset the world." One afternoon a musician was playing the violin and Rumi was listening with great pleasure. A friend entered and said, "Stop this. They are announcing the afternoon prayer." "No," said Rumi, "This is also the afternoon prayer. Both talk to God. He wants the one externally for his service and the other for his love and knowledge."[31]

Visible and invisible: Rumi seems more interested in the flow between them and less inclined to take flight to unseen realms and from there to disdain or even to throw stones at the visible. Rumi was, after all, called to the deepest mystical insights by things that happened in a visible way: first meeting Shams and being with him for several years, second having to recover from the grief and despair he experienced at Shams's sudden death. The visible forced him to go to the invisible as he'd never done before, but he seemed always grateful to the visible for spurring him to do so:

> Invisible, visible, the world
> does not work without both.[32]

The Mystic Path: Archetypes and Journey

Rumi is, therefore, a singular model for exploring the mystic path—how to live attuned to both invisible and visible, how to journey back and forth. From him we can learn what it's like to be on the mystic path, borrowing the modern concept of archetypes to help focus steps along the way.

Archetypes are models or patterns in consciousness that invisibly shape how consciousness flows. They're like the banks of a river, to borrow one of David Bohm's images: if they're narrow and rocky, they create fast currents; if they're wide, the water spreads out in a calm, steady flow. Whatever their form, archetypes set the course.

Not that consciousness is passive in the process. River banks are formed by all the water that's passed through. So, too, with archetypes: their patterns emerge from how consciousness has operated before. Biologist Rupert Sheldrake believes that when individuals engage in some behavior, they create "morphogenetic fields" for their species, patterns in collective consciousness that subsequent individuals can pick up and follow. To use computer images, the new patterns become part of the species' database. Once created, the patterns are online, and anyone can tap into them without having to go through the laborious task of inventing them all over again.

Like the law of gravity, archetypes are invisible, though we can see examples of them. They map an unseen process: how the holomovement unfolds its hidden order and how people have connected with that order—either what they've done with it or what it's done with them. All mystics, and certainly innovative ones like Rumi, contribute to shaping archetypes that in turn shape the mystic's path. Looking at Rumi's life and work, we can detect these archetypal patterns and use them as guides.

The mystic journey begins with some memory of the invisible—a memory that calls us to confront what's amiss in the visible. Mystics aren't immune from what happens around them. Rumi wasn't immune from Genghis Khan's horrific invasions, nor are we immune from physical ills, financial worries, family, school, and business concerns, pollution, or social injustice. The invisible and visible collaborate in calling our inner mystics to the path. Remembering the invisible calls us to turn off the pendulum, while seeing the visible calls us to confront the loss of soul, love, and freedom whenever bargaining prevails.

In the second phase of the mystic path, we turn within to find our invisible Friend, our soul, which provides the ground of change. What's "out there" won't shift as long as "in here" is cut of the same cloth. Only from soul can we find true love and freedom. For healing and transformation, mystics worldwide emphasize soul seeking and soul purification. We cleanse ourselves of all the stuff—the masks, roles, and images, the brokered relationships, and the external-only, money-based freedom—that's come to stand in for soul, love, and freedom but isn't the genuine article.

The third phase explores the "great love" of connectedness. Spending time with the invisible inspires us to reconnect with the visible in ways we hadn't imagined. Our mystics dream new patterns of being to-gether—of creating communities that honor the invisible and visible united, as Rumi did.

In the last phase, our inner mystics live from the invisible and, by so doing, return to our original freedom. Returning to who we are, to the great love inside us, and to our innate freedom, we become a force for transformation, though an inconspicuous one. In Taoist philosophy, the sage does nothing—doesn't meddle, doesn't force things—yet noth-ing is left undone. Cultivating the invisible within oneself encourages the cultivation of it in others. It strengthens the mystic archetype in consciousness, and, as not only every mystic but also every fan of *Star Wars* knows, the invisible is the greatest force for change.

Rumi has more than a little to say about all of this. He even gives some suggestions about how to take what he says—the method of look-ing beyond visible forms to "What's Inside":

> Listen to presences inside poems.
> Let them take you where they will.
>
> Follow those private hints,
> and never leave the premises.[33]
>
>   *
>
> Listen to What's Inside
> anything I say.[34]

And while we're listening to "What's Inside," we don't have to stop having fun. We wouldn't be mystics if we didn't have a few loose screws. Having fun is part of the path:

> Joking is teaching. Don't be fooled by the lightness,
> or the vulgarity. Jokes are serious.[35]

Soul, Love & Freedom Coming Together through the Mystic Path

	SOUL: coming home to who we are (GROUND)	LOVE: connecting from our souls' passions (PATH)	FREEDOM: finding a freedom that is freedom (FRUITION)
1. Confronting the absence of soul, love & freedom	Remembering the unseen and grieving the costs of forgetting it	Leaving loveless habits and following our loves as the way to sanity	Confronting bargaining relations and entering a free flow of need and help
Archetypes that confront loss	1. SEEKER	2. LONER	3. COMPANION
Journey: separation	The call: being called to the inner journey	Crossing the threshold	Accepting help
2. Getting our souls, loves & freedom back	Exploring our inner filters and how they give rise to experience	Moving with reality's two-sided process: into forms and out of them	Healing soul sickness by coming home to who we are
Archetypes that engage the soul	4. SOUL SEARCHER	5. RELEASER	6. HEALER
Journey: purification	Entering the soul's dark night: going within	Learning the art and practice of letting go	Surrendering to our inner authority
3. Soul, love & freedom alive in community	Becoming the empty place where the invisible comes through	Seeing with the Friend's eyes and sharing the visionary method	Building communities on our inner lives and resolving conflicts on that basis
Archetypes that honor love	7. LOVER	8. VISIONARY	9. WANDERER
Journey: reconnecting with the visible	The sacred marriage: wedding the Beloved	Dying to regenerate	Traveling in the world as Lovers and Visionaries
4. Soul, love & freedom open new realms	Moving with the universal principle of transmutation	Moving with the universal principle of attraction	Free as beings of both time and eternity
Archetypes that model freedom	10. ALCHEMIST	11. CONTEMPLATIVE	12. WISE FOOL
Journey: living from the invisible	Going through the refining fire	The return: coming home to our origins	Rolling around anywhere

1

Restless, Hungry, and Dissatisfied

ARCHETYPE   *Seeker*
MYSTIC JOURNEY   *The Call*

Mystics with an Attitude

When we think of mystics, we tend to think of people lost in blissful reverie, above the world and oblivious to problems. But as we've seen, Rumi isn't that kind of mystic:

> How will you know the difficulties
> of being human, if you're always
> flying off to blue perfection?
>
> Where will you plant your grief-seeds?
> Workers need ground to scrape and hoe,
> not the sky of unspecified desire.[1]

Naturally, mystics exist who prefer the clouds, and who can blame them? "Being human" is difficult on good days. But other mystics, like Rumi, prove themselves to be a tough-minded, down-to-earth lot. They don't gloss over the visible. If it's not working, they say so, as Rumi does:

> Things are reversed from what they should be in this place you live
>   now.
> One who should be hung on the scaffold is made emperor.
> People stand and clap.
> Tombs with ornamental plaster, self-conceit everywhere.
> Palm trees made of wax, wax leaves and fruit, wax dirt.[2]

Thanks to Muhammed's life and character, Muslims possess a strong streak of social justice, and Sufis even more so. Since dervishes live outside established institutions, they don't hesitate to say what they think. In Sufi literature, "the dervish is made the mouthpiece of social criticism: he puts his finger on the wound of society and points to the corrupt state of affairs."[3]

Mystics make particularly potent social critics, because their critiques don't stop with visible ills. Straddling visible and invisible, mystics trace outward crises to inward habits. "Outward acts are different from inward feelings," Rumi says, "and their purpose is to show us what's hidden within."[4] The visible doesn't just happen; it comes from something invisible—our philosophy and paradigm—and that can be as deadly as any physical poison:

> Muhammed said, . . .
>
> "I see your prosperity and your falling.
> I see you eating the poison
> that will kill you.
>
> I came to waken everyone to action!
> You hurry like moths toward the fire, while
> I'm waving wildly to keep you from it.
>
> Things you think are triumphs are
> the beginnings of unconsciousness."[5]

The Seeker: Longing for Soul

Mystics manifest this restless dissatisfaction with things, visible and invisible, personal and collective, because that's what starts mystics on the path. Something isn't right, something's missing, and the mystic in us wants to find out what. Though we may not have a clear sense of the unseen Presence of which Rumi speaks, the mystic in us does—enough at least to let us know when it's not there, to hunger for it, and to seek it:

> Everything started with the cry of the craving soul:
> Nourish me for I am hungry and hurry for time is a sword.[6]

With "the cry of the craving soul," the archetype of the Seeker calls us to the mystic path. To respond is to embark on a journey that takes us—who knows where? For sure, it's not directed toward success, rewards, or even self-improvement. It's rather to do with becoming more real, more true to who we are, even though we have no idea what this means. At the least, the path calls us to step outside conventions. We're looking for soul and meaning—ours—and something that's unique to each one of us isn't found in off-the-rack places:

> For a while we lived with people,
> but we saw no sign in them of the faithfulness we wanted.
> It's better to hide completely within
> as water hides in metal, as fire hides in a rock.[7]

"Hiding completely within" to find "faithfulness" to the soul leads the Seeker to inner worlds, where our mystics live. They're hiding, because we're trained to be anything but mystics. From Western science to philosophy, schools to religions and businesses, Western values place the outward before the inward, words and numbers before ideas and qualities. If we can't observe or measure something, it's assumed not to exist. Grades, bottom lines, salaries, bills, schedules, technologies, and consumer goods: everything gears us to the outward and measurable side of life. To achieve the right effects, we've even learned what to think, so that what goes on inside conforms to what's outwardly accepted—what's religiously, academically, socially, financially, or politically "correct."

This isn't easy on our inner mystics, who get tired of externals and bored with outer correctness. Much energy focused on the outward and little on the inward leaves our mystics' lives in shambles, like a magnificent old mansion that's been neglected, left to the rain and snow, mice and spiders.

When the Seeker first opens the door to this dilapidated house, it's a shock, as if we've been robbed of a legacy we forgot we had. What starts as restless dissatisfaction builds to anger—anger at ourselves for neglecting something so valuable, anger at the people and social systems that drove us to abandon our inner homes, anger at God for letting this happen, anger at the mystic path for making us confront our predicament, anger even at our souls for complicating our lives with intangible yearnings. We know the mansion is ours to reinhabit—that no one can reinhabit it but us—yet the job seems overwhelming. Maybe we should just let the invisible stay that way:

> A black sky hates the moon. I am that dark
> nothing. I hate those in power.
> I'm invited in from the road to the house,
> but I invent some excuse.
> Now I'm angry at the road.
>
> I don't need love. Let something break me.
> I don't want to hear anyone's trouble.
> I've had my chance for wealth and position.
> I don't want those.
>
> I am iron, resisting the most enormous Magnet there is.
> Amber pulls straw to it. That makes me angry.
> We're molecules spinning here, four, five, six of us.
> What does that mean, *five, six*?
> I am angry at God.
>
> You don't understand, being out of water.
> You resemble the sun? I hate likenesses.[8]

Inspirational insights aren't helpful at this point. The inner mansion isn't restored with metaphysical statements. All may be one—what else would it be?—yet that's not the point. We're not "interested in how things look different in moonlight"; we want our house—the "artist" inside us—back in our lives:

> Tomorrow you'll see what you've broken and torn tonight,
> thrashing in the dark. Inside you
> there's an artist you don't know about.
> He's not interested in how things look different in moonlight.[9]

Clearly, this path is neither up in the clouds nor for the faint of heart. It challenges us to grapple with outwardly oriented values and how we've internalized them in ways that cut us off from our inner experience. Beneath our culturally adapted personalities, there's something more real that wants out:

> The human shape is a ghost
> made of distraction and pain.
> Sometimes pure light, sometimes cruel,
> trying wildly to open,
> this image tightly held within itself.[10]

Our souls' "image" is "tightly held within," because it finds no place in visible systems, given their demands. Unchallenged, a visible-only paradigm functions like a sleeping pill, dulling us to the invisible and rendering us unconscious of our inner mansions. Yet waking up from a culture-wide paradigm—one we've been inducted into since birth— takes time:

> I run around looking for the Friend.
> My life is almost over,
> but I'm still asleep!
>
> When it happens, if it happens,
> that I meet the Friend,
> will I get the lost years back?[11]

It also takes courage and perseverance. Seeking our inner lives can be painful, more so the longer we've been away from them. It's painful to recall what caused us to board up our souls' homes, to see what's become of our inner worlds as a result, and to consider what it takes to reinhabit them. Will outward pressures once again drive us away?

No wonder Seekers often feel confused. Old answers don't work, nor do existing patterns satisfy. It's as if we have to rebuild our lives from scratch—the midlife crisis that people of all ages are now experiencing. On one hand, we feel as if we're losing our minds; on the other, we feel as if something more sane than anything we've ever experienced is going on inside us:

> This mirror inside me shows . . .
> I can't say what, but I can't not know!
>
> I run from body. I run from spirit.
> I do not belong anywhere.
>
> I'm not alive!
> You smell the decay?
>
> You talk about my craziness.
> Listen rather to the honed-blade sanity I say.[12]

It's no failure to acknowledge pain and helplessness. In fact, these are appropriate responses to encountering dimensions of meaning that go beyond the ordinary and visible. If we feel that we're in over our heads, that only means we're reconnecting with our souls' view of things—something long lost and forgotten—and we're on our way. "Searching like that does not fail":

> When acts of helplessness become habitual,
> those are the *signs*.
>
> But you run back and forth listening for unusual events,
> peering into the faces of travelers.
> "Why are you looking at me like a madman?"
> *I have lost a Friend. Please forgive me.*
>
> Searching like that does not fail.[13]

Searching with our mystics' passion doesn't fail, because our inner mystics know what's at stake. For all the pain and uncertainty, there's no going back. To do so would hurt us more:

What hurts the soul?
To live without tasting
the water of its own essence.[14]

Even so, pain that cuts both ways—pain if we stay on the path and pain if we leave it—tests the mystic's yearnings:

Longing is the core of mystery.
Longing itself brings the cure.
The only rule is, *Suffer the pain.*[15]

Trapped inside Visible Forms

This testing has nothing to do with judgments, passing or failing. Pain arises because the mystic path goes against the grain of outwardly driven cultures. Scholars often describe mystical movements as "true countercultures," democratic and egalitarian. Everyone has an inner experience, and this inner life transcends "sex, age, social class, education and heresy,"[16] race, and even species. Rumi honored slave, beggar, sheikh, king, cow, dog, and parrot with equal respect and kindness, valuing each according to the inner qualities expressed. Very often, the animals in his poetry prove wiser than the humans; they're not so locked into the cultural paradigm.

For outwardly driven cultures, however, the outward is a big deal, and we're to spare no efforts in securing our place in outward worlds. Visible forms determine our standing in society and how we're to be treated. The rich, the expert, and the powerful are emulated, while the poor and common folk are dismissed. If we know what's good for us, we'll place outward concerns first.

Turning to an inward path puts us at odds with this cultural priority. We feel caught between a rock and a hard place. The yearning for meaning is compelling but so is the need to pay bills, support families, and maintain an image of sanity in a society that has little regard for mystical longings. The more the yearnings intensify, the more we feel trapped. Rumi uses images of noble animals caged. In the following story, a falcon wanders away from the king—his soul's realm—only to have his wings clipped and talons cut by an old woman who ties him up, claiming that's the way he should be treated:

> The king had a noble falcon,
> who wandered away one day,
> and into the tent of an old woman,
> who was making dumpling stew
> for her children.
>   "Who's been taking care
> of you?" she asked, quickly tying
> the falcon's foot.
>   She clipped
> his magnificent wings and cut
> his fierce talons and fed him straw.
>   "Someone
> who doesn't know how to treat falcons,"
> she answered herself,
>   "but your mother knows!"
> Friend, this kind of talk is a prison.
> Don't listen!
>   The king spent all day
> looking for his falcon, and came at last
> to that tent and saw his fine raptor
> standing on a shelf in the smoky steam
> of the old woman's cooking.
>   "You left me
> for this?"
>   The falcon rubbed his wings
> against the king's hand, feeling wordlessly
> what was almost lost.[17]

"You left me for this?" We left our inner mansions to do what? to be what? to have what? The falcon escaped, but a gazelle wasn't so lucky:

> A hunter captures a gazelle and puts it
> in the stable with the cows and donkeys.

The gazelle runs about wild with fear and confusion.
Every night the man pours out chopped-up straw
for the barn animals. They love it,
but the gazelle shies quickly from side to side
in the big stall, trying to get away
from the smokey dust of the straw
and from the animals milling to eat it. . . .

For many days this precious animal
wriggles like a fish thrown up on dry ground.
Like dung and rare incense closed
side by side in a box.

One donkey says sarcastically, "This guy is wild!
He must be somebody special!"

Another, "With all his ebb and flow, he must be
making a pearl. Probably a cheap one."

Another, "Why can't he eat what we eat?"

Another donkey gets indigestion and offers
the gazelle his fodder with a formal invitation.

"No thank you. I am unwell too."

The donkey is offended. "Don't be so aloof.
Are you afraid of what people will say
if you're seen eating with me?"

The gazelle doesn't answer, but he thinks,
"Your food is for *you*. It revives your strength.
But I have known a pasture by a creek
where hyacinths and anemones and sweet basil grow.
My food is there. Some destiny put me here,
but I can't forget the other. If my body
gets old and sick, still my spirit
can stay new."[18]

Our souls feel like the falcon and gazelle. They're convinced that we
came from somewhere else—a place where the inward takes the lead,

where qualities of soul and character matter—and our inner mystics
long to return:

> All day I think about it, then at night I say it.
> Where did I come from, and what am I supposed to be doing?
> I have no idea.
> My soul is from elsewhere, I'm sure of that,
> and I intend to end up there.[19]

Accounts of near-death experiences support this view. Where we
came from and where we're going focus on cultivating invisibles: soul,
spirit, wisdom, and compassion. These come first, and manifestations
of them follow. Outward forms aren't the focus, as they are in our cultural donkey stables.

When we come here, because we've "known a pasture by a creek
where hyacinths and anemones and sweet basil grow," the outward
focus seems alien and hard to swallow. Our inner mystics feel as if
we've been put in "a narrow stall" where we can't "get up or take a
breath." Living in the cage of externals is more than our mystics can endure. As long as we're trapped there, it's impossible to meet our
Beloved, our souls:

> Don't punish the old guy. . . .
>
> He's tried to meet the Beloved,
> but he never has.
>
> That's why he acts as he does. That's why
> his eyes are so painful to look into.
>
> He keeps complaining to God, 'All the others
> can fly. Why have you cut my wings?'
>
> Where he lives is a narrow stall
> that a camel might lie down in at night.
>
> He cannot get up,
> or take a deep breath
> in there, in his life.

Never hand such a person a knife.
He'll eventually turn his hatred
on himself and rip open his stomach.[20]

And My Name Is. . . ?

What keeps us in the stall is our loss of memory. We recall neither our mystics nor our inner mansions. At first it's too painful to remember, but then we get used to juggling externals, and what memories remain fall by the way. Remembering soul and meaning doesn't relate to the job at hand. After awhile, our inner experiences seem to hover just beyond our conscious awareness, like dreams we can't quite get back. Who are we, and what are we doing here?—our Seekers don't recall:

Who looks out with my eyes? What is the soul?
I cannot stop asking.
If I could taste one sip of an answer,
I could break out of this prison for drunks.
I didn't come here of my own accord, and I can't leave that way.
Whoever brought me here will have to take me back.[21]

Lacking clear recollections of soul and meaning, we buy the culture's outward definitions. Visible, measurable images stand in as our "best guess" of who we are:

You're from a country beyond this universe,
yet your best guess is
you're made of earth and ashes!

You engrave this physical image everywhere
as a sign that you've forgotten
where you're from![22]

This will never do for mystics. We can't afford to be like "the old guy" who's never met his Beloved. The cost is too high. Without our inner lives, we may as well be dead:

No more muffled drums!
Uncover the drumheads!

Plant your flag in an open field!
No more timid peeking around.

Either you see the Beloved,
or you lose your head![23]

Grieving What's Happened

Perhaps the most compelling way to remember what's been lost is to
grieve it. Grieving opens the inner doors, allowing us to feel what our
souls feel. We connect with something real, something deep within
us. It's as if we walk into our inner mansion, sit down on the floor,
and let the house tell its story. Grieving awakens our souls' passions—
what we've been away from so long. Rumi quotes "the Andalusian
poet, Adi al-Riga":

> I was sleeping, and being comforted
> by a cool breeze, when suddenly a grey dove
> from a thicket sang and sobbed with longing,
> and reminded me of my own passion.
>
> I had been away from my own soul so long,
> so late-sleeping, but that dove's crying
> woke me and made me cry. *Praise*
> to all early-waking grievers![24]

Grieving connects us with our souls on the old rule that "the cure
for pain is in the pain."[25] If we flee from pain—anesthetize it—we don't
hear its message. Whatever is wrong gets worse. But if we allow pain
to surface, we "go beyond the veil" that separates outer and inner, and
we hear the dialogue between them:

> Pain arises when you look within,
> and this pain makes you go beyond the veil.[26]

Being stuck in pain is like being stuck in a river's whirlpool—the image in Edgar Allan Poe's short story "A Descent into the Maelström" (1841). Those who struggle to keep their heads above water exhaust themselves and drown. Only those who allow themselves to be carried to the depths survive, for the whirlpool's currents shoot them out downstream. Not fighting pain but grieving to the depths of our souls works the same way. We come out the other side and remember our souls' story. "Down in that hole," we "find something shining" and feel ourselves being "pulled up the dark way" into light:

> It's the old rule that drunks have to argue
> and get into fights.
> The lover is just as bad: He falls into a hole.
> But down in that hole he finds something shining,
> worth more than any amount of money or power.[27]

> *

> Some nights, stay up till dawn,
> as the moon sometimes does for the sun.
> Be a full bucket pulled up the dark way
> of a well, then lifted out into light.[28]

Understanding what grief and pain do for us, our inner mystics don't fear them. By listening to the stories that pain and grief tell, we ground ourselves in our souls, and that's "a blessing":

> The minute I'm disappointed, I feel encouraged.
> When I'm ruined, I'm healed.
> When I'm quiet and solid as the ground, then I talk
> the low tones of thunder for everyone.[29]

> *

> I saw grief drinking a cup of sorrow
> and called out,
> 　　　　　"It tastes sweet,
> does it not?"

"You've caught me,"
grief answered,
                    "and you've ruined my business.
How can I sell sorrow,
                    when you know it's a blessing?"[30]

As a result, the call to return to "the Friend" may lead us into a "night [that] extends into eternity," but at the same time, knowing that we're on the quest for our souls "is what joy is." Grieving for our souls spares us the greater grief of forgetting our souls:

This night extends into eternity,
like a fire burning inside the Friend.
Truly knowing this is what joy is.
Forgetting it is grief, and a lack of courage.[31]

Called by Our Souls

What we remember through grieving is that our mystics' sense of dis-ease in outwardly focused worlds is not unfounded. Our "deepest soul-instincts" are toward the holomovement, where visible and invisible unite in one process. Given this totality as the ground of our existence, it makes no sense to focus exclusively on visibles, cut off from the un-seen dynamics that give rise to them. Half the picture doesn't satisfy our desire for meaning, just as half of us, the outward half, doesn't make us happy. The half-view is as mystifying as trying to read a book with every other word blacked out. If our source is the whole—if "the Ocean" makes our existence possible moment to moment—then it's our nature to remember wholeness. One way or another, our whole nature calls us.

Rumi says our nature is to move with the Ocean like "a wild Ocean-Duck," yet we've learned to live on land as if we're chickens. Our souls call us to be ducks again, to remember what it's like to have the Ocean touch our chests:

You're a wild Ocean-Duck
that has been raised with chickens!

Your true mother lived on the Ocean,
but your nurse was a domestic land-bird.

Your deepest soul-instincts are toward the Ocean.
Whatever land-moves you have
you learned from your nurse, the hen.
It's time now to join the ducks![32]

*

A duckling may have only just been born,
but the Ocean touches its chest.[33]

Being ducks at heart, we don't make convincing chickens. We keep looking for the Ocean, and a few mud puddles don't do the trick. The restless seeking, dissatisfaction, and hungering for more comes from our nature, origin, and essence. How could we not experience pain and grief at being stranded on strange land? We wouldn't be who we are if we could live only in externals and be happy:

We are the mirror as well as the face in it.
We are tasting the taste this minute
of eternity. We are pain
and what cures pain. We are
the sweet, cold water and the jar that pours.[34]

In other words, the Friend who's lost is also what urges us to seek. Our own souls call to us and make us yearn for our souls' home, until ultimately there's no "distinction of caller and called":

Remember God so much that you are forgotten,
until you are lost in the Call,
without distinction of caller and called.[35]

Because our innermost nature moves us to the mystic path, we become Seekers and respond to the call as naturally as fish respond to the sound of waves or falcons to the falconer's drum. Embarking on the mystic path simply means following our deepest nature and taking the leap:

Why doesn't the soul fly
when it hears the call?

A fish on the beach always
moves toward wave-sound.

A falcon hears the drum
and brings its quarry home.

Why doesn't every dervish
dance in the sun?

You've escaped the cage.
Your wings are stretched
out. Now, fly![36]

2

Love and Madness

ARCHETYPE *Loner*
MYSTIC JOURNEY *Crossing the Threshold*

Fly Where?

The Seeker calls us to fly, but where? Where do we go with our mystics' restless hunger? The old answer is to fly to visible worlds—to channel our yearnings into bargaining systems, those that ask us to check our souls at the door and then take our loves as well. Inner hungerings get replaced with a hunger for a material more. Rumi compares bargaining for visibles to wanting "a small fig from a random tree" but ending up detained by "an old crone," "stinking-mouthed, with a hundred talons"—not a bad portrait of bargaining systems that promise to help us but instead hold us "tight by the belt":

> You miss the garden,
> because you want a small fig from a random tree.
> You don't meet the beautiful woman.
> You're joking with an old crone.
> It makes me want to cry how she detains you,
> stinking-mouthed, with a hundred talons,
> putting her head over the roofedge to call down,
> tasteless fig, fold over fold, empty
> as dry-rotten garlic.
>
> She has you tight by the belt,
> even though there's no flower and no milk
> inside her body.
> Death will open your eyes
> to what her face is: Leather spine
> of a black lizard. No more advice.

Let yourself be silently drawn
by the stronger pull of what you really love.[1]

Drawn by the invisible, our inner mystics take that last verse as a credo. If we don't follow what we really love, then we don't follow our souls either, since they're the source of our loves. Yet how can our lives be fun—much less be right for us—if "what we really love" has no place in them?

Rumi doesn't mince words about what it's like to live cut off from our loves. Not only do we lose what has meaning for us—time for ourselves and those we care about, time for what makes us happy—but worse, in return for that sacrifice, "we feel a rope around our neck." Concerns for visibles dominate:

Already tightly bound, we are wrapped with yet another chain.
We've lost everything, but here's another disaster.
Held in the curls of your hair,
we feel a rope around our neck.[2]

Reason That's "Death to Our Souls"

How do we get into such a fix? By a way of thinking that the culture instills through all its institutions. It's called "reason," but what's meant is a thought process that limits us to observables and countables. This version of rationality sizes up the visible side of things and makes decisions on that basis alone. The visible tells us all we need to know, indeed all we can know.

Any other way of thinking is considered irrational. Using invisible values to decide about visibles? Spending more on a shirt or rug, for instance, because it's not made by forced labor, or leaving a high-paying job because you don't agree with the values that go with it? These responses are considered imprudent, emotional, unscientific, and potentially dangerous.

Why? Because reason says we don't move up in the world by following our loves, and society might fall apart if we all did. Nothing would get done. We need external rewards and punishments to keep us in line doing what systems require. If we know what's good for us, we'll brush aside the "love stories" that our souls write, even if that causes us pain:

> Every day, this pain. Either you're numb
> or you don't understand love.
> I write out my love story.
> You see the writing, but you don't read it.[3]

Our mystics do read it, painful though it is. They don't agree with visible-only thinking. Rationalized "answers" about where to fly don't fly. We're made unhappy (addictive, numb, crazy, depressed, compulsive), and the more we're unhappy, the more our systems reflect our unhappiness. The "wine"—symbolizing life-giving meaning—doesn't go into a glass but slips through our fingers:

> This world hurts my head with its answers,
> wine filling my hand, not my glass.
> If I could wake completely, I would say without speaking
> why I'm ashamed of using words.[4]

If we're numb from bargaining, not we but the notion of reason has gone awry. By dismissing inner for outer, visible-only reasoning factors out half our being, and the most meaningful half. "Conventional knowledge is death to our souls, and it is not really *ours*. It's laid on"— laid on by a cultural way of thinking that says we're here to "take little steps and peck at the ground":

> There are many guises for intelligence.
> One part of you is gliding in a high windstream,
> while your more ordinary notions
> take little steps and peck at the ground.
>
> Conventional knowledge is death
> to our souls, and it is not really *ours*.
>
> It's laid on. Yet we keep saying
> that we find "rest" in these "beliefs."[5]

What's missing from ground-pecking reason is the big picture. Confined to tangibles, it misses the intangibles, the biggest one being "whether we're in harmony with that which has no definition." Are we in sync with the holomovement, so that we're being who we came here to be? Ground-pecking reason can't touch this question. It's good at cleverness and manipulating figures, but it can also waste our minds trying to untie sacks that turn out to be empty:

> A peaceful face twists with the poisonous nail
> of thinking. A golden spade
> sinks into a pile of shit.
>
> Suppose you loosen an intellectual knot.
> The sack is empty. You've grown old
> trying to untie such difficulties.
> So loosen a few more, why knot!
>
> There is a big one fastened at your throat,
> the problem of whether you're in harmony
> with that which has no definition.
> Try solving that.[6]

Crossing the Threshold and Becoming Loners

Because visible-only thinking doesn't work for our inner mystics, we face a choice. Every journey begins with crossing a threshold, and this choice marks the mystic's. Either we abandon our longings for meaning, that is, abandon the journey before we start, or we abandon the culture's concept of what's rational.

Choosing the first isn't an option for our inner mystics. Without a quest for meaning, we'd see only the outward side: worlds of injustice, an economic survival of the fittest, the rich getting richer and the poor poorer, bureaucracies grinding out bought decisions, people doing things only if they're rewarded, and everywhere the haunting fear of not making it—a picture that leaves us feeling disillusioned and cynical about the world. On top of that, without our mystics' connectedness to meaning, we'd bargain away our destinies in exchange for external rewards. We'd end up using the same cynical and disillusioning methods that create the worlds we despise, leaving us cynical and disillusioned about ourselves as well.

This choice will never do for our inner mystics. Without our souls and our quests for meaning, who are we? As Rumi sees it, we need our yearnings for the unseen—our inner mystics—to "continue being human":

> There's no love in me without your being,
> no breath without that. I once thought
>
> I could give up this longing, then thought again,
> *But I couldn't continue being human.*[7]

Nonetheless, the second choice—choosing to abandon the cultural concept of what's rational, of who we should be and what we should do with our lives—is a big one. Crossing this threshold takes us out on our own. Others may not understand our choice and, for that matter, we may not understand it ourselves. Our mystic Loner is profoundly that—alone in the holo-ocean:

> Late, by myself, in the boat of myself,
> no light and no land anywhere,
> cloudcover thick. I try to stay
> just above the surface, yet I'm already under
> and living within the ocean.[8]

The holo-ocean isn't such a bad place to be, though, since in it, we have a freedom that we don't have in bargaining systems. If what we want most isn't "out there" but within, then we don't have to bargain to get it. We have it already in who we are—"already under and living within the ocean"—and we just need to learn how to access it. Our inner mystics fire a passion in us to do this—to cross this threshold—and if the passion doesn't fit in both worlds, "No matter":

There is a passion in me
that doesn't long for anything
from another human being.

I was given something else,
a cap to wear in both worlds.
It fell off. No matter.[9]

Loves Connect Us with the Mystery

Choosing to abandon not our souls but not-us, bargaining-system concepts about what to do, we can now return to the original question:
where do we go with our mystic yearnings? As Loners, we're not following official reason—not led by visibles and countables. Yet what
guides us in their place? Rumi's answer is that of the classic mystic: our
loves do. Our loves possess a wisdom about why we're here that nothing else has.

Next to our souls, our loves are our greatest treasures. Not only do
they hold the secret to our reason for being, but more, they're our link
to the whole—how we connect with the big picture and how it connects with us. Both Rumi and Plato claim that what we long for in our
heart of hearts connects us with God:

Muhammed related that God said, "I am not in
the atmosphere, or in the void of space,
or in the most brilliant intelligences.
I live more clearly and brightly
as a guest in a humble worker's heart.

There I am, without qualification, or
definition, or description. I am there,
in that person's loving, so that my qualities
and powers can flow out into everything else.

In such a mirror, time and matter
can bear my beauty. Such a person is

a vast mirror, within which, every *second*,
fifty wedding banquets appear!

Don't ask me to describe it!"[10]

How does this work? Rumi says that our loves are actually God moving in us—the holomovement unfolding through the language of our deepest longings:

Love is the way messengers
from the mystery tell us things.[11]

In Plato's terms, the Good operates in us as our longings for the good. What we love beneath all we've learned to want is something divine. "God lives between a human being and the object of his or her desire," Rumi says. "It's all a mystical journey to the Friend."[12]

In Plato's *Symposium*, a wise woman named Diotima tells Socrates that "Love" is the go-between from ignorance to knowledge, since it's the love of wisdom that leads us from one to the other. In the same way, "Love" is the "envoy" and "interpreter" between heaven and earth, "welding both sides together and merging them into one great whole."[13] Our love for the good draws us to it, or more, is the Good drawing us to itself—"lover and Beloved pull themselves into each other." Either way, love connects "what lives in time" with "what lives in eternity" and directs us on the mystic path:

What characteristics do God and human beings
have in common? What is the connection between
what lives in time and what lives in eternity?

If I kept talking about Love,
a hundred new combinings would happen,
and still I would not say the Mystery.

The fearful ascetic runs on foot, along the surface.
Lovers move like lightning and wind.

No contest.
Theologians mumble, rumble-dumble,
necessity and free will,
while lover and Beloved
                    pull themselves
into each other.[14]

No wonder mystics across cultures go nuts over love in their writings; it's the mystic's element, the exact point of interface between the seen and the unseen. Love is how the visible and invisible converse in us, and to follow our loves is to pursue the dialogue between visible and invisible through our lives.

Love's dialogue turns first to who we are. Our essence is invisible and ineffable, not something we can pin down. Yet in spite of our souls' elusive quality, our loves connect us with them. We, who live in time, and our souls, who live in eternity, are lover and Beloved, drawing each other closer. Following our loves, we move with our essence, just as a flower moves with the wind:

God only knows, I don't,
what keeps me laughing.

The stem of a flower
moves when the air moves.[15]

Psychologist James Hillman suggests that our "soul's code" is seeded in us from the beginning and that our interests and inclinations reveal who we'll be. What we're drawn to from our earliest years indicates our souls' hand in our lives from the start.[16] Far from being trivial or insignificant, then, our loves guide us to our destinies. Our souls are our buried treasures and our loves the maps to find them. Our loves sort out which "calls" are ours and which aren't. "Every call that excites your spirit" is from our loves—hence our souls—whereas "those that make you fearful and sad" are not ours to follow:

Be patient.
Respond to every call
that excites your spirit.

Ignore those that make you fearful
and sad, that degrade you
back toward disease and death.[17]

Our mystics' answer about where to fly, then, is simple: wherever our loves take us. They're our guides. When we're on our own in the holo-ocean, the Loner archetype tells us to turn to our loves and let them "shine inside us." "Love is the mother." By trusting our loves, we trust the holomovement unfolding in us, and we give birth to the lives we were born to live:

Love is the mother.
We are her sons.

She shines inside us,
visible-invisible, as we trust
or lose trust, or feel it start to grow again.[18]

Because we all have different souls, the loves that spring from them are different too. Following our loves can take us down paths where we feel very much the Loner. But instead of living "empty and frightened," our inner mystics take heart in living our loves—in letting "the beauty we love be what we do":

Today, like every other day, we wake up empty
and frightened. Don't open the door to the study
and begin reading. Take down a musical instrument.

Let the beauty we love be what we do.
There are hundreds of ways to kneel and kiss the ground.[19]

Trusting our loves to guide us—to be our "falconer" and "king"— makes us come alive. Bargained lives are deadening, but living from our loves, that's exciting. Our loves take off the "falcon's hood" that keeps us from seeing our souls' meaning at work:

> When a handful of dirt was taken from the hoofprint
> of Gabriel's horse and thrown inside the golden calf,
> the calf lowed! That's what the guide can do
> for you. The guide can make you *live*.

> The guide will take your falcon's hood off.
> Love is the falconer, your king.[20]

Reason in League with Love

What Rumi suggests marks a break with how we've been trained to calculate our lives. It's not a break with reason, though, but only with a certain concept of reason, the "minutiae-collecting" kind. For Rumi, that's not real knowing anyway. Knowing has to do with the whole, visible and invisible. Far from being at odds with love, this knowing embraces love as a powerful source of wisdom. Because love links the seen and the unseen, "Knowing-Love" is "a rising light, a happiness in both worlds":

> There is a kind of Knowing that is a love.
> Not a scholarly knowing. That minutiae-collecting
> doesn't open you. It inflates you, like a beard
> or a fancy turban. It announces you, saying,

> *There are certain plusses and minuses*
> *which we must carefully consider.*

> This other Knowing-Love is a rising light,
> a happiness in both worlds.[21]

Rumi is actually a great advocate of "Reason," as many mystics are. His idea of reason, though, has nothing to do with constructing arguments to rationalize outward advantage. He wouldn't argue for downsizing a company to boost next quarter's earnings, for instance, nor would he debate how much of a toxic chemical we can tolerate in our air or water before we get sick. These uses of the mind "blind" us to the big picture, in which case, how rational are they?

> An eye is meant to see things.
> The soul is here for its own joy.
> A head has one use: For loving a true love.
> Legs: To run after.
>
> Love is for vanishing into the sky. The mind,
> for learning what men have done and tried to do.
> Mysteries are not to be solved. The eye goes blind
> when it only wants to see *why*.[22]

"A head has one use: For loving a true love"—that's Rumi's reason. Reason joins with love, because the ultimate purpose of reason is to unite us with the Good—our souls' good as well as good within the whole—and only our loves can show us how. To this end, reason helps us discover our loves, which are present in us but hidden. Their "intelligence" exists already as "a freshness in the center of the chest," "a fountainhead from within you, moving out." What Rumi calls "plumbing-learning" can't hold a candle to the knowing "already completed and preserved inside you":

> There are two kinds of intelligence: One acquired,
> as a child in school memorizes facts and concepts
> from books and from what the teacher says,
> collecting information from the traditional sciences
> as well as from the new sciences.
>
> With such intelligence you rise in the world.
> You get ranked ahead or behind others
> in regard to your competence in retaining
> information. You stroll with this intelligence
> in and out of fields of knowledge, getting always more
> marks on your preserving tablets.

There is another kind of tablet, one
already completed and preserved inside you.
A spring overflowing its springbox. A freshness
in the center of the chest. This other intelligence
does not turn yellow or stagnate. It's fluid,
and it doesn't move from outside to inside
through the conduits of plumbing-learning.

This second knowing is a fountainhead
from within you, moving out.[23]

Thanks to how we're schooled, though, we seldom trust inner sources of knowing. What we know from our souls and loves—"this second knowing"—doesn't count compared to "acquired" intelligence, collecting and memorizing information. That's the official view, but it's not our mystics'. For them, the door to sanity isn't out there; it opens "from the inside":

I have lived on the lip
of insanity, wanting to know reasons,
knocking on a door. It opens.
I've been knocking from the inside![24]

Leaving Old Habits

Because this second knowing springs from our essence, it draws us, as moths to a flame, consuming whatever is "not really *ours.*" Compared to love-knowing, the acquired kind seems trivial—data to be keyed into computers. As we cross the threshold to real knowing, the intellect that helps us "rise in the world" may be left in ruins, but what we really love emerges in its place:

Soul serves as a cup for the juice
that leaves the intellect in ruins.

That candle came and consumed me,
about whose flame the universe
flutters in total confusion.[25]

When love and reason join, they leave many things "fluttering in total confusion." That's the mystic Loner again—separate not only from people and cultural institutions but also from cultural beliefs. Whatever inclines us to visible-bound reason can't come with us "to the big watertank," where invisibles and visibles move together as one story that surpasses our concepts:

> Wash off all wonderings-why
> and workings-out-however.
> Don't take those with you
> to the big watertank.[26]

For our mystic Loners, leaving belief-habits is natural. Having been asked to bargain away our souls and loves to fit into the culture, our Loners are savvy about what to leave and what to keep. They don't abandon anything that holds meaning, only habits that get in the way of it—two in particular.

First, Loners abandon *dependence on thinking*. They're not impressed with mental maneuverings, since they know what follows. Aspirations go on the shelf, while official reasoning persuades us to do what's efficient or profitable.

Second, Loners abandon *dependence on external rewards*. External factors have no secret knowledge of what's good in the grand scheme of things or what makes us happy. If anything, they lure us into lives we despise. As long as external rewards dominate, our loves—our true guides—don't get a hearing.

Breaking habits in a culture dependent on them, though, isn't easy, even for Loners. These are thresholds that take some doing to cross.

1. Abandoning the Smoke of Thinking

Seneca, the Roman Stoic philosopher, reflected on his life and the emptiness of thinking when it's not connected to something deeper: "All your debates and learned conferences, your scholarly talk, and collection of maxims from the teachings of philosophers are in no way indicative of genuine spiritual strength."[27] Thomas Aquinas, a contemporary of Rumi's, was a walking encyclopedia of Christian doctrines—until the end of his life, when he ceased to speak and write, saying, "All that I have written seems to me nothing but straw . . . compared to what I have seen and what has been revealed to me."[28] According to these thinking-pros, thinking falls short, because it gives off smoke and then plays with smoke patterns, ignoring the real action in the flames:

> A thinker collects and links up proofs.
> A mystic does the opposite.
> He lays his head on a person's chest
> and sinks into the answer.
>
> Thinking gives off smoke
> to prove the existence of fire.
> The mystic sits within the burning.
>
> Imagination loves to discover shapes
> in rising smoke, but it's a great mistake
> to leave the fire for that filmy sight.[29]

Without a great love to guide it, thinking gets lost. Preoccupied with planning the next move, our thinking-side hopes that if only we can think harder or faster, we'll get somewhere. Meaning within the big picture eludes us. The mystic path doesn't begin until our Loners break with visible-bound thinking:

> Tie together all human intellects.
> They won't stretch to here.[30]
>
> *
>
> Nothing happens until you quit contriving
> with your mind. Quit your talking.[31]
>
> *
>
> You can't understand this with your mind.
> You must burst open![32]

Not that thinking doesn't have its function. It's valuable in a supportive role. But for setting the course of our lives, thinking isn't up to the job. To find our way on the mystic path, we need "the wholeness of the sun," and if we have that, "it's an impudence to light lamps":

> Leave, with your scholarship
> and your philosophies.
>
> Even if you reduced them
> to a single hair's breadth,
>
> there'd be no room here for those,
> as now the dawn comes up.
>
> In the wholeness of the sun,
> it's an impudence to light lamps.[33]

2. Finding a "Fire in My Chest"

In contrast to visible-only thinking, "wholeness"-reason wants us moving in the currents of our souls' loves. It's not interested in "subtle discussions"—theological or psychological, political or economic—that snare and resnare us. Instead, love-guided reason reminds us "how it feels to sail the mountain air":

> Don't be addicted to subtle discussions,
> tying and untying knots, posing difficulties
> that then you resolve.
>
> Doing that, you're like a bird
> who learns how to loosen the snare
> and then fastens it again,
> to show off his strange, new skill.
>
> Don't forget that the point is to escape!
> Remember how it feels to sail the mountain air
> and smell the sweetness of the high meadows.[34]

"Sailing the mountain air," we recall our souls' destiny. We see carrots and sticks for what they are, namely, devices that trap us in the visible. For the Loner, "the point is to escape." Once we've broken the habit of snaring, unsnaring, and resnaring ourselves with thinking, our Loners start dismantling the second habit: depending on external rewards for motivation.

Visible-only thinking traps us with external rewards and their promises of security and comfort. These are what Loners lose when they become Loners, and they're the hooks that thinking uses to reel us in. Even though we know on some level that the desire for externals "is not really *ours*, . . . we keep saying that we find 'rest' in these 'beliefs'"—something about recognition, retirement, and saving for a rainy day. After all, doesn't God smile on the righteous by giving them wealth and prosperity? And if those are God's rewards, isn't it good to work for them? Thinking that "old theology" way, we don't respond to what we really love, and we "sleep on" in externals:

> Those who don't feel this Love
> pulling them like a river,
> those who don't drink dawn
> like a cup of springwater
> or take in sunset like supper,
> those who don't want to change,
>
> let them sleep.
>
> This Love is beyond the study of theology,
> that old trickery and hypocrisy.
> If you want to improve your mind that way,
>
> sleep on.
>
> I've given up on my brain.
> I've torn the cloth to shreds
> and thrown it away.
>
> If you're not completely naked,
> wrap your beautiful robe of words
> around you,
>
> and sleep.[35]

The good news is that our Loners are restless creatures. If we sleep, they don't let us sleep long. When we finally embrace the archetype of the mystic Loner—"alone in a circle of himself," like "a glob of oil on water"—we get wise to the hooks. External rewards don't bring the security they promise. Pension funds can disappear overnight from corporate raiding, and the insurance we pay for decades has a way of not applying in our particular moment of need. But even if externals were reliable, our Loners ask, how much of ourselves must we pay to gain them? Is what we get outwardly worth the inner cost?

When we wake up, we agree with our mystic Loners: life isn't about being comfortable; it's about being alive moment-to-moment to the "messengers from the mystery"—our loves—and following them. "Comfortable lives always end in bitterness."[36] Our loves promise something greater, something that's continually dissolving the visible self into some new, unimagined being:

> An intellectual is all the time showing off.
> Lovers dissolve and become bewildered.
>
> Intellectuals try not to drown,
> while the whole purpose of love
> is drowning.
> Intellectuals invent
> ways to rest, and then lie down
> in those beds.
> Lovers feel ashamed
> of comforting ideas.
> You've seen a glob
> of oil on water? That's how a lover
> sits with intellectuals, there, but alone
> in a circle of himself. . . .
>
> To the intellectual mind, a child must learn
> to grow up and be adult.
> In the station of love,
> you see old men getting younger and younger.[37]

That's when the fun begins. By sticking to our loves, our Loners protect what's alive in us and attuned to our souls' meaning. Instead of giving up our mystics' longings, our Loners stay inside the fire that "Love lights in our chests." The result is that we get "younger and younger" as not-loves burn away:

> Love lit a fire in my chest, and anything
> that wasn't love left: intellectual
> subtlety, philosophy
> books, school.
>
> All I want now
> to do or hear
> is poetry.[38]

In the end, what our mystics want is for our lives to unfold from our loves. Outward rewards can't equal this. As our loves emerge, we know where to fly—we "walk out into the indications of where you must go":

> Inside wisdom, a bright-flowing, analytic power.
> Inside love, a friend.
> One a psychic source, the other plain water.
>
> Walk out into the indications
> of where you must go.[39]

Following Our Loves: The Path to Sanity

By living from our loves, our mystic Loners redefine sanity. Sanity isn't being able to fit into a loveless, bargained norm. John Gatto, educator and author of Dumbing Us Down, left public school teaching after twenty-nine years, realizing, "I teach how to fit into a world I don't want to live in." His is a Loner's insight, and with it he crossed the threshold into new worlds of education.

Crossing the threshold to a new understanding of sanity is inevitable on the mystic path, since conforming to externals will never do for our inner mystics. Returning to the "sanity" that Freud described as "an ordinary state of unhappiness" isn't an option. Our mystics would rather die—"humiliate" themselves and "gnaw on their chains"—than conform to a loveless way of life:

What's the lover to do,
but humiliate himself,
and wander your rooms?

If he kisses your hair,
don't wonder why.

Sometimes in the madhouse
they gnaw on their chains.[40]

That's why becoming Loners is equally inevitable. Faced with bargaining systems, our inner mystics stay sane by remaining true to our loves, even if it means bucking systems, leaving them, or being considered a failure by them.

Rumi's friend, Shams of Tabriz, fit the Loner archetype relative to his culture, and he made the Loner's choice. By all accounts, he was unconventional to the bone. No one knew his credentials in mystical initiation, which were a big deal in Sufi societies. Nor was he famous or a pillar of the community as Rumi was. For all appearances, he was just another wandering dervish, and a strange one. Conforming to official systems or norms was the last thing on his mind.

Shams was, however, committed to following his loves. His passion for the eternal Beloved fired Rumi's passion, which had been frozen inside Rumi's proper and prestigious life. A poem attributed to Shams discusses loveless worlds and how real loves don't bother themselves "with someone just wandering through." The heart is what counts and what brings wisdom and sanity:

I went inside my heart
to see how it was.

Something there makes me hear
the whole world weeping.

Then I went to every city and small town,
searching for someone who could *speak* wisdom,
but everyone was complaining about love.

That moaning gave me an idea: *Go back inside*
and find the answer. But I found nothing.

The heart acts as translator between
mystical experience and intelligence.

It has its own inhabitants who do not talk
with someone just wandering through.

And remember what Muhammed said of the place
in human beings we call the heart,
This is what I value.[41]

Shakespeare—who alluded to Shams in his plays—agreed: being true
to our loves is the key to sanity. Shakespeare's plays often turn around
love stories, and the lovers coming together marks the wise resolution of plots that show how crazy and hellish the world gets when we
mistrust or abandon our loves.

In *Romeo and Juliet,* for instance, who's more sane: the scores of
adults locked in family feuding or the two teenage lovers? By contrast,
in *Othello,* the esteemed leader goes insane with jealousy when he stops
trusting his wife. If we abandon our loves, we're lucky if we only get
caught in "much ado about nothing"; more likely, we'll end up like
Othello, murdering our loves and then killing ourselves. Rumi would
prefer we didn't have to "die to see this." Love is the "real mount" that
can "lift the baggage [of thinking] rightly." Directed by our loves, our
"knowledge-load" "will give joy" instead of snaring us:

Don't wait till you die to see this.
Recognize that your imagination and your thinking
and your sense-perception are reed canes
that children cut and pretend are horsies.

The Knowing of mystic Lovers is different.
The empirical, sensory, sciences
are like a donkey loaded with books,
or like the makeup woman's makeup.
                                   It washes off.

But if you lift the baggage rightly, it will give joy.
Don't carry your knowledge-load for some selfish reason.
Deny your desires and willfulness,
and a real mount may appear under you.[42]

Daring to Seem Insane

What's sane according to our loves, however, can seem insane to
worlds that measure actions outwardly. Going where our loves lead
seems foolish, as if we're throwing away our lives:

The mystic dances in the sun,
hearing music others don't.

"Insanity," they say, those others.
If so, it's a very gentle,
nourishing sort.[43]

The music of our souls and loves—and our mystics' ability to hear
it—is unsettling to those in power, since they don't control the tunes.
To a paradigm that seeks power over people, nothing is more threatening than for us to follow our loves. Of Gandhi, for instance, Gilbert
Murray wrote:

Persons in power should be very careful how they deal with a man who
cares nothing for sensual pleasure, nothing for riches, nothing for comfort or praise, or promotion, but is simply determined to do what he believes to be right. He is a dangerous and uncomfortable enemy, because
his body, which you can always conquer, gives you so little purchase
upon his soul.[44]

The sanity of adhering to our loves is precisely what control systems
consider "dangerous and uncomfortable." Paradigms of power become
the "slaughterhouse" to our loves, and if we walk there, we find the
floor "running with blood." For Rumi and Shams, this wasn't only
metaphoric:

This love is beyond the range of language,
but you come in asking, "How's your heart?"

holding your robe up slightly.
I answer, "Hold it higher!

This slaughterhouse floor
is running with blood."[45]

That's when our mystics need our Loners the most—the part of us that isn't afraid to step outside systems and go it alone. Sooner or later, because love's sanity is true sanity, people recognize the wisdom of Loners and say "There's daylight"—a way out of insanity:

I am insane, but they keep calling to me.
No one here knows me, but no one chases me off.
My job is to stay awake like the nightwatchman.
When they're drunk enough, and it's late enough,
they recognize me. They say, *There's daylight.*[46]

Before Shams came along, Rumi disdained music and dancing. He was satisfied giving lectures at the college. After Shams, Rumi could do little but listen to music, dance, and recite poetry. Some historians believe Rumi went mad after his contact with Shams—not surprising given what Rumi says about intellectuals. Yet madness doesn't produce mystical poetry that's stood for centuries as among the best if not *the* best ever composed. More likely, Shams awakened Rumi to his soul's passions. After he met Shams, whatever Rumi did, he did from his heart, from "this present-thirst" that is "your real intelligence":

This present-thirst is your real intelligence,
not the back-and-forth, mercurial brightness.
Discursiveness dies and gets put in the grave.

This contemplative joy does not.
Scholarly knowledge is a vertigo,
an exhausted famousness.
Listening is better.[47]

Granted, this is pretty radical stuff, as Rumi well knew. The more sane we are, the more we challenge bargaining systems. If we've grown up in slaughterhouses, familiarity with them makes them seem comfortable. But when we realize it's our souls, hearts, and loves that are being killed, they no longer feel so safe, and it's insane to stay there longer. To do so would be to "spill the springwater of your real life." If leaving slaughterhouses is insane, "I'll be mad":

> We must become ignorant
> of what we've been taught,
> and be, instead, bewildered.
>
> Run from what's profitable and comfortable.
> If you drink those liqueurs, you'll spill
> the springwater of your real life.
>
> Distrust anyone who praises you.
> Give your investment money,
> and the interest on the capital,
> to those who are actually destitute.
>
> Forget safety.
> Live where you fear to live.
> Destroy your reputation.
> Be notorious.
>
> I have tried prudent planning
> long enough. From now
> on, I'll be mad.[48]

That's the Loner and happy to be so. But there's a surprise. Once Loners cross the threshold, they find they're not so alone. Help is all around.

3

Free Help Wanted

ARCHETYPE   *Companion*
MYSTIC JOURNEY   *Accepting Help*

Help at a Price

Help may be all around, but in a bargaining world, it comes at a price, and we're drawn to the Loner archetype precisely because we're not willing to pay what's asked. For our inner mystics, the incessant quid pro quoing that goes on in outward affairs costs us our freedom:

> . . . In this marketplace world
> people sit on benches waiting to be paid.
>   The child won't give up
> the onion in one hand until it has the apple tightly
> in the other. Nobody says, "The Peace of God be with you,"
> without some ulterior motive about making money.
>   Very seldom
> do you hear a true *Salaam*, one that means it. I listen
> to hear God saying, *God's Peace be with you*,
> but it's rare.[1]

For our Loners, the solution is easy: we stay free by going it alone. Otherwise receiving help translates into being controlled. Those who receive help must answer to those who give it. This control notion reflects marketplace thinking, giving rise to mercantile law based on who owns what and whom, as opposed to civil law based on justice. Whereas justice appeals to invisible ideals such as rights, freedom, and fairness, ownership doesn't. In mercantile law, only owning counts—hence the need for "two angels praying in the market":

72

The Prophet said that there were always two angels
praying in the market. One said, "Lord,
give the poor wanderer help." The other, "Lord,
give the miser a poison."[2]

Islam's angels are tough on misers, because they epitomize what's
wrong with the mercantile model. When help becomes a means of
control, we not only avoid seeking help but also stop giving it, afraid
that if we do, we'll deplete our help reserve, and we won't be able to
help ourselves when we need it.

Before long, a marketplace model infects all human interactions. To
accept help on any level is to become indebted, whether the source is
people (parents, spouses, colleagues) or institutions (banks, companies,
religious organizations). We live under a cloud of indebtedness, and
almost anything can create a debt. If someone is simply nice to us or
willing to overlook our shortcomings, seeds of indebtedness start to
grow. No wonder Loners choose as they do.

Companions on the Way

Though we need the Loner's courage to follow our loves, the issues sur-
rounding marketplace help aren't about love; they're about freedom.
Loners aren't actually as free as they seem, since they have to do everything for themselves. They're not free to get help when they need it.
Once we become Loners and follow our loves, the very next challenge
on the mystic path is to find a way to connect—to enter into a flow of
helping—and still be free.

The archetype of the mystic Companion takes on the challenge
by assuming an invisible bill of rights that applies to all beings. This
invisible credo grants every being, among other things, freedom, self-
determination, equality, innate worth as the holomovement expressed,
and a right to participate in the universe of interconnectedness without being enslaved along the way.

Thanks to these assumptions, every relationship starts off with a
mutual understanding that's rooted in the invisible. Status relative to

outward forms—race, sex, class, material possessions, even species, two-legged or four-legged—doesn't define the relationship. Visible forms are incidental to the invisible joining of souls on a shared quest for meaning.

In practice, this means that Companions coexist as free beings, each continuing in the relationship for no other reason than that they delight in the other's presence. Their desire in being together is that they each experience good as their own souls seek it. Owning, controlling, or manipulating each other doesn't come up, because the Companion model doesn't inspire it.

Outward forms being incidental, Companions sense in each other a beauty and treasure that persists no matter what. Though Shams looked wild and unkempt and had a bluntness that annoyed people, none of that fazed Rumi. Companions see through everything to the soul's core. They have a sense of destiny about their being together—that sharing the path somehow serves the grand scheme of things beyond what could be measured outwardly.

And help does flow both ways, each Companion giving and receiving it. One isn't always needy with the other always helping, nor are they two Loners rubbing shoulders. Going along together benefits both. Without Companions, the journey would be far more difficult and far less fun. Indeed, "a wall standing alone is useless, but put three or four walls together . . .":

> This road demands courage and stamina,
>
> yet it's full of footprints! Who *are*
> these companions? They are rungs
> in your ladder. Use them!
> With company you quicken your ascent.
>
> You may be happy enough going along,
> but with others you'll get farther, and faster.
>
> Someone who goes cheerfully by himself
> to the customs house to pay his traveler's tax
> will go even more lightheartedly

when friends are with him.

Every prophet sought out companions.
A wall standing alone is useless,
but put three or four walls together,
and they'll support a roof and keep
the grain dry and safe.³

Companions help each other without having clouds of indebtedness gather, because mutual respect remains foremost. An equality of spirit prevails regardless of who's helping whom—an equality that resides on inner, soul levels, independent of circumstances. Between Rumi and Shams, "the categories of Teacher and student, lover and Beloved, Master and disciple, dissolved."⁴

For Rumi, no relationship proved more powerful. As he saw it, Companions are a source of sublime joy. Indeed they're gifts of "grace," enabling us to fulfill our life's purpose. To exist at all—much less to fulfill our destinies—we must allow our lives to be *"woven"*:

When ink joins with a pen, then the blank paper
can say something. Rushes and reeds must be *woven*
to be useful as a mat. If they weren't interlaced,
the wind would blow them away.

Like that, God paired up creatures,
and gave them friendship.⁵

*

The Friend will become bread and springwater for you,
a lamp and a helper, your favorite dessert
and a glass of wine.
                   Union with that one
is grace.⁶

The model of mystic Companion, by removing indebtedness from relationships, makes it possible for us to be together freely, and that's something divine: "The One who acts without regard to getting anything back is God. Or a Friend of God."[7] A free exchange is truer to our invisible nature, our divine side, because the free atmosphere allows the holomovement to flow through our relationships unhindered, not forced into quid pro quo boxes:

> A mouse and a frog meet every morning on the riverbank.
> They sit in a nook of the ground and talk.

> Each morning, the second they see each other,
> they open easily, telling stories and dreams and secrets,
> empty of any fear or suspicious holding-back.

> To watch and listen to these two
> is to understand how, as it's written,
> sometimes when two beings come together,
> Christ becomes visible.[8]

We're drawn to Companions—and they to us—by our souls' longing for the highest and best in relationships. It was Shams's longing for a Companion that led him to Rumi. "Shams wandered the world looking for a companion, a Friend on his level of attainment."[9] As Coleman Barks explains, Shams was willing to give up his head—his calculating mind—to find "a companion to his soul":

> [Shams] prayed for a companion to his soul. "What will you give in return?" a voice asked. "My head!" "The one you seek is Jelaluddin of Konya." So a bargain was struck in the invisible world. Fire met fire, ocean ocean, in a small square in south-central Anatolia. There is no explaining the place of pure being they went to together. Perhaps a fragrance comes in the poetry.
>
> Theirs is the story of longing for company on the Way. The searching, the meeting, the enjoyment of mysterious conversation, the wrenching away, and the transmutation of absence to another level of presence.[10]

Social roles can't compare with this. Whereas the Companion model invites us to go beyond outer forms, social roles do the opposite. They make us adapt to external circumstances—the culture and our place in it. Through social roles, cultures work out the quid pro quos for us. Roles offer prepackaged relating—help with the prices clearly marked. Adopting roles puts us in a dealing mind-set—"how do I have to behave to get what?" To advance ourselves financially, socially, professionally, or even spiritually, all we have to do is behave thus and so. Our story gets told in clichés, and we "forget completely what companionship is":

> Sometimes I forget completely
> what companionship is.
> Unconscious and insane, I spill sad
> energy everywhere. My story
> gets told in various ways: A romance,
> a dirty joke, a war, a vacancy.[11]

The good thing about roles is that we outgrow them. If a relationship exists only to barter, we don't need the relationship—nor do the others need us—once the deal is done: our "five-day buddies," our trading partners, leave us:

> All faces turn back into dirt.
> The moist-dry, hot-cold parts
> rejoin their kinfolk, and our spirits
> receive a letter from the world
> of pure intelligence. It says,
>
> > *So your five-day buddies left you!*
> > *Learn who your true friends are.*[12]

With Companions, we "rest from wanting," since the experience isn't about maneuvering to get something. Instead of being "that selfishness again"—the old quid pro quoing—we go on a "strange journey to the ocean of meanings," where the flow of meaning determines the course of our relationships:

> Don't give me back to my old companions.
> No friend but you. Inside you
> I rest from wanting. Don't let me
> be that selfishness again.[13]

*

Rise up nimbly and go on your strange journey
to the ocean of meanings where you become one of those.
From one terrace to another through clay banks,
washing your wings with watery silt,
follow your friends.[14]

Invisible Companions

Companions come in all shapes and sizes, and not all are visible. Rumi's cosmology includes many dimensions of beings, and invisible Companions are every bit as close, active, and helpful as the visible kind. Coleman Barks writes:

> Rumi often mentions the reality of a helpful in-knowing. Sometimes he calls it "the voice," sometimes a kind of "magnetism," a being-drawn together that friends feel. The *abdals* [the invisible beings in the hierarchy of saints] . . . are another level of helpers. Rumi is always clear about the collaborative nature of any action. Many beings, visible and invisible, are involved in what we do, an entire community.[15]

Nor is Rumi alone in this view. Socrates spoke of his Muse, who never told him what to do but always intervened to prevent him from doing something unwise. Shamans, the medicine people of indigenous cultures, work with spirits, guides, and power animals in their healing rituals. In their view, the invisible helpers are the ones with the power to heal and transform; shamans only provide the visible channels for healing energies to flow. Judaism, Christianity, and Islam describe invisible Companions as angels, who accompany us from birth to death, while Hinduism describes the invisible team as gods and deities.

But if angels, gods, and deities seem a bit magnificent for everyday confidants—Nora Ephron's film *Michael* goes a long way toward offsetting this image—there are always pookas to pal around with, the large and mischievous invisible animal-Companions of Celtic mythology. In the film *Harvey*, Elwood P. Dowd enjoyed the companionship of a six-foot invisible rabbit named Harvey. Instead of conforming to an ordinary state of unhappiness, Mr. Dowd, through his relationship with

Harvey, invited everyone else to live in a world of gracious regard that happened to have pookas in it.

However we conceive of invisible Companions, they're "all around you, bumping, trying to help," though it takes patience to sense their presence and hear "their singing":

> The world is an ocean. The body, a fish.
> Jonah is your soul, which cannot see the dawn,
> until you glorify God like Jonah did.
>
> Then you'll be released. There are spirit-fishes
> all around you, bumping, trying to help,
> but you can't see them.
>
> Listen to their singing. Hear how they praise,
> and be patient. Patience is your way to glory.[16]

Because of these invisible Companions, changes occur in our lives that don't lend themselves to outward explanations. Of millions of people, we're drawn to just the Companions we need—those whose quest dovetails with ours. Or visible Companions leave us, and though it may feel right for us to go our own ways, we can't explain why. "A hand shifts our birdcages around." "You can't see it, but . . . it's there":

> What draws Friends together
> does not conform to Laws of Nature.
> Form doesn't know about spiritual closeness.
> If a grain of barley approaches a grain of wheat,
> an ant must be carrying it. A black ant on black felt.
> You can't see it, but if grains go toward each other,
> it's there.
>
> A hand shifts our birdcages around.
> Some are brought closer. Some move apart.
> Do not try to reason it out. Be conscious
> of who draws you and who not.[17]

The Ultimate Source of Help

Just as visible Companions provide channels for invisible ones, so too both visible and invisible Companions provide channels for the ultimate source of help, the "Unseen Presence . . . that gives the gifts." Rumi perceives a rich multiplicity of helping Companions, but he also perceives them as emanating from one source. The origin is "Spirit," and "we're the opening and closing of our hands," or it's "Joy," and "we're all the different kinds of laughing":

> There is an Unseen Presence we honor
> that gives the gifts.
>
> You're Water. We're the millstone.
> You're Wind. We're the dust blown up into shapes.
> You're Spirit. We're the opening and closing
> of our hands. You're the Clarity.
> We're this language that tries to say it.
> You're the Joy. We're all the different kinds of laughing.
>
> Any movement or sound is a profession of faith,
> as the millstone grinding is explaining how it believes
> in the River! No metaphor can say this,
> but I can't stop pointing
> to the Beauty.
>
> Every moment and place says,
> "Put this design in Your Carpet!"[18]

However we describe the origin, it's God, the holomovement, the ultimate context from which all help comes.

> A famous saint once said
> that the meaning of the Name of Allah is,
> that worshipers should take refuge there.
> In times of sudden danger all people call out, *O my God!*
>
> Why would they keep doing this, if it didn't help?
> Only a fool keeps going back where nothing happens. . . .

All giving comes from There, no matter who
you think you put your open hand out
toward, it's That which gives.[19]

Help That's Freeing

God as the source of help nullifies the model of indebtedness once and
for all and transforms how we experience help, whether we're giving
or receiving it. On the receiving side, if people are agents of help to us
but not its source, then they're channels for things that aren't theirs to
possess. We may be grateful for the channels, but we don't become indebted to them, body and soul. Tracing help back to its origin keeps
our relationships free and happy. Sticky indebtedness doesn't infect
what's otherwise something wonderful—an act of kindness:

> Whenever some kindness comes to you, turn
> that way, toward the source of kindness.
>
> Love-things originate in the ocean.
> Restlessness leads to rest.[20]

Staying connected to the source of help, our inner mystics live like
"one of God's fish who receives what it needs directly from the ocean
around it":

> The day and the daily bread that comes
> are not to be worshipped for themselves.
>
> Praise the great heart within those,
> and the loving ache in yourself
> that's part of that.
>
> Be one of God's fish
> who receives what it needs
> directly from the ocean around it—
> food, shelter, sleep, medicine.[21]

On the giving side, if the capacity to help comes from the holo-ocean,
then the help we give doesn't belong to us either; we're stewards of it.

The things we assume to be ours and give as ours are borrowed goods, whether it's money, objects, talents, opportunities, ideas, energies, or even love. We're not the source. What fills our "wicker basket" doesn't come from us. If we try to live independently of the source, we'll come up empty:

> A wicker basket sank in the Ocean,
> and saw itself full of seawater, and decided
> it could live independently.
>
> It left the Ocean
> and not a drop stayed in it.
> But the Ocean took it back.
>
> For no reason, the Ocean took it back.
> For God's sake, stay near the sea![22]

Our inner Companions stay in the Ocean. Thanks to them, our models of relating shift, and we're happy to let the water flow in and out of our baskets freely. To do otherwise would take us out of the Ocean and "kill" us. By drinking from "the inspired spring," we join those who, moving in the open field of infinity, draw on the infinite:

> You have read about the inspired spring.
>
> Drink from there. Be companions with those
> whose lips are wet with that water.
>
> Others, even though they may be your father
> or your mother, they're your enemies.
> Leave, before they kill you!
>
> The pathless path opens
> whenever you genuinely say,
>
> *There is no Reality but God.*
> *There is only God.*[23]

An Ultimate though Ineffable Companion

Between Rumi and the mystic path, there's no way to avoid bringing God into the story. Nor would it make sense to leave God out. That would be like trying to discuss physics without mentioning energy or music without harmony. God is the bottom-line "Reality," the holo-movement ground that sustains everything—"all subsist, exist, in God":

> The whole world lives within a safeguarding: fish
> inside waves, birds held in the sky, the elephant,
> the wolf, the lion as he hunts, the dragon, the ant,
> the waiting snake, even the ground, the air,
> water, every spark floating up from the fire,
> all subsist, exist, in God. Nothing
> is ever alone for a single moment.[24]

Yet God isn't easy to discuss. It's not as if we all agree on what we're talking about. Fortunately, Rumi knows the difficulties. Instead of trying to pin down who or what God is, he starts from the first pillar of Islam: "There is no Reality but God. There is only God." Everything is a quest to find out what this means and how it transforms us. But if we want more than that—specific theories or doctrines, for instance—Rumi isn't much help:

> If anyone wants to know what "spirit" is,
> or what "God's fragrance" means,
> lean your head toward him or her.
> Keep your face there close.
> *Like this.*[25]

The reason Rumi is so cagey is that reality surpasses the words and concepts we use to talk about it—an insight as old as the first mystic thinkers. God isn't an image or idea in our heads; God is reality as it is. Language is useful to point us toward this reality, but the Unseen Presence is more:

God has said,
              "The images that come
with human language
do not correspond to me,
but those who love words
must use them to come near."

Just remember,
              it's like saying of the king,
"He is not a weaver."
                        Is that praise?
Whatever such a statement is,
words are on *that* level
of God-knowledge.[26]

From a purely visible perspective, the word *God* doesn't mean any-thing, since we can't point to some object and say that's God. But mys-tics don't think that way. Behind the visible they look for patterns, and behind the patterns orders, behind the orders principles, and behind all of it some underlying unity or wholeness. To the visible-only way of thinking, Rumi has this to say:

Who says the eternal being does not exist?
Who says the sun has gone out?

Someone who climbs up on the roof, and closes his eyes tight,
and says, *I don't see anything*.[27]

For mystics, visible-only thinking is like putting on goggles and then declaring that nothing exists except what's in front of us:

There are those that say, "Nothing lasts."
They're wrong. Every moment they say,
"If there were some other reality,
I would have seen it. I would know about it."

Because a child doesn't understand a chain of reasoning,
should adults give up being rational?

If reasonable people don't feel the presence of love
within the universe, that doesn't mean it's not there.[28]

Whatever God is, the reality behind the term is our most constant Companion, since we're never outside the holomovement. For Rumi, God is the Friend and Beloved that's closer to us than breath, nearer than the "big vein in our necks." Yet what does this mean? The Companion relationship is expansive by nature, but with God? It's hard to imagine. To feel that we're the friend of God and God of us, for instance, that the Whole purposes the greatest good adapted to us, that we have access to all the resources we need, that reality isn't dumb matter moved by blind chance but has consciousness, intention, and a plan of good that includes us: such implications of companionship with God free us to learn "what we really are." From that expansive ground, we grow:

Through companionship with the ground a grapevine
grows. It opens into the earth's darkness
and flies. It becomes selfless
in the presence of its origin and learns
what it really is.[29]

Accepting the ultimate as our Companion opens us to a passionate connectedness—a "burning" union—that frees us to express that unity as we see fit, to grow as the ground inspires us. We go beyond obeying people, institutions, or doctrines and set our sights on exploring reality, whatever it is. Rumi tells a story about Moses and a shepherd:

Moses heard a shepherd on the road praying,
                                        "God,
where are You? I want to help You, to fix Your shoes
and comb Your hair. I want to wash Your clothes
and pick the lice off. I want to bring You milk,
to kiss Your little hands and feet when it's time
for You to go to bed. I want to sweep Your room
and keep it neat. God, my sheep and goats

are Yours. All I can say, remembering You,
is *ayyyy* and *ahhhhhhhhh*."

       Moses could stand it no longer.
"*Who* are you talking to?"

      "The One who made us,
and made the earth and made the sky."

        "Don't talk about shoes
and socks with God! And what's this with *Your little hands
and feet*? Such blasphemous familiarity sounds like
you're chatting with your uncles.

       Only something that grows
needs milk. Only someone with feet needs shoes. Not God!
Even if you meant God's human representatives,
as when God said, 'I was sick, and you did not visit me,'
even then this tone would be foolish and irreverent.

Use appropriate terms. *Fatima* is a fine name
for a woman, but if you call a man *Fatima*,
it's an insult. Body-and-birth language
are right for us on this side of the river,
but not for addressing the Origin,

       not for Allah."

The shepherd repented and tore his clothes and sighed
and wandered out into the desert.

      A sudden revelation
came then to Moses. God's Voice:

     *You have separated Me
from one of my own. Did you come as a Prophet to unite,
or to sever?*

    *I have given each being a separate and unique way
of seeing and knowing and saying that knowledge.*

*What seems wrong to you is right for him.
What is poison to one is honey to someone else.*

*Purity and impurity, sloth and diligence in worship,
these mean nothing to Me.*

I am apart from all that.
Ways of worshipping are not to be ranked as better
or worse than one another.
                         Hindus do Hindu things.
The Dravidian Muslims in India do what they do.
It's all praise, and it's all right.

It's not Me that's glorified in acts of worship.
It's the worshippers! I don't hear the words
they say. I look inside at the humility.

That broke-open lowliness is the Reality,
not the language! Forget phraseology.
I want burning, burning.
                         Be Friends
with your burning. *Burn up your thinking*
and your forms of expression!
                         Moses,
those who pay attention to ways of behaving
and speaking are one sort.
                         Lovers who burn
are another."[30]

When the revelation concluded, Moses ran after the shepherd:

         . . . "I was wrong. God has revealed to me
that there are no rules of worship.
                         Say whatever
and however your loving tells you to. Your sweet blasphemy
is the truest devotion. Through you a whole world
is freed.
                         Loosen your tongue and don't worry what comes out.
It's all the Light of the Spirit."
                         The shepherd replied,
"Moses, Moses,
                         I've gone beyond even that.

You applied the whip and my horse shied and jumped
out of itself. The Divine Nature and my human nature
came together.
                    Bless your scolding hand and your arm.
I can't say what has happened.
                              What I'm saying now
is not my real condition. It can't be said."[31]

The Companion Within

The shepherd jumped into the deepest companionship: "The Divine
Nature and my human nature came together." To be Companions with
God is to be Companions with our own being, with the Ocean as it
"splashes inside" us:

When the Ocean surges,
don't let me just hear it.
Let it splash inside my chest![32]

Having the unseen Presence as a source of help can't mean being
dominated from without, because it's not without. When, to paraphrase Step Three of Alcoholics Anonymous, we turn our will and our
lives over to the Truth of all that is, we turn our will and our lives over
to the truth that's us as well—to "a hidden love-center in human beings" that we "savor and nourish ourselves with":

As when a baby stops nursing and grows interested
in solid food. As when seeds break open in the ground
and act differently.
                    There is a hidden love-center
in human beings that you will discover and savor
and nourish yourself with. That will be your food.[33]

This "hidden love-center" supplies us with a wisdom, guidance, and
encouragement that takes us by surprise, unaccustomed as we are to
having such a Friend so close. Invisible though it is, our inner Companion never ceases to come and help us:

My spirit saw how dull and down
I was and came and sat laughing

on my bed. Holding my brow,
"Sweetheart, I can't bear
to see you like this!"[34]

Learning to Accept Help—Surrender

The trick to benefitting from all the help at hand is learning to accept it,
but that's not easy. For one thing, we're not accustomed to trusting invisible sources. The invisible has its own timing, and that's hard to trust
when visible schedules demand action now:

Sheikh Ahmad was continually in debt.
He borrowed great sums from the wealthy
and gave it out to the poor dervishes of the world.
He built a Sufi monastery by borrowing,
and God was always paying his debts, turning sand
into flour for this Generous Friend. . . .

For years, until his death, he scattered seed profusely.
Even very near his death, with the signs of death clear,
he sat surrounded by creditors. The creditors in a circle,
and the great Sheikh in the center gently melting
into himself like a candle.

The creditors were so sour-faced with worry
that they could hardly breathe.

"Look at these despairing men," thought the Sheikh.
"Do they think God does not have four hundred gold dinars?"
Just at that moment a boy outside called,
                                    "Halvah, a sixth
of a dirhem for a piece! Fresh halvah!"
                                    Sheikh Ahmad,
with a nod of his head, directed the famulus
to go and buy the whole tray of halvah.

"Maybe if these creditors eat a little sweetness,
they won't look so bitterly on me."

The servant went to the boy, "How much for the whole lump
of halvah?"
                 "Half a dinar, and some change."

"Don't ask too much from Sufis, my son.
Half a dinar is enough."

The boy handed over the tray, and the servant brought it
to the Sheikh, who passed it among his creditor-guests.
"Please, eat, and be happy."

The tray was quickly emptied, and the boy asked the Sheikh
for his half a gold dinar.

"Where would I find such money? These men can tell you
how in debt I am, and besides, I am fast on my way
into non-existence."
                 The boy threw the tray on the floor
and started weeping loud and yelling,
                       "I wish
I had broken my legs before I came in here!
                           I wish
I'd stayed in the bathhouse today. You gluttonous,
plate-licking Sufis, washing your faces like cats!"

A crowd gathered. The boy continued, "O Sheikh,
my master will beat me if I come back without *any*thing."

The creditors joined in, "How could you do this?
You've devoured our properties, and now you add this
one last debt before you die.
                 Why?"

The Sheikh closes his eyes and does not answer.
The boy weeps until afternoon prayers. The Sheikh
withdraws underneath his coverlet,
                     pleased with everything,

pleased with Eternity, pleased with death,
                              and totally
unconcerned with all the reviling talk around him. . . .

At afternoon prayers a servant comes with a tray
from Hatim, a friend of Ahmad's, and a man
of great property. A covered tray.

The Sheikh uncovers the face of the tray, and on it
there are four hundred gold dinars, and in one corner,
another half a dinar wrapped in a piece of paper.

Immediately the cries of abasement, "O King of Sheikhs,
Lord of the Lords of Mystery! Forgive us.
We were bumbling and crazed. We were knocking lamps over.
We were . . . "
                    "It's all right. You will not be held
responsible for what you've said or done. The secret here
is that I asked God and the way was shown

that until the boy's weeping, God's merciful generosity
was not loosened.
                    Let the boy be like the pupil of your eye.
If you want to wear a robe of spiritual sovereignty,
let your eyes weep with the wanting."[35]

Thanks to our inner mystics, we have times when we trust the unseen source as the Sheikh did, but we also have times when we feel
closer to the boy and the creditors. When we do, the boy's desperate
weeping is the right response. It's true to where we are, and, as Rumi
says, it "loosens" "God's merciful generosity," broadcasting our need of
help to the unseen helpers.

Granted, the boy's desperate weeping isn't a place we like to go, so
much so that even if we're there, we'll pretend we're not. We don't like
it when the visible pushes us up against a wall and we see no way out.
It suggests things about us that the visible-minded consider bad: poor
judgment, mistakes, weakness, vulnerability. "What's the matter with
you, boy? You should know better than to trust those wily old Sufis!"

But worse, it's scary. Who enjoys the sinking feeling that we've chosen a road from which there's no return?

Yet as far as the mystic path is concerned, the wits-end place is closer to our reality than we realize, and acknowledging this place in us works like a potent medicine, connecting us with just the help we need. If we think we're on top of things, then we'll also think we need neither help nor Companions. We may as well stay Loners and stop the mystic journey at the second stage. But the path doesn't stop. In the dynamics of consciousness, our intense crying out creates a vacuum that both draws to us the help we need and prepares us to accept it. Feeling like the boy—"the total helplessness inside"—pushes us to a truly open consciousness, which is the essence of prayer:

> . . . pray the prayer
> that is the essence of every ritual: *God,*
> *I have no hope. I am torn to shreds.*
> *You are my first and my last*
> *and my only refuge.*
>
> Don't do daily prayers like a bird
> pecking its head up and down.
>
> Prayer is an egg.
> Hatch out
> the total helplessness
> inside.[36]

Admitting our profound need of help raises the issue of surrender, which is the meaning of the word *Islam*. As a religion, Islam doesn't say we're miserable wretches born in sin, but it does say we have no existence apart from God—"There is no Reality but God. There is only God." "All subsist, exist, in God." Without the ocean, what existence has a wave? The wave may think it's rolling along on its own, but it needs more ocean-help than it knows:

> You are so weak. Give up to Grace.
> The ocean takes care of each wave

till it gets to shore.
You need more help than you know.[37]

     *

We are beggars. Everything a beggar has
was given to him by the Rich and All-Sufficient.
We're total darkness. God is light.
Sun comes in our houses and mixes with shadows.
Climb out on the roof if you want more light.
If you don't want to live depressed any longer,
move into the sun. The sun.[38]

When Rumi describes us as "beggars" and "total darkness," he's not saying that we're no good but rather that all that we are comes from God. Buddhism states something similar, only without the God language: we have no separate self—no "own being"—apart from the movements of consciousness. Or in physics language, things don't exist in isolation; fields form things. That's as true for egos, personalities, and souls as it is for atoms and planets.

Surrender is our giving ourselves over to this truth and letting it change how we live. Companions surrender a notion that can be a temptation for Loners; namely, that we exist as self-sufficient, separate beings, expressed in an everyday way as believing we can get along without help. As we abandon this notion, we realize how big the idea of surrender is and how profoundly it changes our concepts of existence:

Science and theology would be just whims of the wind,
if you knew full surrender.

These beautiful world-birds would seem like flies,
if that wing-shadow fell across you.

The famous drums would sound like tapping sticks.
If that dawn rose, you'd be released
from whatever is holding you.

What you thought was ahead
would be behind.

One word, one *letter,* from that book,
and you'd understand.[39]

Trying always to be on top of things doesn't serve us as well as we'd imagine. Not only does it render Companions unnecessary, but more it obscures our true dependence on the holomovement. Surrender suggests we "stop swimming so hard" and give our Companions a chance:

What are these terms *wakefulness* and *sleep*?
Don't answer. Let God answer.
Don't speak, so the Speakers can.
Not a word, so Sun-Light can say
what has never been in a book, or said.
Don't *try* to put it into words,
and the Spirit will do that through you,
in spite of you,

> beside you,

> > among you.

Stop swimming so hard,

> > and climb in the boat

with Noah.[40]

Not that surrender leaves us blithering idiots, or as it's said, "disempowered." Rather it gives us a gentleness of spirit, a humility, and a flexibility before life and the big picture. Surrender says there's more going on with everything, ourselves included, than we can possibly imagine, so why not admit this and allow ourselves the inner openness to say *"Lead us"*?

Be helpless and dumbfounded,
unable to say yes or no.

Then a stretcher will come
from grace to gather us up.

We are too dulleyed to see the beauty.
If we say *Yes we can*, we'll be lying.

If we say *No, we don't see it,*
that *No* will behead us
and shut tight our window into spirit.

So let us not be sure of anything,
beside ourselves, and only that, so
miraculous beings come running to help.

Crazed, lying in a zero-circle, mute,
we will be saying finally,
with tremendous eloquence, *Lead us.*

When we've totally surrendered to that beauty,
we'll become a mighty kindness.[41]

The Free Flow of Need and Help

For Rumi, the free flow of need and help, of helplessness and helper, is
as natural to the cosmic order as yin and yang are in Taoist philosophy.
Haves and have-nots are part of the cosmic rhythm not as social groups
but as polarities in consciousness with a dynamic flow between them.

To seek only the have side throws the cosmic order out of balance
or, more accurately, throws us out of balance with the cosmic order.
When, for instance, Socrates said the beginning of wisdom is to know
that we don't know, he was reintroducing the have-not side of knowing to the Sophists' emphasis on have. For knowledge to grow into wisdom, we need both. So, too, with need and help. In the cosmic order,
the presence of one draws the presence of the other:

Whatever comes, comes from a need,
a *sore distress*, a hurting want. . . .

And every need brings in what's needed.
Pain bears its cure like a child.

Having nothing produces provisions.
Ask a difficult question,
and the marvelous answer appears.

Build a ship, and there'll be water
to float it. The tender-throated
infant cries and milk drips
from the mother's breast.

Be thirsty for the ultimate water,
and then be ready for what will
come pouring from the spring.[42]

Just as we'd throw the cosmic order out of balance if we only want yang and reject yin, so also we'd gum up the free flow of helping if we only want to be a have/helper and can't abide the experience of have-not, of needing help. The helping universe requires both. To participate in that universe—to honor the two sides—we have to be willing to "cry out":

Give your weakness
to One Who Helps.

Crying out loud and weeping are great resources.
A nursing mother, all she does
is wait to hear her child.

Just a little beginning-whimper,
and she's there.

God created the child, that is, your wanting,
so that it might cry out, so that milk might come.

Cry out! Don't be stolid and silent
with your pain. Lament! And let the milk
of Loving flow into you.[43]

The more we cry out from our souls—cry out that we don't know what to do with our lives, cry out that we don't know how to help someone we love who's in pain, cry out that we don't know what's happening to our planet, cry out that we don't know where to begin to help ourselves and our world—the more profoundly we experience our need, and the more help comes our way. "Where lowland is, that's where water goes." The crying out triggers help's flow.

Keeping track of the help that follows—who helps whom and how much—puts cotton in our ears, so that we don't hear "the sphere-music." By tossing out the scorecard, Companions listen to the cosmic flow of need and help and give themselves over to it, knowing that, from an invisible perspective, need and help are simply two sides of one reality in action:

> A dragon was pulling a bear into its terrible mouth.
>
> A courageous man went and rescued the bear.
> There are such helpers in the world, who rush to save
> anyone who cries out. Like Mercy itself,
> they run toward the screaming.
>
> And they can't be bought off.
> If you were to ask one of those, "Why did you come
> so quickly?" He or she would say, "Because I heard
> your helplessness."
> Where lowland is,
> that's where water goes. All medicine wants
> is pain to cure.
> And don't just ask for one mercy.
> Let them flood in. Let the sky open under your feet.
> Take the cotton out of your ears, the cotton
> of consolations, so you can hear the sphere-music.[44]

Learning what it is to be true Companions to each other; learning how many Companions we have; learning to participate in the helping universe in a way that expands our freedom; learning to cry for help when we need it; learning that crying for help isn't a failing but part of the cosmic order—all these things that the Companion archetype teaches are necessary for the next three stages which focus on soul and inner purification: Soul Searcher, Releaser, and Healer.

4

Going Within

ARCHETYPE   *Soul Searcher*
MYSTIC JOURNEY   *Entering the Soul's Dark Night*

Pulled in Two Directions

Moving in a Companion atmosphere changes our self-awareness. It awakens memories of feeling different about ourselves—of not needing to measure or calculate, of being accepted as we are and not having to put on fronts to keep that acceptance. The personalities we've developed for quid pro quoing in families, schools, jobs, and the culture no longer seem necessary. We can be freer than that, and once we've had a taste of what it's like to interact more freely, we find ourselves rethinking what it is to be us.

On one hand, it's liberating to experience ourselves in a more open context. Instead of feeling like dried-up wicker baskets vying for drops of water, we slip into the Ocean and have all the water we need. With the holomovement as our Companion, the habits, roles, and defenses that go with the marketplace model become unnecessary.

On the other hand, we're still in a culture whose dominant paradigm is anything but oceanic. In line with its outward orientation, we assume that we must build a strong ego and fortify it with knowledge, accomplishments, and possessions to demonstrate our worth. Presenting ourselves as separate beings is both what we do and what's expected.

There's truth to both perceptions, yet it's not clear how to bring them together. For our mystics' sensibilities, our culturally packaged personalities weigh heavily on us—too many expectations about how we should be. In cages of separateness, we behave at our worst, full of fears. The walls that go up between us lead to misunderstandings, competitions, jealousies, and conflicts.

Yet regardless of the problems it causes us, we nonetheless perceive ourselves as separate creatures, and we're not sure we'd like to give that up. Our sense of separateness may get us into trouble, but it also makes up who we are in time, space, and society.

The gap between these two perceptions—our ocean-being and our cultural persona—precipitates an inner crisis. Sometimes it erupts as upheavals in relationships or jobs as we try to escape the cages, but it can also cook behind the scenes as creeping frustration and unhappiness. Pulled in opposite directions, we start questioning what we're doing here: Who is this creature called *us*?

> We're like the four different birds,
> that each had one leg tied in
> with the other birds.
>
> A flopping bouquet of birds!
> Death releases the binding, and they fly off,
> but before that, their pulling is our pain.
>
> Consider how the soul must be,
> in the midst of these tensions,
> feeling its own exalted pull.
>
> *My longing is more profound.*
> *These birds want the sweet green herbs*
> *and the water running by.*
>
> *I want the infinite! I want wisdom.*
> *These birds want orchards and meadows*
> *and vines with fruit on them.*
>
> *I want a vast expansion.*
> *They want profit and the security*
> *of having enough food.*[1]

One obvious way to resolve the crisis is to ignore our mystical side. The crisis arises only insofar as we feel mystic yearnings: "*I want the infinite! I want wisdom. . . . I want a vast expansion.*" If we suppress that part of us—if we dismiss the mystic pull as naive or unrealistic, which cultural conditioning claims it is—then there's no crisis. Our bargaining self is all we know.

Perhaps we can avoid the crisis by doing as the culture advises, but our inner mystics aren't convinced. They don't go away so easily—we still feel their yearnings for soul, love, and freedom—and the crisis keeps coming back. Who we are in our mystic bones doesn't jibe with who we are in a bargaining culture. The only way to sort out our "flopping bouquet of birds" is to go within, to draw on the archetype of Soul Searcher and explore our inner landscape.

The Soul's Dark Night

Going within is an ancient discipline, recommended by virtually every spiritual tradition. The Dalai Lama, for instance, suggests that we spend as much time exploring inner space as we do outer space. He characterizes Tibetan Buddhism as the practice of working on ourselves—confronting the self in all its forms and how it gives rise to experience.

That's how Buddhism brought peace to the fierce warrior culture of Tibet twelve centuries ago: working on ourselves is better than working on everyone else. Not only does it avoid the distress that comes with meddling, proselytizing, and attempting to put others right, but it's a better use of energies. As the Roman Stoic Epictetus argued, changing ourselves is within our power, whereas changing others isn't. This was Gandhi's method: the battle lies within. In the middle of complex relationships, inner practice comes as a relief. We can do our inner work, and that's the most effective course.

Even so, working on ourselves is scary. Mystical literature refers to inner searching as the "dark night of the soul," so named by sixteenth-century mystic John of the Cross in the poetry he started writing in prison—and it's not called "dark night" for nothing. Our Soul Searchers call everything into question. Beliefs and practices we thought we'd never doubt start wavering in our minds, whereas feelings and perceptions we thought we'd never have emerge as our truth. The sifting of what's us and what's not can feel like "sheer terror":

A self-sacrificing way,
but also a warrior's way, and not
for brittle, easily-broken, glass-bottle people.

The soul is tested here by sheer terror,
as a sieve sifts and separates
genuine from fake.[2]

Part of the terror comes from what arises inwardly. After years of being outwardly focused, feelings surface that have waited a long time for a hearing. Once the door is open, the gamut of emotions pours through. We can be happy one moment, depressed the next, peacefully magnanimous then ready for blood:

The inner being of a human being
is a jungle. Sometimes wolves dominate,
sometimes wild hogs. Be wary when you breathe!

At one moment gentle, generous qualities,
like Joseph's, pass from one nature to another.
The next moment vicious qualities
move in hidden ways. . . .

At every moment a new species rises in the chest—
now a demon, now an angel, now a wild animal.[3]

It's as if we're sitting on a Pandora's box, and we wonder if we'll be able to cope with the "demons" and "wild animals" inside. If roles and cultural conditioning keep the lid on, maybe they're not such a bad idea—maybe we can get by without "soul-water." In the dark night of the soul, though, we realize this will never work. We can't ignore what's within, no matter what's there, because the inner is our "living water." Let night come, Rumi says, since that's when "we night-thieves go to work" and take the lid off:

People focus on death and this material earth.
They have doubts about soul-water.
Those doubts can be reduced!

Use night to wake your clarity.
Darkness and the living water are lovers.
Let them stay up together.

When merchants eat their big meals and sleep
their dead sleep, we night-thieves go to work.[4]

Going Within:
Not about Judging or Rejecting Ourselves

Fears about going within also come from the judgments we make about our inner content. We're allowed to think and feel only in ways that are considered good. Pain, sadness, regret, anger, fear, confusion: not only do we find these inner experiences unpleasant but worse we judge ourselves negatively for having them. When we discover these feelings within, we feel bad because of the feelings, and we feel worse because we have them. Only bad people have such feelings, we think, people with some flaw, defect, or weakness.

Judging our inner content deepens the darkness, but it's not what going within is meant to do. Going within seeks the value of what's there, whereas judging rejects it. If our souls have been traded for visibles, pain, regret, and anger are precisely how our souls feel, and to judge these feelings as bad is to reject our souls' genuine experience. It denies what's most essentially us:

I must have been incredibly simple or drunk or insane
to sneak into my own house and steal money,
to climb over the fence and take my own vegetables.
But no more. I've gotten free of that ignorant fist
that was pinching and twisting my secret self.[5]

Whatever we find within is an expression of our souls' dynamics. Soul Searchers assume that our souls have their own healing principle, or in Viktor Frankl's terms, their own meaning-driven logic. What we feel, we feel for a reason. Pain hurts, as does anger and grief, but they're not bad; they express what our souls feel. Like the have and have-not of help, what's called good and bad serve as poles of our inner process.

Both give us feedback. Both tell stories that come from the invisible levels of our being. To feel our souls' "enthusiasm," we have to embrace the spectrum and "jump off that good-and-bad":

> Stretch your arms and take hold the cloth of your clothes
> with both hands. The cure for pain is in the pain.
> Good and bad are mixed. If you don't have both,
> you don't belong with us.[6]

*

> Don't analyze this enthusiasm!
>
> The wheel that lifts some up
> and drags others down,
> we're not riding it anymore.
>
> We've jumped off that
> good-and-bad.[7]

Allowing only what's considered good freezes the soul's dynamics. Rejecting some part of ourselves is a form of self-hatred, and if we were to step back and observe it, we'd see it as such. We'd hate that hidden habit of self-rejection "openly":

> You say you have no sexual longing any more.
> You're one with the one you love.
>
> This is dangerous.
> Don't believe that I have a love like that.
>
> If one day you see a picture of how you think,
> you'll hate yourself, openly.[8]

Of course, we get habits of self-rejection honestly. Everything about the culture—parenting rules, school structures, job hierarchies, religious doctrines, media subliminals—conveys the message: who we are is unacceptable, and only when we're remade in the images that families, schools, religions, employers, the media, and the culture set for us will we become acceptable. That we're prone to judge and reject our-selves merely reflects what we've experienced.

Going within, however, requires that we leave behind these cul-turally instilled messages. The way of the Soul Searcher is beyond judg-ments, "beyond ideas of wrongdoing and rightdoing." That's where our souls agree to meet us, and from there they take us to completely new levels of self-awareness:

> Out beyond ideas of wrongdoing and rightdoing,
> there is a field. I'll meet you there.
>
> When the soul lies down in that grass,
> the world is too full to talk about.
> Ideas, language, even the phrase *each other*
> doesn't make any sense.[9]

The Method: Unconditional Self-Acceptance

Because habits of judging and rejecting ourselves are so ingrained, though, our Soul Searcher's method of going within seems impossible at first—beyond dark night to black void—because it calls us to do the culturally unthinkable, namely, to accept ourselves, Pandora's box and all. Not rejecting our inner material is one thing, but going the whole nine yards and embracing everything we feel as an integral part of our souls' journey—that's another.

Self-acceptance is culturally discouraged, even taboo, because in-sofar as we accept ourselves, we become free agents answering to our inner truth—a quality that's made mystics unpopular with religious and political authorities since the rise of patriarchies. Mystics have paid for accepting their inner truth with imprisonment, torture, and death.

The acceptance we don't find in cultural institutions, we do feel with Companions. Among true Companions, acceptance is a given. We don't need to deny our inner truth to get it. Even cosmically, the mys-tical sense of God as Companion affirms us as we are in the universe, contrary to the patriarchal image of God as Judge or punishing Parent.

Our Soul Searchers appeal to our Companion experiences to model the unconditional acceptance we can cultivate for ourselves.

Unconditional acceptance is our Soul Searchers' method, because for our inner mystics, what's within is holy ground. There may be pain and rage in there, but these feelings are not our enemies. Our inner world is attuned to the holomovement and so contains "a guide from beyond." Once we accept what's within unconditionally, everything we experience becomes part of our souls' story, and every thought and emotion connects us more deeply with who we are. Instead of censoring the help our inner world offers, our Soul Searchers "welcome and entertain them all":

> This being human is a guest-house.
> Every morning a new arrival.
>
> A joy, a depression, a meanness,
> some momentary awareness comes
> as an unexpected visitor.
>
> Welcome and entertain them all!
> Even if they're a crowd of sorrows,
> who violently sweep your house
> empty of its furniture,
>
> still, treat each guest honorably.
> He may be clearing you out
> for some new delight.
>
> The dark thought, the shame, the malice,
> meet them at the door laughing,
> and invite them in.
>
> Be grateful for whoever comes,
> because each has been sent
> as a guide from beyond.[10]

Naturally, happy feelings are easier to "invite in" than "mean thoughts" or "sourness." Yet for Soul Searchers, our inner dynamics use both poles of the spectrum, the high yang and the low yin, to work out our souls' purpose: "What seems to be keeping you from joy may be what leads you to joy." Depression, for instance, may not be a failure of our psyches but a time to inwardly restructure. Breakdown comes only when we reject our need to move into a yin/inward-turning phase, which is when our psyches turn up the volume.

For Rumi, as for Eastern meditative philosophies, emotions represent phases of our souls' self-evolving dynamics, just as physical sensations represent phases of our bodies' self-regenerating powers. The more we embrace our souls' dynamics in all phases—go within and accept what's there—the more powerfully our souls operate in us as "a healing root":

> Pay close attention to your mean thoughts.
>
> That sourness may be a blessing,
> as an overcast day brings rain for the roses
> and relief to dry soil.
>
> Don't look so sourly on your sourness!
> It may be it's carrying what you most deeply need
> and want. What seems to be keeping you from joy
> may be what leads you to joy.
>
> Don't call it a dead branch.
> Call it the live, moist root.
>
> Don't always be waiting to see
> what's behind it. That wait and see
> poisons your Spirit.
>
> Reach for it.
> Hold your meanness to your chest
> as a healing root,
> and be through with waiting.[11]

Accepting our inner experience means accepting where we are right now, even if it's a dark night of upheaval. Wishing ourselves to be elsewhere—thinking we should be better or feel better—is self-rejecting. From our mystics' perspective, where we are inwardly is how the holomovement is unfolding at this moment in time and space. A story attributed to Shams and which he told for "the inner meaning" teaches the wisdom of accepting where we are as "the best place" to be:

> A great caravan arrived at a certain place where they found no habitation and no water. There was a deep well, but no bucket and no rope. To test for fresh water, they tied a kettle to a rope of their own and let it down. It struck something, and they pulled, but the kettle broke away. They sent down another and lost it too. After that they lowered thirsty volunteers from the caravan, but they also disappeared.
>
> There was a wise man there. He said, "I will go down." He was nearly to the bottom when a terrible dark creature appeared. "I can never escape from you," said the man to the monster, "but I hope at least to stay aware, so I can see what's happening to me."
>
> "Don't tell me long stories! You're my prisoner. You'll never leave unless you answer one question."
>
> "Ask it."
>
> "Where is the best place?"
>
> The wise man reflected, "I am totally helpless here. If I say Baghdad or some other beautiful place, it may be that I will insult his hometown by not mentioning it." So he replied, "The best place for someone to live is where he feels at home. If that's a hole in the middle of the earth, then that's it."
>
> "Well said. You are a rare human being. Because of your blessing, I'll set the others free in your care and give you authority over the world. I'll take no more prisoners, and I'll release the waters of this well."[12]

Going within and accepting what's there, we leave the Critic, Judge, and Moralist behind. We don't even judge the self-rejection that's kept us "unconscious." We go within to "feel the motions of tenderness" and to "listen to the sound of waves within you," whether they're crashing or gently lapping:

> Why should we grieve that we've been sleeping?
> It doesn't matter how long we've been unconscious.

We're groggy, but let the guilt go.
Feel the motions of tenderness
around you, the buoyancy.[13]

*

Give up subtle thinking, the twofold, threefold
multiplication of mistakes. Listen to
the sound of waves within you.[14]

Seeking What's Hidden Within

With the method of unconditional self-acceptance, our Soul Searchers
explore our inner lives. Whereas our visible forms usually get most of
our attention, it's our invisible side that gives rise to them. The unseen
is the greater, because it's generative, the powerhouse behind the visible. To know our inner side is to know our essence, "the original cause":

A True Human Being is the essence,
the original cause.

The world and the universe
are secondary effects.

Don't trade yourself for something worth less!
Existence is in service to you.

And yet you look in books for knowledge.
Ridiculous.

You buy halvah to have some sweetness.
Absolutely absurd!

Everything you want and need
is inside you.

What is wine?
What is music?
What is sex?

When you look to those for delight,
it is as though Venus, the source
of poetry and song and all feasting,
came and begged to have a cup
of the raw, bitter wine that
people drink on the streets.

You are the unconditioned spirit
trapped in conditions,
the sun in eclipse.[15]

For all our inner powers, we'd think soul-searching would be a culturally supported activity, but it's not. The cultural bias interprets self-reflection as self-involvement, self-acceptance as narcissism, and inner work as a nonproductive waste of time. Good, healthy people don't need inner work; they're too busy handling the real job of life, which is outward. In this cultural climate, no wonder our inner lives aren't known:

No intellect denies that you are,
but no one gives in completely to that.

This is not a place where you are not,
yet not a place where you are seen.[16]

*

Our eyes do not see you,
but we have this excuse: Eyes
see surface, not reality,
though we keep hoping,
in this lovely place.[17]

Nonetheless, our souls "keep hoping" to be known, because they're manifestations of the holomovement—God's "Hidden Treasure"—and they come into existence out of God's "desire to be known." Reflecting this origin, our souls have purposes that they want known as well. What's hidden in us wants out:

> The forms and the creatures have a purpose.
> God said, *I was a Hidden Treasure,*
> *and I desired to be known.*
>
> Manifestation contains that Desire
> to be known. Like a deep truth
> inside a lie, like the taste of butter
> in buttermilk, that's how Spirit
> is held in form.[18]

With these poems, Rumi sketches the hidden dynamics that give rise to who we are. We're "unconditioned spirit," but we're also "held in form." We're moving with the Ocean, but we're also manifesting as specific waves with specific purposes. Our Soul Searchers explore this hidden process—how our forms emerge out of formlessness and what shapes our forms as we go.

Perception Follows Filters

Coming into form has to do with focusing the holomovement, or with the holomovement focusing itself, by using filters. From a mystical perspective, rocks, plants, animals, humans—the whole world and universe—function as different filters for the holomovement. Through different ways of filtering, all creation brings reality's infinite nature into focus.

Consider humans: our minds, bodies, and personalities filter infinite reality. The holomovement being a bit much to swallow, we bring it into focus in a two-legged, cultural, racial, gender way and then in our own personal ways, so that we have some sense of what's going on. Maybe from another level, we come into being and filter reality as we do so that the holomovement can know itself through the incredible diversity of all of us. Mystics tend to think so. Whatever, our very existence functions as a filter of reality, screening the invisible brilliance so that it becomes visible without being overwhelming:

> The universe and the light of the stars come through me.
> I am the crescent moon put up
> over the gate to the festival.[19]

*

The body itself is a screen
to shield and partially reveal
the light that's blazing
inside your presence.[20]

Through our ways of "filtering spirit," we bring "furniture to this invisible place, so we can live here." In other words, we develop a shared language of forms that creates consensus reality, which we then use to learn and evolve:

Days are sieves to filter spirit,
reveal impurities, and too,
show the light of some who throw
their own shining into the universe.[21]

＊

Since we've seen each other, a game goes on.
Secretly I move, and you respond.
You're winning, you think it's funny.

But look up from the board now, look how
I've brought in furniture to this invisible place,
so we can live here.[22]

According to the filters we use, some facets of reality come into focus and others not. With survival-of-the-fittest categories, for instance, we perceive life, especially economic life, as a brutal struggle. With other categories—for example, sharing the earth as stewards who work together for a common good—we perceive life's challenge differently. Our filters determine which:

Know that created beings are as diverse as Z
and A. From one perspective unified.
From another, they seem opposites.

To one being, resurrection is laughter.
To another, it's a deadly judging-time,
when all frauds will be exposed.[23]

＊

To an Egyptian, the Nile looks bloody.
To an Israelite, clear.
What is a highway to one is disaster to the other.[24]

Our experience of reality follows our filters. Because of our diverse filtering systems, we perceive one reality many ways. To us, tables and chairs look solid and don't move; to a quantum physicist, they're empty space filled with high-energy particles flying about, while to Rumi, they "have knowledge" and "make decisions":

For you, it may be the middle of the night.
For me, dawn is very near. To my eyes,
every night looks like daytime.

To you, this gate feels like iron,
but to the hands of a great artisan
it feels workable like wax.

To you, a mountain is solid matter piled up.
To David, a mountain is a master-musician
he can learn from. To you, a column
is inanimate stone. To Muhammed,
it is a friend about to surrender to God,
that alive! To some, the particles
of this world seem dead, but they're not.
They have knowledge. They make decisions![25]

Inward Filters Projected Outward

If one reality appears so different relative to our filters, though, how much of our experience comes from our filters and how much reflects reality? This question is as old as ancient Hindu thinkers and as modern as philosopher Immanuel Kant or physicist Werner Heisenberg. Kant argued that everything we perceive is shaped by our filters—our "categories"—time, space, energy, and mass being some of the most basic. We don't know reality as it is in itself; we know it only as our filters package it for us. Hindu thinkers came to much the same conclusion millennia ago, as have physicists ever since Einstein.

If that's so, then reflecting on our filters and how they give form to our experience is the most important work we can do. Otherwise, though we're in the holomovement—the Ocean—we perceive ourselves as separate from it, not realizing that our filters make it seem that way. We believe that the filter-packaged world is all there is and our filter-packaged forms are all we are:

> Mad with thirst, he can't drink from the stream
> running so close by his face. He's like a pearl
> on the deep bottom, wondering, inside his shell,
> "Where's the Ocean?"
> His mental questionings
> form the barrier. His physical eyesight
> bandages his knowing. Self-consciousness
> plugs his ears.[26]

> *

> An ant drags its one grain fearfully, blind
> to the vastness of the threshing floor it walks on.
> The owner of the harvest looks down at the trembling ant.

> "Hey, how about this grain over here, or this?
> Why are you so devoted to that particular one?"

> This is how we are before we realize
> that we are not this body.[27]

> *

> . . . A lover of world-things
> has put himself in just such a box.
> Though he appears to be free, he can see nothing
> but the inside of his chosen chest.
> He moves from tomb to tomb.[28]

Soul Searchers break out of the closed worlds—"tombs"—that filters create by observing the relation between filters and our perceptions. Filters are the original spin doctors. Reality appears the way they spin it:

Many people travel to Syria and Iraq
and meet only hypocrites.

Others go all the way to India
and see just merchants buying and selling.

Others go to Turkestan and China
and find those countries filled
with sneak-thieves and cheats.

We always see the qualities
that are living in us.[29]

Knowing the relation between behind-the-scenes filters and per-
ceived experience is where mysticism proves most practical. If certain
filters make reality look a certain way, then we can't change that way
of experiencing reality—as filled with competition, hostility, and greed,
for instance—until we change our filters, the ones doing the packaging.
Our perspective must first shift, otherwise we keep seeing the same filters projected everywhere:

. . . To change,
a person must face the dragon of his appetites
with another dragon, the life-energy
of the soul."
When that's not strong,
the world seems to be full of people
who have your own fears and wantings.

As one thinks the room is spinning
when he's whirling around.[30]

*

You're seeing things reversed
as from the top of a pear tree,
the pear tree of phenomena.

All you see from there is a thorn thicket
full of scorpions. When you climb down,

you'll see a crowd of rosy children
with their nurses.[31]

As advertisers, politicians, and the media are quick to notice, we can use filters to play with other people's perceptions—to give reality a spin that serves our agenda. Rumi has a story to illustrate, one that's by no means his earthiest:

> Once there was a woman
> who wanted to make love with her lover
> in the presence of her gullible husband.
> She says to him,
> "Lucky you, I'm going to climb
> the tree and gather some fruit."
> In the top of the tree
> she starts screaming and pointing at her husband,
> "Who is that woman you're lying on top of?"
> "You've lost your mind," says the husband.
> "I'm standing here by myself."
> "I see what you're doing,
> you humping bastard!"
> "Come down," he says,
> "You're getting senile. I'll pick the fruit."
>
> She climbs down, and he climbs up. Immediately
> she and her lover begin what they enjoy.
> "Hey whore, what's going on?"
> "Don't be silly,"
> she says from underneath. "I'm here by myself.
> It must be the tree making the illusion.
> When I was up there, I saw things just as weird.
> Climb down, so you can see right."[32]

If filters generate our experience of reality by spinning it, then we're never sure how much of an experience reflects our filters and how much reality as it is. What's coming to us from where? Is it all our own inner stuff being reflected back to us, or are we dealing with a reality beyond our filters?

Faced with this dilemma, Soul Searchers turn within. We can't resolve the dilemma until we first look at our filters, and even then we can't know with certainty, since filters operate on many levels. Given this inevitable uncertainty, we adopt the working assumption that everything we perceive has some relation to our filters. That way, we keep working on ourselves—reflecting on our filters and recognizing the spin they give things:

> You're like a child that has turned round and round,
> and now you think the house is turning.[33]

It may be, as Rumi suggests, that far more of our experience reflects our filters than we realize. When we comment on people and things, for instance, we think we're talking about something "out there," but we're really giving voice to what's "in here":

> If someone's trickery seems charming to you,
> remember he is only *your* saint, not a real one.
> Someone who is like you will often sound prophetic.[34]

>   *

> What the sayer of Praise is really praising is
> himself, by saying implicitly,
> "My eyes are clear."

> Likewise, someone who criticizes is criticizing
> himself, saying implicitly, "I can't see very well
> with my eyes so inflamed."[35]

For our Soul Searchers, projecting our inner filters outward is a help. By doing so, we have a mechanism for seeing them—for making invisible filters visible. What psychologists call *projection* is simply our psyches' mechanism for uncovering what's within. Once we get the hang of how our souls use projection to bring our filters to light, we make the connection, and our Soul Searchers get busy investigating filters that "we sometimes know, and then not":

> Water, stories, the body,
> all the things we do, are mediums
> that hide and show what's hidden.
>
> Study them,
> and enjoy this being washed
> with a secret we sometimes know,
> and then not.[36]

Beyond Filters to Our Souls

As useful as filters are, though, we're more than our filters. Personalities, professions, bodies, and roles all serve as filters for us, but they're not us. Our "daylight" is beyond thoughts and words, "before thinking and imagining." Compared to our souls who draw on the whole, filters get wearisome—they trap us in the same projected patterns, and "thirsty" ones at that:

> Thoughts take form with words,
> but this daylight is beyond and before
> thinking and imagining. Those two,
> they are so thirsty, but this gives smoothness
> to water. Their mouths are dry, and they are tired.[37]

Our origins being in formlessness, our essence isn't bound by forms. When we tire of our filters' projected worlds, our inner mystics go back to our origins and explore new ways of coming into form. We're the entire coming-into-form process, and the filters we use are but one phase of that activity.

It's as if the holomovement is a river and our souls specific currents. In this analogy, filters may be the rocks that cause ripples so we can see the currents better, but the currents are more than the rocks they flow around. Why reduce ourselves to rocks—to gender, family, economic, professional, religious, or political filters—when they're "dust-motes" compared to the reality we are?

> You are the whole ocean.
> Why send out for a sip of dew?
>
> It's like the sun asking for help with shining
> from a dust-mote that only sparkles
> a moment in an open window.[38]

Identifying with our filters obscures our souls' greater-than-filters reality. Confining ourselves to filter-defined images is like groping "in a dark lane" or washing "our eyes with blood":

> Imagining is like feeling around
> in a dark lane, or washing
> your eyes with blood.
>
> You *are* the truth
> from foot to brow. Now,
> what else would you like to know?[39]

As Rumi says, "You *are* the truth," and filters are just different "ways of talking" about it. The words don't matter compared to the meaning:

> We have this way of talking, and we have another.
> Apart from what we wish and what we fear may happen,
> we are alive with other life, as clear stones
> take form in the mountain.[40]

Keeping Filters Fluid

Accepting ourselves as more than our filters makes it easier to change them. We put filters on like clothes, but we can take them off again and still be us. Here's where the method of unconditional self-acceptance comes in handy. By accepting our feelings without judging or rejecting them, we get a clear reading on the fit between our souls and our filters.

If, for instance, we're feeling pain, anger, or frustration, chances are our souls aren't happy with the filters we're using. The more we observe our feelings and accept their genuine response to our filters, the more fluidly we move with our souls and follow their lead on making filter shifts. We "give up opinions on all matters" and "become the reed flute for your breath":

> When I see you and how you are,
> I close my eyes to the other.
> For your Solomon's seal I become wax
> throughout my body. I wait to be light.
> I give up opinions on all matters.
> I become the reed flute for your breath.[41]

Since our filters color everything, nothing could be more important than having ones that serve our souls. If our souls want to explore new dimensions of meaning, for instance, but our filters tie us back to decades-old meaning, we won't be happy. Or if our souls say we're ready to do inner healing but our filters stand in the way, we're in for a rough inner ride.

Staying attuned to our souls is the key. Unconditional self-acceptance—coming and sitting "in front of" our souls as we "would at an altar"—opens us to what our souls have to say and how they intend to guide us in managing our filters. In their presence, we find ourselves breaking "every promise" we had with our filters. The filter-shifting that follows makes us either "laugh out loud" or "explode in pieces," as the stones of our filter prisons fall away:

> I came and sat in front of you
> as I would at an altar.
> Every promise I made before
> I broke when I saw you.[42]
>
> *
>
> Someone who sees you and does not laugh out loud,
> or fall silent, or explode in pieces,

is nothing more than the cement
and stone of his own prison.[43]

Not that we give up filters altogether. As long as we're involved with focusing the holomovement, we need filters; they're our means of focusing. Even though our filters are never absolute or final—how could they be, since new dimensions of the holomovement require new filters to focus them?—they're nonetheless useful to help us "uncover pearls in oyster shells":

> The field itself sprouts new forms,
> while the camel dances over them, imaginary
> plants no one has thought of,
> but all these new seeds, no matter how they try,
> do not reveal the other sun.
> They hide it.
> Still, the effort is joy,
> one by one to keep uncovering
> pearls in oyster shells.[44]

Adapted to our souls, filters bring the holomovement into focus through the language of our lives. By leading us through the soul's dark night, our Soul Searchers show us how to read our life's language and see what's at work there—our souls, our filters, and the holo-ocean behind them: we "look through that astrolabe . . . ":

> The body is a device to calculate
> the astronomy of the spirit.
> Look through that astrolabe
> and become oceanic.[45]

5

Breathing Out

ARCHETYPE   *Releaser*
MYSTIC JOURNEY   *Letting Go*

Releasing

Moving with the ocean means not only going where it takes us but also leaving where we've been. Leaving, letting go, releasing: these qualities of the fifth stage on the mystic path make it somewhat hard to define. For one thing, it concerns a phase of mystical life that's not much practiced in the West. When it is, it's often considered negative or harsh—as asceticism, for instance, or worse, as self-flagellation, beating up on ourselves for our "sins" or failings.

This stage is also elusive because it has so many faces: Destroyer, Creator, Griever, Player, Remover, Opener, Purifier, Dissolver. These faces seem incompatible—destroying and creating both? grieving and feeling playful together?—but from a mystical perspective, they're different manifestations of one process.

The core idea is simple: Before new forms can emerge, old ones must be cleared away. Before we can develop new filters, we must release the ones we have. Jesus talked about not pouring new wine into old wineskins, because the new wine causes the old, stretched-out containers to burst. Eastern philosophies build entire meditative practices on letting go, claiming that it's as natural as breathing: we must breathe out before we can take fresh air into our lungs. Yogic techniques even suggest breathing out twice as long as we breathe in to make sure all the old air is expelled.

Buddhism grows from this root awareness of releasing. The Buddha's Four Noble Truths explain that suffering comes from being attached to things that are impermanent. Forms come and go—that's their nature—whether they're tangible forms such as bodies or possessions or less tangible forms such as personalities, relationships, jobs, beliefs, or paradigms.

On one hand, all the different ways we filter reality into forms have a purpose. They serve as containers for our lives and channels for our energies. Through them, the holomovement comes into focus. Even the defenses we develop for keeping filters in place have their value, enabling us to cope with stress and trauma. We couldn't be here without many levels of containers, and it's only right to be grateful for them.

On the other hand, containers have an end, a time when their purpose is fulfilled. A right form at the wrong time is the wrong form. If we don't know how to release forms as they pass away, we experience pain—physical, emotional, marital, family, social, financial, ecological.

But pain can cease, the Buddha realized, if we learn the art of letting go. How much pain would we be in, for instance, if we decided to hold on to the air in our lungs and refused to let it out for new? That's how basic releasing is.

Culturally, though, we're geared to do the opposite. Western life turns around collecting, establishing, and making things fixed, from building solid ego structures to accumulating belongings, from creating self-perpetuating institutions to building empires. If something lasts a long time, we assume it must be good. And there's truth to that. The question is, what makes something enduring: its ability to stay fixed or its ability to let forms go?

Our inner mystics believe the latter. They're mindful of the rhythm that moves from formlessness to forms back into formlessness, out of which new forms arise. Accordingly, they're as happy to leave forms behind once they've served their purpose as they are to create new ones. Our mystics move with the two-sided process, which makes us "sometimes crescent, sometimes full":

> Leave and don't look away from the Sun as you go.
> Through him you are sometimes crescent, sometimes full.[1]

Otherwise, our mystics reason, we'd get backlogged with filters which we no longer need and which clog the channels for new patterns emerging. Releasing forms is as much a sacred discipline as creating them. In the end, the point isn't having or releasing but moving with "the invisible river" whose "turning" includes both sides as part of "the same motion":

> . . . I am a millstone
> turning day and night, moaning and creaking.
>
> By turning, you know the power and motion
> of the invisible river. The beloved friend
> is a river. The nightsky is a waterwheel
> revolving in that. The love-river
> doesn't rest. In it, if you grab a branch,
> the river breaks it. Any attachment you have,
> take hold strongly and let it be snapped off!
>
> If you can't see the huge sky-turnings,
> look at the broken sticks moving by,
> and the foam-bubbles around you.
>
> The giddy wind, the constantly reaching up
> of the ocean, these are parts of the same motion.[2]

Nor need releasing be labored or wrenching. Our inner mystics don't focus on what's no longer there—either as something good that we've lost or as something bad that we're ashamed to have had—but on staying attuned to the two-sided "motion" that's the source of re-generation. Valuing forms and then releasing them, using "filtered light" and then taking away "personal coverings," is basic to life:

> When a baby is taken from the wet nurse,
> it easily forgets her
> and starts eating solid food.
>
> Seeds feed awhile on ground,
> then lift up into the sun.
>
> So you should taste the filtered light
> and work your way toward wisdom
> with no personal covering.

> That's how you came here, like a star
> without a name. Move across the nightsky
> with those anonymous lights.[3]

Tripping over Forms

As natural as the releasing side of the motion is, though, it must be a conscious practice. Somewhere along the line our inner mystics' link to the two-sided motion gets obscured and we slip into a habit of doing only the first half—the getting, building, attaching, forming part. Some say this is human nature. Given how we're constructed with eyes and ears focused outwardly, forms fascinate us, and we lose sight of the flip side. After awhile, the letting go part seems alien. We forget how to do it.

But there's more involved with our fears about letting go. For at least six thousand years, humans have struggled under the one-sidedness of patriarchy, which puts a priority on controlling forms. Outward forms are all there is, according to this paradigm, and those who possess the biggest or most forms control the rest. The desire to gain forms and the fear of losing them become driving passions on which our security, happiness, and autonomy depend. Voluntarily letting go of things we've worked hard to attain seems unthinkable.

We know human nature only under this one-sided influence, not as we may otherwise be. Unfortunately, as Buddhists observe, when we're "clinging" to forms, we're not at our best. That's when we're most competitive, jealous, and ready to fight, because that's also when we're most afraid and insecure, therefore most desperate to gather forms around us to fortify our position. The form-only paradigm puts us on a course that generates afflictive and violent emotions and then traps us there. As Rumi suggests with the image of a nomad's watchdog, seeking protection in forms ends up making us prisoners to them:

> . . . you've seen a nomad's dog
> lying at the tent entrance, with his head
> on the threshold and his eyes closed.

Children pull his tail and touch his face,
but he doesn't move. He loves the children's
attention and stays humble within it.

But if a stranger walks by, he'll spring up
ferociously. Now, what if that dog's owner
were not able to control it?

A poor dervish might appear: the dog storms out.
The dervish says, "I take refuge with God
when the dog of arrogance attacks,"
and the owner has to say, "So do I!
I'm helpless against this creature
even in my own house!

Just as you can't come close,
I can't go out!"[4]

Caught in forms, we trip over them. Caught in roles, for instance, we find them confining, leading us to behave in ways we ourselves don't like. Or, caught in family or career ambitions, we make choices based on outward advantages without making sure our choices are also inwardly right. A form-only perspective lacks the big picture of why forms come to be and when it's time for them to pass away. If we pursue forms without a big-picture awareness, we're misled. We get lost in the quest for forms, and our bodies record our doings:

On Resurrection Day your body testifies against you.
Your hand says, "I stole money."
Your lips, "I said meanness."
Your feet, "I went where I shouldn't."
Your genitals, "Me too."[5]

If we're not moving with the "huge sky-turnings" that balance form and formlessness, having and letting go, we fall out of sync. The changes we make to get "what we want" backfire:

Who makes these changes?
I shoot an arrow right.
It lands left.
I ride after a deer and find myself
chased by a hog.
I plot to get what I want
and end up in prison.
I dig pits to trap others
and fall in.

I should be suspicious
of what I want.[6]

Borrowed Robes

According to Rumi, we fall out of sync by taking forms—outward appearances—too seriously, as if the forms define who we are. Bodies, roles, personalities: we assume they're us, but they're really "borrowed robes." We put them on when we come into this time-space dimension, as we must to participate in consensus reality. The mistake comes only if we "pretend" they're ours:

What fault was committed?

God answers,
                    "The crime is
that they put on borrowed robes
and pretended they were theirs.

I take the beautiful clothes back,
so that you will learn the robe
of appearance is only a loan."[7]

The robes are borrowed from families, societies, and cultures, and they show it: they're woven from shared, collective patterns. We add our own touches, but collective influences persist. As useful as the robes are to get around, they don't do justice to the side of us that's linked to formlessness. To reduce ourselves to the formed side, the robe, is to forget the dynamic being who's wearing it, and to act exclusively from our form side is as logical as doing what our clothes tell us to do. Sufi scholar Idries Shah writes:

> In order to approach the Sufi Way, the Seeker must realize that he is, largely, a bundle of what are nowadays called conditionings—fixed ideas and prejudices, automatic responses sometimes which have occurred through the training of others. . . . "If you follow the ways in which you have been trained, which you may have inherited, for no other reason than this, you are illogical." [Rumi][8]

Indeed, the borrowed robes are made up of "attachment to beliefs and bloodties and desires and comforting habits,"[9] of which Rumi says:

> Don't listen to them!
> They seem to protect,
> but they imprison.
>
> They are your worst enemies.
> They make you afraid
> of living in emptiness.[10]

"Afraid of living in emptiness": that's what ties us to robes and that's what our inner Releasers ease by shifting our focus to deeper levels. Attuned to the holomovement, our souls bring a lightness to forms, a practice of not being confined to any one outfit.

On soul levels, we know formlessness is our origin, and we go into it easily as part of our nature. From soul levels, we know we're more than appearances—more than jobs, net worth, social images, personalities, relationships, and coping devices. Compared to "that presence within," the borrowed robes are expendable—the fewer the better:

> I can break off from anyone,
> except that presence within.
>
> Anyone can bring gifts.
> Give me someone who takes away.[11]

Even so, the form side of us finds this difficult. When forms "pass away," we grieve. But as Rumi says, we should grieve even more for "forgetting what doesn't" pass away—for forgetting the holomovement's two-sided process, its unfoldings and enfoldings as one activity. True spirituality, as far as Rumi is concerned, embraces both, whereas doing only the first half imitates spirituality and puts "a lock on your chest":

> Wherever people grieve over anything,
> you should sit with them and grieve louder,
> because you have an even better right to moan.
>
> They lament for what passes away. You cry
> for your forgetting what doesn't.
>
> You have been imitating spirituality.
>
> Imitation is a lock on your chest.
> Dissolve it with tears.[12]

The "lock" of imitation—trapping ourselves in borrowed robes, even spiritual-looking ones—is a problem, because when we hold on to forms, we bottle up "the energy of the sun." As natural as flowing in and out of forms is to us by virtue of our origin, feeling bound to existing forms seems equally natural once we're in forms. Yet it's this attached feeling that "knots up" the process. Rumi alludes to the yogic chakra system, which, like many ancient healing systems, conceives of health as energy-flows: are they blocked or moving freely?

> You sit here for days saying, *This is strange business.*
> You're the strange business.
> You have the energy of the sun in you,
> but you keep knotting it up at the base of your spine.[13]

Breaking Up Ground

Whatever blocks the "moving river" causes imbalances which build until the blockage breaks. Nor is the breaking a bad thing. When containers stop channelling "Living Water," they cut us off from it, and the only way to move with the river again is to break the "clay pitchers":

> . . . The pitcher breaks.
> You're in the moving river. Living Water,
> how long will you make clay pitchers
> that have to be broken to enter you?[14]

Rumi uses an image from nature to show what must occur when our relation to forms gets rigid: we have to break up hardened soil before plants can grow in it. Tilling the ground looks as if something negative, even devastating is happening, but without that loosening, the new can't take root:

> A man was breaking up the soil,
> when another man came by, "*Why*
> *are you ruining this land?*"
>
> "Don't be a fool! Nothing can grow
> until the ground is turned over and crumbled.
>
> There can be no roses and no orchard
> without first this that looks devastating.
>
> You must lance an ulcer to heal it.
> You must tear down parts of an old building
> to restore it, and so it is with a sensual life
> that has no spirit in it."[15]

In view of this breaking-up process, even things that look like mistakes can serve the rhythm, because they jolt us out of fixed patterns. The Fifth Step of AA functions this way. By admitting wrongs, we reflect on our thoughts, actions, and habits with an eye to releasing them. If we use mistakes for leaving old patterns, what seems to "take us backward" instead leads "toward shelter":

> . . . When you prune
> weak branches, the remaining fruit
> gets tastier. Lust can be re-directed,
> so that even when it takes you backward,
> it goes toward shelter.[16]

As far as our souls are concerned, overturnings are necessary; they create the space we need to move and grow. Our souls like to "tear down houses" not to give us pain but to loosen the hold that forms have on us. We're cautious when it comes to forms and fearful of losing them, but when they actually go, after the weeping, our souls "get brighter," less dulled by heaviness:

> Why are you so blind to what the soul needs?
> Weep for yourself as when a cloud weeps,
> and then the branch freshens. As when a candle
> releases tears and gets brighter.[17]

> *

> Your face is a garden that comes up where the house was.
> With our hands we tear down houses and make bare places.[18]

> *

> Beloved, take our self-restraint
> and strangle it.

> Burn our houses. A lover's house
> is better burnt! A candle gets more pointed
> and brighter as it burns. Stay up
> this one night. Walk the sleepless
> precincts. Be with those
> being killed in union.[19]

Upheavals don't occur to destroy us. "Being killed in union" is Rumi's way of saying "being released for new ways of moving with the whole." Behind the upheavals and releasing lies the truth that we need "a place to live with . . . dimensions" as great as our souls. Shelters that can be "knocked down with one kick" aren't worthy of us:

> You reach out wanting the moon with your eyes,
> and Venus. Build a place to live
> with those dimensions. A shelter that can be

knocked down with one kick,
go ahead and knock it down.[20]

Not Minding the Sparks

Mindful of the freedom and clarity that comes with releasing forms, our mystic Releasers welcome the flames. It's a relief to be rid of forms we no longer need. We feel cleared and open to the new, like after a shower or spring cleaning. What's burned up isn't our essence—our connectedness to the holomovement—but only what obstructs it. We're purified of shelters whose dimensions are too small anyway. Between "world-consuming" fire and "world-protecting" water, our inner Releasers choose fire any day, as Rumi explains in a story:

> One dervish to another, *What was your vision of God's presence?*
> I haven't seen anything.
> But for the sake of conversation, I'll tell you a story.
>
> God's presence is there in front of me, a fire on the left,
> a lovely stream on the right.
> One group walks toward the fire, *into* the fire, another
> toward the sweet flowing water.
> No one knows which are blessed and which not.
> Whoever walks into the fire appears suddenly in the stream.
> A head goes under on the water surface, that head
> pokes out of the fire.
> Most people guard against going into the fire,
> and so end up in it.
> Those who love the water of pleasure and make it their devotion
> are cheated by this reversal.
> The trickery goes further.
> The voice of the fire tells the *truth*, saying *I am not fire.*
> *I am fountainhead. Come into me and don't mind the sparks.*
>
> If you are a friend of God, fire is your water.
> You should wish to have a hundred thousand sets of mothwings,
> so you could burn them away, one set a night.

> The moth sees light and goes into fire. You should see fire
> and go toward light. Fire is what of God is world-consuming.
> Water, world-protecting.
> Somehow each gives the appearance of the other. To these eyes
>   you have now
> what looks like water burns. What looks like
> fire is a great relief to be inside.[21]

Instead of waiting for upheavals to wrench forms loose, our inner mystics let forms go before their narrowness precipitates a crisis. By walking into the flames, we surrender our attachments to forms, whether they're habits of mind or behavior. We invite inner tilling, "so wildflowers will come up where we are":

> Weep, and then smile.
> Don't pretend to know something
> you haven't experienced.
>
> There's a necessary dying,
> and then Jesus is breathing again.
>
> Very little grows
> on jagged rock.
> Be ground.
>
> Be crumbled,
> so wildflowers will come up
> where you are.
>
> You've been stony for too many years.
> Try something different.
> Surrender.[22]

Not that we don't grieve as forms pass away. Letting go is tough, especially given years of conditioning in a forms-define-who-you-are paradigm. Rumi doesn't ask the superhuman of us. Having grieved his heart out over the loss of Shams, he wouldn't be one to advocate stoically ignoring or suppressing what we feel during upheavals. If we feel grief and pain, we should weep and let it out: "Cry easily like a little child." Feeling what we feel to the depths, we embrace the releasing process not only in our heads but in our emotions as well. As a result, our lives "stay fresh":

> The cloud weeps, and then the garden sprouts.
> The baby cries, and the mother's milk flows.
> The Nurse of Creation has said, *Let them cry a lot.*
>
> This rain-weeping and sun-burning twine together
> to make us grow. Keep your intelligence white-hot
> and your grief glistening, so your life will stay fresh.
> Cry easily like a little child.[23]

Getting Naked

To improve the Grim Releaser's image or maybe just to have fun with us, Rumi likens letting go to getting naked: off with the borrowed robes! Even before Rumi, though, some ascetics, men and women, lived naked (or almost) to experience union with God without masks or coverings. The ascetic spin may take some of the fun out of it, but the idea is good, namely, that lovers don't want layers of coverings between them, and the Releaser is just the archetype for getting rid of them. All the caution that keeps forms wrapped around us goes to the wind, as we connect with our Beloved, our formless, unfolding side:

> The Beloved we want is always awake,
> and always meets us when we arrange to meet.
>
> True lovers . . . don't sleep. They stay up
> walking on the roof. They're wildly awake.
> They can't be tied down.
>
> Love and a respectable hesitation
> don't mix. It's time to strip,
> and quit being bashful.[24]

*

You've been walking the ocean's edge,
holding up your robes to keep them dry.

You must dive naked under, and deeper
under, a thousand times deeper![25]

*

Come to this street with
only your sweet fragrance.

Don't walk into *this* river
wearing a robe!

Paths go from here to there,
but don't arrive from somewhere!
It's time now to live naked.[26]

One of the values of forms is that they function as a language for us. Forms distinguish this and not that, here and not there, me and not you. Too often, though, the language medium becomes the message, as Marshall McLuhan observed. When the language of forms stops telling our story of moving with the holomovement and lures us into telling its story of separateness, lovers draw the line—we're better off "naked":

Walk the beach.
Your face is pale
with being so separate,
but it will get redder.
Paleness wants Union.

Be lean with wanting that.
Walk out where there's no shade.
The network of shadows is a filter
that you no longer need.

Lovers want each other completely naked.[27]

Attuned to the flow from invisible to visible back into the invisible, our mystics have no problem with living in the inner buff. In the spirit of adventure, our mystics take on personalities in this marketplace world, but they also know how to take the robes off again with a free, even care-free, spirit. Specific forms—personalities, concepts, images, bodies—are "born once," whereas our inner mystics are born "many times":

> Personalities are born once,
> a mystic many times.
>
> Wearing the body-robe, I've been busy
> in the market, weighing and arguing prices.
>
> Sometimes I have torn the robe off
> with my own hands and thrown it away.[28]

Cleared for New Forms

Whether we experience this process as traumatic or liberating, sober-ing or playful, releasing is for a good cause. Not only are we relieved of dead wood—forms that no longer carry "Living Water"—but we're also cleared for new growth. The cycle begins again, bringing with it re-generation and renewal. As the "tight knot" of holding on to forms loosens, our being lightens naturally, and we and everyone around us "fly up like doves":

> When the house of the brain fills with a wanting,
> your heart gets crowded with anxieties.
> The rest of the body may be undisturbed,
> but in your chest there's constant traffic.
>
> Find a safe haven instead
> in the strong autumn wind of awe.
> Let last year's peonies blow off their stems.
> Those flowers must go, so these new buds can grow.[29]

>   *
>
> A tight knot loosens.
> Something which died in December

lifts a head out,
and opens.[30]

*

If you could untie your wings
and free your soul of jealousy,

you and everyone around you
would fly up like doves.[31]

So important is this fifth stage that, from a Buddhist perspective, if we practice this one stage well, the rest will take care of themselves. Releasing as a lifelong method is a challenge, but it's not negative or nihilistic, as Buddhism itself has often been mischaracterized. Instead, it clears the way for us to be unconditionally open to reality. What could be more positive, more affirming? By releasing old filters, we open ourselves to life in its fullness and spontaneity—"with each striking we change":

We break what holds us, each one a blacksmith
heating iron and walking to the anvil.
We blow on the inner fire.
With each striking we change.[32]

*

Whatever You break finds itself more intelligent
for being broken. Every second a new being
stands in the courtyard of Your chest
like Adam, without a father or a mother,
but the beginning of many generations to come.

I should rhyme that fifty times![33]

With releasing also comes inner peace. The traffic of forms doesn't disturb us so much, which is why images of the Buddha depict him as being serene. Releasing forms releases us from the anxiety of figuring out how things should be and then trying to make them happen that

way. We allow ourselves the peace of moving with reality's process—
of letting "a streaming beauty flow through us"—without the stress of
trying to control its course:

> A certain sufi tore his robe in grief,
> and the tearing brought such relief,
>
> he gave the robe the name *faraji*,
> which means *ripped open*, or *happiness*,
> or *one who brings the joy of being opened*. . . .
>
> If you want peace and purity,
> tear away your coverings.
>
> This is the purpose of emotion, to let
> a streaming beauty flow through you.
>
> Call it spirit, elixir, or the original
> agreement between yourself and God.
>
> Opening into that gives peace,
> a song of being empty,
> pure silence.[34]

Trusting the Process

From this fifth stage, a deep trust in reality's two-sided process emerges.
The more we let go, the more we learn how releasing works and we
begin to trust the process. In turn, the more we trust the process—trust
that it won't annihilate us, for instance, or trust that it brings good beyond our current awareness—the easier it is to let go.

Rumi's poetry conveys this trust. Sometimes Rumi is read as if he's
a fatalist, yet he's not that at all. He's trusting the holomovement—
both sides of it. The part of him that's focused on forms may feel "like
a cat in a bag . . . whirled around overhead," but that's because he's
also open to the part of him that's yet emerging, a part he doesn't control. Not knowing what the new looks like, he doesn't want to force
it into preconceived channels. Existing forms may be too narrow for

what's unfolding. He'd rather have "whitewater," the holomovement river, carry him along:

> Resurrection is happening now!
>
> Should I worry about whether
> I'm strong willed enough to obey
> some rule of behavior?
>
> In the hand of love I'm like a cat in a bag,
> lifted up and whirled around overhead.
>
> That's how much control I have over circumstances.
> Whitewater carries me along.[35]

The deeper the trust in reality's two-sided process, the easier releasing is. That's why Sufism was once defined as "the feeling of joy when sudden disappointment comes." The joy comes from trusting that something good is going on, no matter how things appear. What looks like a disaster may in the big picture prevent greater "disasters from happening."

Granted, these are astonishing conclusions for people witnessing the massive destruction of their culture, as Sufis were then from Mongol invasions. Tibetan Buddhists have talked the same way under similar circumstances for the last half century. That both traditions emphasize releasing as a life practice may be why both inspire such a profound trust in reality's unseen process, no matter what the theater of outward forms throws their way:

> Someone once asked a great sheikh
> what sufism was.
>   "The feeling of joy
> when sudden disappointment comes."
>
> The eagle carries off Muhammed's boot
> and saves him from snakebite.
>
> Don't grieve for what doesn't come.
> Some things that don't happen
> keep disasters from happening.[36]

As these traditions demonstrate, a practice of releasing forms gives rise to different attitudes toward life. We do what's ours to do and let it go. For our inner mystics, results don't matter as much as moving with the process. Whatever we're doing, our mystics "give in completely to it," "learn from it," and then release it. That way, our lives become "happier friends":

> When you start some new work,
> you give in completely to it.
>
> You're excited,
> because the Creator keeps you
> from seeing what's missing.
>
> Your heatedness hides that,
> so you do the work, and then look back
> and see the nature of it.
>
> If you'd seen that at first,
> you wouldn't have done anything!
>
> Don't worry about repenting.
> Do the work that's given,
> and learn from it.
>
> If you become addicted to looking back,
> half your life will be spent in distraction,
> and the other half in regret.
>
> You can live better than that!
> Find happier friends.[37]

Love behind the Releasing

What does all this have to do with love, love being the focus of the fifth stage? Simple: we release forms not because we don't love them but because we love being connected to the larger process more. Even if the process brings "devastation," it's still "the way of love," of moving with the holomovement. By loving that path and staying with it, we're "given wings":

The way of love is not
a subtle argument.

The door there
is devastation.

Birds make great sky-circles
of their freedom.
How do they learn it?

They fall, and falling,
they're given wings.[38]

Behind grief and loss, therefore, always lies "love's mystery." It's the story of how we're in love, how we experience reality's two-sided process as first filling us and then emptying us. It's not an evil force at work. We're so at-one with the process—feeling it "nearer than our jugular veins," as the *Qur'an* also says—that it moves through our lives unhindered. That's true even if, to our ordinary ways of thinking, we're left "stunned like the dead":

A poet tries to say love's mystery,
why the reed flute grieves.

Listen and obey
the hushed language.
Go naked.[39]

    *

There is a tall tower that Love builds.
Live there in Silence.

The One who knows all secrets
is here *now*, nearer
than your jugular vein.[40]

    *

Tonight remove whatever remains.

Last night we lay listening to your one story,
of being in love. We lay around you,
stunned like the dead.[41]

Turning our lives around forms wears thin anyway. As far as our mystics are concerned, we're not here for that. We're holders for the holomovement, places where reality's process goes on, and we don't need to plant flags—a long line of forms—to prove that's happening. "Only love," only moving with the process, counts for our inner mystics:

I'm so tired of what I've been doing.

Then one image without form came,
and I quit.

Look for someone else to tend the shop.
I'm out of the image-making business.

Finally I know the freedom
of madness.

A random image arrives. I scream,
"Get out!" It disintegrates.

Only love.
Only the holder the flag fits into,
and wind. No flag.[42]

6

A Treasure beneath the House

ARCHETYPE   *Healer*
MYSTIC JOURNEY   *Surrendering to Our Inner Authority*

Soul Sickness and the Healer

Going within and releasing (stages four and five on the mystic path) provide the tools for getting our souls, loves, and freedoms back. With these tools, we tackle the root ill: soul sickness. Mystics are practical, and for them, soul sickness is the number one ill to remedy. Heal soul sickness, they say, and all the other problems take care of themselves.

That's why the Healer archetype emerges prominently at this stage. Curing fixes symptoms, whereas healing goes to the root of breakdown. Unless the root is healed, one set of symptoms diminishes only for another to arise, since the source of pain continues untreated. For mystics, the root of "the manifest world" is our inner life. If that's in shambles—full of "thorn-roots"—the outer will be a mess as well, a mess that can't be put right until the inner ill is healed. In practice, this means our inner Healers won't let up in presenting us with increasingly intense forms of soul sickness until we take notice and work toward genuine healing:

> . . . Roots produce branches.
>
> Your inner opening and closing
> is the underworld, the ground
> that feeds the manifest world.
>
> Tear out the thorn-roots quickly.
> When you feel held in, find out why.
> Dig for the cause.[1]

Soul-sick means soul-disconnected. If we use our souls as bargaining chips—a coping habit that starts under duress, pain, or trauma—we lose our link to them. After years of bargaining, our souls get pushed so far into the background that we no longer have access to them. Instead of being guided by the inner gyroscope that our souls provide, we throw our energies outward, seeking validation from outward sources—people, jobs, or circumstances.

This can't work, of course, as the study of addiction testifies. Disconnected from who we are, we slip into self-destructive behavior. If we can't be united with our "Beloved"—our souls—we "die of our desiring." Soul sickness comes to a crisis in various patterns of self-destruction. It's truly the most deadly disease, destroying not only people but also communities, species, even the planet's life-support systems—all because we've lost touch with who we are:

> Whose idea was this,
> to have the lover visible
> and the Beloved *in*visible!
>
> So many people have died of their desiring
> because of this. The lover cannot kiss
> the lips he wants, so he bites himself![2]

For our inner mystics, nothing can take the place of our souls. That's why, if we're soul-sick, we can possess the best material goods and still be unhappy, whereas if we're soul-grounded, we can have nothing and be "in rapture":

> One man curls up in rapture
> in an outside nook of a mosque.
>
> Another walks disappointedly
> his elegant gardens.[3]

Soul sickness makes us "walk disappointedly," because no amount of outward validation satisfies. What gives meaning to life is still missing. There's a hole in us that must be filled for our lives to have meaning.

With outward methods, though, we don't fill it with what belongs there. External validations aren't oatmeal—and certainly not chicken soup— for the soul. They're too thin and temporary to fill the void that our souls left, which means we seek more and more outward diversions to try to fill it. Before we know it, we're swallowed up in visibles, carried away by the pursuit of forms:

> There is a duck inside you.
> Her bill is never still, searching through dry
> and wet alike, like the robber in an empty house
> cramming objects in his sack, pearls, chickpeas,
> anything. Always thinking, "There's no time!
> I won't get another chance!"
>
> A True Person is more calm and deliberate.
> He or she doesn't worry about interruptions.
>
> But that duck is so afraid of missing out
> that it's lost all generosity, and frighteningly expanded
> its capacity to take in food.[4]

Thanks to our cultural paradigm—duck-thinking from the top down—soul sickness is everywhere. We're not raised to know who we are and then encouraged to "build a place to live there." Instead, kindergarten through graduate school and onto the job, we're trained first to run after "raisin-and-walnut snacks" and then to put ourselves in charge of who gets what:

> . . . Blessed is anyone
> who knows who he or she really is
> and builds a place to live there.
>
> A child loves walnuts and raisins more than anything.
> A mature spirit sees those delights for what they are.
>
> To your deepest being the body
> is like a raisin-and-walnut snack.
> Your soul has no doubts about
> what's more real.

Every man has testicles and hair,
as every male goat has a beard and balls.

One goat, though, leads the group to the butcher.
He combs his beard and says,
"I'm in charge here."

Yes, in charge of death and worrying![5]

Duck-thinking produces "death and worrying"—every form of unhappiness. Dismissing inner for outer concerns, duck-thinking obscures our link to the whole, thereby depriving us of the means for finding a meaningful place in it. Our souls have an agenda in life or, as Eastern philosophies put it, definite reasons for incarnating. Remove our "souls' code," and we haven't a clue what our purpose here may be. We become like donkeys stuck in a mudhole:

Soul-drunk, body-ruined, these two
sit helpless in a wrecked wagon.
Neither knows how to fix it.

And my heart, I'd say it was more
like a donkey sunk in a mudhole,
struggling and miring deeper.[6]

We try to make the best of things by piecing together lives that have the appropriate elements in them—family, friends, education, religion, career, success, possessions, children—but without our souls to breathe life into all of this, it's as if we're trying to put a "bit and halter" on a sick donkey:

What you've been wanting is a donkey lying sick
on the ground. What you've been doing
is the bit and halter on that donkey.[7]

The result is misery. From one seed of soul loss come "many trees" of suffering. When our lives are gutted from within, "no one lives here anymore":

With one glance many trees grow from a single seed.
Your two eyes are like a Turk born in Persia.
He's on a rampage, a Persian shooting Turkish arrows.
He has ransacked my house so that no one lives here anymore,
just a boy running barefooted all through it.[8]

"A boy running barefooted all through it"—that's what our Healers build on. Our souls' development may have been put on hold by duck-and-donkey living, but our souls persist. They "still live inside us":

The manner and appearance of a prophet,
our secret origins, these are born
of a woman who still lives inside us,
though she's hiding from what we've become.[9]

The only cure for soul sickness is reclaiming our souls. Only then are we free beings—neither trapped in externals nor driven by soul loss but free to live who we are from the inside out. Rumi tells a story about a caged parrot:

There was a merchant setting out for India.

He asked each male and female servant
what they wanted to be brought as a gift.

Each told him a different exotic object:
A piece of silk, a brass figurine,
a pearl necklace.

Then he asked his beautiful caged parrot,
the one with such a lovely voice,
and she said,
            "When you see the Indian parrots,
describe my cage. Say that I need guidance
here in my separation from them. Ask how
our friendship can continue with me so confined
and them flying about freely in the meadow mist.

Tell them that I remember well our mornings
moving together from tree to tree.

Tell them to drink one cup of ecstatic wine
in honor of me here in the dregs of my life.

Tell them that the sound of their quarreling
high in the trees would be sweeter
to hear than any music."

This parrot is the spirit-bird in all of us,
that part that wants to return to freedom,
and is the freedom. What she wants
from India is *herself!*[10]

Using Our Soul Searchers to Get Back Who We Are

But who are we? Who is that "spirit-bird in all of us"? Our inner Healers call on our Soul Searchers for help, since soul-searching methods are precisely what we need for healing soul sickness.

Soul Searchers respond by reframing our lives. We're not here to do daily life and fit soul-searching in on the side; soul-searching is what we're really doing here, and all of life—both the big stuff and the details—provides a forum for that activity. Not that soul-searching has to be ponderous. We can do it "with speech, with silence," or "with sniffing about." Soul-searching is an awareness that everything relates to who we are and to the stories our souls want to tell. By maintaining this perspective, we "keep moving toward the Friend":

Anyone who genuinely and constantly with both hands
looks for something, will find it.

Though you are lame and bent over, keep moving
toward the Friend. With speech, with silence,
with sniffing about, stay on the track.[11]

Another method our Soul Searchers use builds on the interweaving of soul and life. If what's going on in our souls is reflected everywhere—

in our relationships with people, events, and circumstances—then even
outward experiences can serve to connect us with them. Wherever we
are and whomever we're with, our souls speak to us:

> Friend, our closeness is this:
> Anywhere you put your foot, feel me
> in the firmness under you.[12]

Through experiences, our souls' messages are "at once obvious and
obscure": obvious in what's presented, obscure in the inner meaning.
It's the obscure part that our Soul Searchers explore, and they do it by
tracing our feelings and responses back to some dynamic arising from
soul levels—in many cases, to some inner pain or conflict that our souls
want healed. Soul Searchers assume that there's a soul-reason for
everything, that we are who we are, feel what we feel, and react as we
do, because "the Friend" "is like that":

> The Friend comes clapping, at once obvious
> and obscure, without fear or plans.
>
> I am like I am
> because this one is like that.[13]

If our souls feel lost and rejected, we feel that way too, even if we sit
on top of the world in money, power, or position. Whatever the condition of our souls, we "take on those qualities." Understanding this
"mirroring" helps us reconnect with who we are and heal the inner rift:

> Of these two thousand "I" and "We" people,
> which am I?
>
> Don't try to keep me from asking!
> Listen, when I'm this out of control!
> But don't put anything breakable in my way!
>
> There is an Original inside me.
> What's here is a mirror for that, for You.

If You are joyful, I am.
If You grieve, or if You're bitter, or graceful,
I take on those qualities.[14]

A third method of soul-searching involves paying attention to our souls' guidance. Feeling what our souls feel, Soul Searchers then take those feelings seriously and act on them. Our souls sense, for instance, whether a relationship is good for us, whether we should look for a new job, whether we should have children, even whether we should attend a party. They sense when we're ready to heal some trauma embedded in our psyches and bodies. They also sense when our egos are getting too small for what our souls want to do. All this wisdom and practical help is present in everyone, yet we're trained to dismiss it in favor of conventional wisdom or the opinions and expectations of others.

Getting back to our "Original" begins with honoring our souls' wisdom and heeding its messages. If we feel a certain way, it's more than "just a mood." Soul Searchers assume that our souls are taking the opportunity to raise issues, heal old wounds, or move our lives in more soul-nourishing directions.

Granted, re-attuning ourselves to our souls is tricky. Even if we're fairly certain that our souls are the force behind a feeling, their choices don't always coincide with what's outwardly advantageous. That's when our Healers step in. While our Soul Searchers put us back in touch with our souls, our Healers use the connection to restore wholeness, urging us to choose our souls' course. As difficult as this course may be, choosing against it is worse. For our Healers, being "locked-in" on our souls' path is better than going a more comfortable route. Their "rejection" of what's not in harmony with our life's purpose is "wanted more than anyone else's acceptance":

Satisfaction is always two bow-shots away,
and yet something in the soul
prefers this unreachable Lover
to anyone reachable.

This being locked-in,
is better than having the keys
to any consolation-house.

The Beloved's rejection is wanted more
than anyone else's acceptance.[15]

A fourth soul-searching method involves accepting our souls' dynamics unconditionally, trusting that they're working for healing, even if this involves "anger and desire." Soul Searchers don't judge inner responses according to preconceived notions of how "a true human being" ought to behave. If a response comes from the root of our being, that's sufficient grounds for accepting it—for assuming it bears some soul message and has a role to play on our path:

A man was wandering the marketplace at noon
with a candle in his hand, totally ecstatic.

"Hey," called a shopkeeper. "Is this a joke?
Who are you looking for?" "Someone breathing *Huuuuuu*,

the divine breath." "Well, there are plenty
to choose from." "But I want one who can be

in anger and desire and still a true human being
in the same moment." "A rare thing! But maybe

you're searching among the branches for what appears
only in the roots."[16]

This method is especially important for healing soul sickness. By not arbitrarily censoring our inner content, Soul Searchers allow our souls to come through, emotions being a primary means for our souls to communicate. "Every emotion has a source," Rumi says, "and a key that opens it."[17]

Once our Soul Searchers open the door to our inner experience, though, painful and conflicted emotions often surface—shame, fear, regret, anger, grief, frustration. These so-called negative emotions are our souls' way of getting our attention—of saying something is doing or has done violence to us. They serve to warn and protect us, like guard dogs, even if they get confused in their mission and bark at the wrong thing. Confused or clear, though, the barking comes from our "Beloved," who's not someone to be muzzled:

> Let the Beloved come
> and sit like a guard-dog
> in front of that tent.[18]

That's when we need our Healers. Attempting to rid ourselves of negative emotions while we continue to live immersed in soul-sick structures cannot work. Emotions have purposes that Healers respect. Jesus wasn't being emotionally unenlightened when he got angry at the money changers. He was acting from his Healer who cared about society's spiritual roots.

Instead of killing the messengers, Healers trace negative emotions back to their roots—all of them. Some roots lie in personal history and development, while others lie in social, religious, economic, and other cultural structures. Healers aren't picky about which roots to address. They don't, for instance, focus exclusively on personal roots and ignore collective ones, or vice versa. Whatever contributes to soul sickness, Healers want to heal. They want us living from our souls, and they want cultures and philosophies where that's allowed.

With these methods, our Soul Searchers instill a passion for the search—for finding the lives our souls want to live and not settling for less. Our Healers then fire this passion with an awareness both of what's possible and what's at stake:

> If I find my life, I'll never let go,
> holding and twisting the cloth of your coat
> as in that dream when I saw you.[19]

Using Our Releasers to Get Back Our Souls' Freedom

Finding our lives, though, means letting go of what hides them. Rumi says, "There's sweet syrup here where you've been buying vinegar and unripened fruit.[20] The Releaser's job in healing soul sickness is to get rid of the vinegar and sour fruit—to help us release attitudes, roles, images, belief systems, conditionings, expectations, habits, or whatever else covers our souls. We don't have to make our souls come into existence. We do, however, need to remove what Buddhists call "obscurations," so that our innate being can emerge:

> You sweep the floor like the man
> who keeps the doorway.
> > When you brush
> a form clean, it becomes
> what it truly is.[21]

Unfortunately, we're more familiar with the coverings than with what's underneath. Accustomed to defining ourselves in terms of assets and résumés, we "tremble like leaves" at the thought of letting familiar forms go. Fortunately, by this stage on the mystic path, tremblings aren't a problem, since we also have "a green-winged longing" for our Friend. Our longing for what's most real about us carries us through the "pain," "exile," and "taste of dust":

> . . . We tremble like leaves
>
> about to let go. There's no avoiding pain,
> or feeling exiled, or the taste of dust.
>
> But also we have a green-winged longing
> for the sweetness of the Friend.
>
> These forms are evidence of what
> cannot be shown. [22]

"What cannot be shown" is our invisible side. Personalities are great for adapting to a culture, but they're not the whole of us. We're invisible and visible moving together, and only from this whole-process perspective can we value the props and furniture of our lives as our souls see them. Without this view, we get stuck inside our local identities, our time-space, culturally molded personalities:

What I most want
is to spring out of this personality,
then to sit apart from that leaping.
I've lived too long where I can be reached.[23]

With our Releasers in gear, we start "the work of demolishing."
Rumi likens a soul-sick personality to a rented house built over a treasure. The house doesn't belong to us. We can't own all the conditionings and traumas that shape our local side, because we're not the
source of those conditionings and traumas. Social systems and cultural
paradigms hold the greater share of that deed.

But even if we drew traumatic experiences to us by our mind-set or
karma, where did patterns of soul sickness start? Not in personal but in
collective ignorance—*avidya*, the Sanskrit term for root ignorance in
Hindu and Buddhist philosophies. Avidya doesn't belong to any of us;
we may suffer from it, but it's not our personal possession. The treasure, by contrast, does belong to us, because it's our being. We just have
to do some "pick and shovel work" to get to it:

> Some commentary on *I was a hidden treasure,*
> *and I desired to be known:* tear down
>
> this house. A hundred thousand new houses
> can be built from the transparent yellow carnelian
>
> buried beneath it, and the only way to get to that
> is to do the work of demolishing and then
>
> digging under the foundations. With that value
> in hand all the new construction will be done
>
> without effort. And anyway, sooner or later this house
> will fall on its own. The jewel treasure will be
>
> uncovered, but it won't be yours then. The buried
> wealth is your pay for doing the demolition,
>
> the pick and shovel work. If you wait and just
> let it happen, you'll bite your hand and say,

"I didn't do as I knew I should have." This
is a rented house. You don't own the deed.

You have a lease, and you've set up a little shop,
where you barely make a living sewing patches

on torn clothing. Yet only a few feet underneath
are two veins, pure red and bright gold carnelian.

Quick! Take the pick-axe and pry the foundation.
You've got to quit this seamstress work.

What does the patch-sewing *mean* you ask. Eating
and drinking. The heavy cloak of the body

is always getting torn. You patch it with food,
and other restless ego-satisfactions. Rip up

one board from the shop floor and look into
the basement. You'll see two glints in the dirt.[24]

How do we do the demolition? With the help of two parrots, one
outward, one inward. The outward-oriented parrot uses experiences
to burn up coverings—"trash"—and train us to think of the Friend. In
practice, this irksome bird makes things not work out as we hoped. We
realize that the best laid plans don't always have much soul wisdom in
them. What's really happening behind disappointments is our parrot-
souls teaching us releasing as a life practice. They're Releasers bent on
healing soul sickness and, as such, they're "raging lions" that "cannot
be contained by any meadow":

There is a parrot in you that God speaks through.
What the parrot says, you see reflected

in phenomena. The parrot takes away what you think
you like and gives joy. She hurts you and you feel

the perfect justice of the pain. You were burning
up your soul to keep the body delighted,

but you didn't know what you were doing. I am
another kind of fire. If you have trash

to get rid of, bring it here. My kindling is always
on the verge of catching. How can such things be

hidden? How can I talk with a raging lion inside me?
The lion that wants union cannot be contained by

any meadow. I try to think of different rhyme-words,
but the Friend says, "Think only of me. Sit and rest

in my presence, where you yourself rhyme with me!"[25]

The second parrot—the one who sent a message to her friends in
India via her merchant owner—teaches the liberating power of releasing inward blocks. Inward blocks can be self-limiting attitudes, images, habits, and belief systems, or they can be qualities we're proud
of—talents, skills, and abilities—that, as good as they are, prevent us
from going beyond them. According to this parrot, any inward pattern
that stands in the way of our souls' freedom must go. When we finally
release such patterns, it may look as if we're dying to one way of
being, but we're really discovering our freedom to be more:

So this parrot gave her message to the merchant,
and when he reached India, he saw a field
full of parrots. He stopped
and called out what she had told him.

One of the nearest parrots shivered
and stiffened and fell down dead.

The merchant said, "This one is surely kin
to my parrot. I shouldn't have spoken."

He finished his trading and returned home
with the presents for his workers.

When he got to the parrot, she demanded her gift.

"What happened when you told my story
to the Indian parrots?"

"I'm afraid to say."
    "Master, you must!"

"When I spoke your complaint to the field
of chattering parrots, it broke
one of their hearts.

She must have been a close companion,
or a relative, for when she heard about you
she grew quiet and trembled, and died."

As the caged parrot heard this, she herself
quivered and sank to the cage floor. . . .

When the merchant threw the "dead" parrot
out of the cage, it spread its wings
and glided to a nearby tree!

The merchant suddenly understood the mystery.
"Sweet singer, what was in the message
that taught you this trick?"

"She told me that it was the charm
of my voice that kept me caged.
Give it up, and be released!"

The parrot told the merchant one or two more
spiritual truths. Then a tender goodbye.

"God protect you," said the merchant
"as you go on your new way.
I hope to follow you!"[26]

As this parrot suggests, we don't lose who we are when we release forms. Letting go of what no longer serves our essence, we're free to move with our essence freely, like an uncaged bird. Instead of diminishing us, "this giving up" is "a deep honoring" of who we are, making it possible for us to "feel the treasure hiding inside us":

You've been fearful
of being absorbed in the ground,
or drawn up by the air.

Now, your waterbead lets go
and drops into the ocean,
where it came from.

It no longer has the form it had,
but it's still water.
The essence is the same.

This giving up is not a repenting.
It's a deep honoring of yourself.[27]

*

With our faces so close to the love-mirror,
we must not breathe, but change
to a cleared place where a building was
and feel the treasure hiding inside us.[28]

Meeting the Friend

Healing roots is seldom a smooth course, though. Just as we open the door to finding who we are, we get cold feet. Are our souls good enough? Everyone else's soul is surely special, a treasure lying under a rough-hewn house, but maybe ours isn't. Can we face who we are without the bells and whistles we've depended on to feel good about ourselves? "I may not have a good temperament, but at least I make money," or "I may not like myself, but my kids depend on me," or "No one thought I'd amount to anything, but look at all I've done." Without these extras, who are we? Maybe the rented house is worth more than the treasure under it. These fears translate into anger at our mystics' suggestion that we look deeper.

Our souls aren't persuaded. They're not put off by our doubts and insecurities:

> *Look here. If you angrily turn away now,*
> *you will do the same on the day you die. Be pale*

for the One who created color. Don't put saffron
on your face for the sake of shadows.
Be a rooster, conscious of time and the leader.
Don't change your rooster to a hen.
Bend and sit crookedly, but tell the straight truth.
Truth is enough. I am the Friend, your spirit.
Why look for someone else?[29]

Meeting "the Friend, your spirit" isn't a judgment but a coming home, even if we have to face all the pain our souls have experienced. Feeling pain is a testament to our souls' character. It's the gentleness of our souls that makes our encounters with soul-sick people and worlds, as well as with soul sickness within, hurt so much. Under all the pain, confusions, and toughness—"nine layers of illusion"—we find that "gentleness" in our souls:

In pain, I breathe easier.
The scared child is running from the house, screaming.
I hear the gentleness.

Under nine layers of illusion, whatever the light,
on the face of any object, in the ground itself,
I see your face.[30]

For our inner mystics, we're not here to win tough games by fighting tough people; we're here to live from our souls. Inner, soul qualities are what we bring into the visible world, and they're what we take out of it. While we're here, the things we want most in life—sustenance, happiness, a sense of fulfillment, peace, joy—grow from our relationship with "the Friend," our core being:

Remember there's only one reason
to do anything: A meeting with the Friend
is the only real payment.[31]

*

There is no food
but meeting face to face
with the Friend.[32]

As Rumi conceives of it, we have an amazing Friend—one with whom we can share our most intimate thoughts, who knows our needs and helps us meet them, and who values who we are in time and eternity. This Friend is with us day and night, though we're unaware of it. We believe either we have no Friend or our Friend is remote from us. Rumi says we're in for a surprise:

> During the day I was singing with you.
> At night we slept in the same bed.
> I wasn't conscious day or night.
> I thought I knew who I was,
> but I was you.[33]

Surrendering to Our Inner Authority

Our Friend functions like an ideal king or queen in our lives—a wise but also compassionate authority. Over our entire realm of experience and beyond, our Friend commands knowledge and offers guidance. Nothing in the world can compare with what our own souls give us:

> The unity of the soul
> has no likeness.
>
> Just remember, Solomon lives nearby!
> Don't scout the horizon for his presence.
>
> As a man sleeping in a house
> is not aware of the house, in that same way
> you are not conscious of Solomon,
> even though he's your shelter.[34]

Given this powerful inner authority, we'd be foolish not to trust it, yet that's exactly how we're raised. What we feel in our bones is unreliable, we're trained to think, and we should consult those more "expert" than we. In soul-sick cultures, external authorities have more clout than our own inner guidance:

> You were inside my hand.
> I kept reaching around for something.

I was inside your hand, but I kept asking questions
of those who know very little.[35]

More insidious, we're trained to use a way of thinking that excludes
our souls' input. Our inner authority is bumped not so much for experts as for how they think, which we then adopt—the official reasoning that deals only with visibles. Being sensible means ignoring
intangibles and "bowing to sensuality." When we consult that way of
thinking, Rumi says, "the advice is poisonous":

> The inner king is your spirit.
> The inner advisor, your intelligence.
>
> When that counselor bows to your sensuality,
> the advice is poisonous, but when he looks further
> than just getting what's wanted at the moment,
> then you're connected with Solomon.[36]

That's our inner authority. Why brush aside a built-in Solomon?
If we do what "thinking" demands instead of what our "spiritual
guide" suggests, our lives feel labored, endless work without much joy.
But if we go with our inner authority, we "move with fresh intelligence," effortlessly:

> Sacrifice your mind
> to be with the Friend.
>
> You do have a spiritual guide,
> in whose presence you move
> with fresh intelligence.
>
> It's not like "thinking."
> There's no effort.[37]

Of course, sacrificing our minds—or the way they've been programmed to think—may lose us the good opinion of others. Rumi certainly lost it, while Shams's wild iconoclasm never had it. But that's the
way of mystics:

> We're not afraid of God's blade,
> or of being chained up, or
> of having our heads severed.
>
> We're burning up quickly, tasting
> a little hellfire as we go.
>
> You cannot imagine
> how little it matters to us
> what people say.[38]

It's also the way of "free human beings." How can there be free thought if we all defer to expert opinion and doubt our own truth? Children are required to defer to adults, but then we forget to grow up. There's always some new external authority to say we're not there yet. Instead of parents, teachers, or older siblings, we have the media, statistics, computer-tracked trends, government and corporate experts, employers, clergy, tradition—all of which tell us with complete seriousness that "sticks and pieces of broken pottery" are valuable.

As far as Rumi is concerned, if we're old enough to tell our right from our left, we're old enough to listen to our inner authority:

> How many years, like children,
> do we have to collect sticks and pieces
> of broken pottery and pretend they're valuable?
>
> Let's leave childhood and go
> to the banquet of free human beings.
>
> Split open the cultural mould.
> Put your head up out of the sack.
>
> Hold this book in the air
> with your right hand. Are you old enough
> to know your right from your left?
>
> God said to clarity,
>   *Walk,*

and to death,

> *Help them with discipline.*

To the soul,

> *Move into the invisible.*

Take what's there,

> *and don't sing*

the pain anymore.

> Call out that

you are now the king.[39]

The Healer: Accepting Who We Are Heals

Soul-searching, releasing, meeting the Friend, and surrendering to our inner authority are profoundly healing methods. Not only do they re-attune us to our souls and point the way out of soul sickness, but more, they show what healing is all about.

Healing is a mystery. Doctors do biological plumbing and chemistry, but whether or not a body heals depends on something intangible. Everything can be in order, but the patient doesn't get better, or conversely, the body can be a wreck and healing still happens. In psychology, healing is even more mysterious. Some people with horrendous early experiences are able to recover, while those apparently less traumatized can suffer all through life.

As our Healers see it, the intangible factor in healing is our relation to our souls: are we connected with them or not? If we are, even if our bodies die, we're healed; but if we're not, we can be cured in body yet remain ill inside:

> Seeing you heals me.
> Not seeing you, I feel the walls closing.
> I would not wish for anyone else
> such absence.[40]

Breath is an ancient and cross-cultural symbol for the soul, since when we stop breathing, our souls have left. Behind sickness or health, Rumi says, lie different "ways of breathing." One breathes us into soul

sickness. The other frees us to go wherever our souls take us, and that's
health:

> There is a way of breathing
> that's a shame and suffocation.
>
> And there's another way of expiring,
> a love-breath that lets you open infinitely.[41]

Breathing "that lets you open infinitely" does so by reversing the
priorities of soul sickness. As long as our souls' well-being takes a back-
seat, we'll be angry that what's most deeply us is granted least worth.
When our Healers put inner concerns "at the head," our wounds heal,
and we "sing about joy":

> I was a tiny bug. Now a mountain.
> I was left behind. Now honored at the head.
>
> You healed my wounded hunger and anger,
> and made me a poet who sings about joy.[42]

In other words, not something outside us but our own souls are our
Healers; without them, sickness just assumes different forms. Healing
occurs as we honor "what we most deeply want," and let our souls'
longings take the lead:

> The one who heals us
> lets whatever hurts the soul
>
> dissolve to a listening
> intelligence, where what we most
>
> deeply want, union with eternity,
> grows up around and inside us now![43]

Sometimes what our souls "most deeply want" is to wrestle with
demons. Just because individuals, families, or cultures are having a
rough time of it doesn't mean they're soul-sick. Their souls may have

chosen to confront thorn-roots embedded in collective consciousness—
the bodhisattva choice in Mahayana Buddhism—and that's not an easy
job. To assume the soul sickness is theirs would be to judge things outwardly, and mystics don't do that. They wait for the inside story, and
until that's told, they don't venture opinions.

For Rumi, it's our souls that catch "the sun's light" and reveal what's
really going on. Their telling of our stories makes our "raggedness silky"
and inspires a gratitude for our life's course, no matter what it's been.
Not something bad but something healing has been at work:

> You are the fountain of the sun's light.
> I am a willow shadow on the ground.
> You make my raggedness silky.
>
> The soul at dawn is like darkened water
> that slowly begins to say *Thank you, thank you.*[44]

Such unconditional self-acceptance heals soul loss. We reclaim our
souls, and they reclaim us. We feel happy to be the person we are, and
we sense a rightness about what's gone on in our lives. Our souls took
us down this path for a reason, in fact, for reasons that interweave our
lives with the big picture. We're able to reclaim that we have a purpose
here, and our souls are the keys to discovering what our individual
purpose may be—the "pearl hidden in the chest." As we call on our
souls to help us find our pearl, they respond with a knowing that we
feel "in every cell of the body":

> The universal soul touches
> an individual soul and gives it
> a pearl to hide in the chest.
>
> A new Christ lives in you
> from that touch, but no one
> can say why or how.
>
> Every word I say
> is trying to coax a response
> from that.

"Lord," I call out,
and inside my "Lord" comes,
                    "Here I am,"
a "Here I am"
                    that can't be heard,
but it can be tasted and felt
in every cell of the body.[45]

Coming Back to Life

The search for our pearl makes us come alive to who we are. Whereas soul sickness traps us in "lust and dead living," our souls' "Here I am" brings us back to life. It doesn't matter how confused or pain-filled our soul-sick period has been either. Our souls don't care about that, because they don't perceive experiences as fixed absolutes divorced from the larger process:

A shout comes out of my room
where I've been cooped up.
After all my lust and dead living I can still live with you.
You want me to.
You fix and bring me food.
You forget the way I've been.[46]

Whatever has happened, our Soul Healers say, has been part of healing—experiences that one way or another have brought us to the realization that our souls are our lives, and that without them, we're neither happy nor alive:

Water has been drawn and poured in a skin
to drink from. Call it your life,
or call it your Friend.[47]

Living from our souls or trying to get by without them is truly a life-or-death issue. Addiction is a "progressive, fatal disease," because soul sickness is. As our Healers dissolve soul sickness, we die to addictions

and come alive to our real being. Every "limb" and "bone" our souls
touch feels energized with meaning. "Weaknesses" don't matter, neither does the past. Longing for our souls opens the door for our souls
to come through, so that "what died last night can be whole today":

> . . . Forget your weaknesses.
> Your longing is everything.
>
> People will say, "So-and-so is dead."
> But you'll know how alive you've become.[48]

*

> Without you the instruments would die.
> One sits close beside you. Another takes a long kiss.
> The tambourine begs, *Touch my skin so I can be myself.*
> Let me feel you enter each limb bone by bone,
> that what died last night can be whole today.[49]

7

Emptiness Music

ARCHETYPE   *Lover*
MYSTIC JOURNEY   *The Sacred Marriage*

There's Lovers and There's Lovers

As we come home to who we are—the culmination of the first six stages—we're ready to explore our relatedness through the next six stages, first with people and communities (chapters 7, 8, and 9), then with reality and consciousness (chapters 10, 11, and 12).

The Lover kicks off this half of the mystic journey with a jolt. Being a mystic Lover isn't what we might think. What Shams was to Rumi, Rumi's Lover is to our notions of love and community—lightning and thunderbolts, which clear the air for a new foundation.

The subject of love can use the mystic treatment. Where there's soul sickness, there's love sickness, since love engages the soul. Given that soul bargaining pervades our culture, we inherit sick habits of the heart: game playing, falling in love with images, gender roles that crush individual expression, using love to control and manipulate, associating love with boundary violations and dependence, craving love to compensate for self-hate—all of which attempt to make love take the place of being soul-connected.

Rumi knows about love sickness and, though it's not what he has in mind when he talks about the Lover, he sees what's moving behind it. Even through the warping lens of soul sickness, love is a powerful force. In one of Rumi's poems, a caliph falls in love with a sketch of a king's concubine and sends a captain to storm a walled city to get her—a little obsessive?—whereupon the captain falls in love with her, too, and knows her in the biblical sense (though the Bible doesn't tell it the way Rumi does). Rumi comments:

. . . Don't laugh at this.
This loving is also part of infinite Love,
without which the world does not evolve.[1]

By restoring our souls, our Healers also restore our capacities to love. But even healthy love doesn't capture what Rumi means with Lover. Though he loves love in all its expressions, Rumi's mystic Lover is different. Two lovers are two forms, and their love is made visible through rituals of relating: courtship, shared householding, joint vacations. The cultural concept leans on what's visible about love, whereas mystic Lovers are drawn by love's invisible side:

Young lovers like to drink red wine
and listen to love songs,
                    but there's another
Lover, another Wine, another Lovesong,
another Tavern.
                    Hand me, says the mystic poet
to the One he can't see, *Your Cup.*
You are my face. No wonder I can't see You.
You are the intricate workings of my mind.
You are the big artery in my neck.
When I call out in the desert, O God,
I'm only pretending, to distract the others,
so they won't notice Who sits beside me.[2]

The Invisible-Visible Dance

Mystic Lovers envision a dance going on within reality—like the dance of Shiva in Hindu mythology—a dance they take to be not only the source of love but also the essence of love itself. Love is the attraction of everything to everything within the holomovement, because it's all of a piece. How this dance of mutual attraction moves from formlessness into forms back into formlessness makes up the story of our lives—"Their dance is our dance":

You that love Lovers,
this is your home. Welcome!

In the midst of making form, Love
made this form that melts form,
with love for the door, and
Soul, the vestibule.

Watch the dust grains moving
in the light near the window.

Their dance is our dance.

We rarely hear the inward music,
but we're all dancing to it nevertheless. . . . [3]

The dance moves two ways. First, the invisible is drawn to the visible and generates new forms—a birth from nonbeing into being. Behind the curtain of the visible, the invisible is always cooking up new ways of expressing meaning—a new idea, a shift in life direction, or a new relationship. Through this behind-the-scenes dance, the invisible infuses the visible with heightened significance and new life. When we yearn for love, that's what we really want:

There is some kiss we want
with our whole lives,
the touch of Spirit on the body.[4]

That's what happens when we fall in love—"Spirit touches the body." Invisible qualities transform our perception of a person, making that one special to us out of millions. A complete stranger becomes dear to us, even when no one else can see why. Out of invisible meaning, a relationship is born.

Second, the visible is drawn back to its source. It returns to the invisible for renewal. When partners focus only on externals, the spark of love goes out of the relationship. Children feel it too. If their material needs are met but not much more, they don't feel loved. To keep love alive, we need to let the invisible dance through the relationship, reinfusing it with meaning and purpose.

For our mystic Lovers, love is moving with love's two-way process. It's being neither all-visible nor all-invisible but living inside the dialogue between them. Mystic Lovers hear the holomovement's conversation back and forth as it calls different meanings into existence, which then take shape in our lives.

Love is the mutual attraction within reality which, like the forces of physics, keeps the dialogue moving. It's the unity within the holomovement that's always looking to have children—to bring forth new forms of expression. And it's the force, the unseen unity dancing in our bones, that draws us to the invisible path of Lovers. We feel attraction going on, and we want to be part of it.

Granted, our experience of love gets focused around forms, just as thoughts get expressed in words. But more than forms are involved. Whether or not we experience love, therefore, isn't determined by an object—"I need 'x' in my life to experience love"—but by our capacity to engage in love's process. We find love in the "making"—in moving with love's two-way dance—more than in what's "made," the shadow or echo that trails behind:

> . . . Anyone who loves
> Your making is full of Glory. Anyone who loves
> what You have made is not a true believer.[5]

Sufis know how to make a point. In the next poem, a Sufi expresses ecstatic love for an empty food-sack. If you didn't know about love's invisible-visible dance, you'd think the guy was nuts. Instead, it's clear he loves the dance that moves from formlessness into form back into formlessness, and he doesn't need the physical "bread" to celebrate what's going on. Most of love's process goes on in the unseen anyway—love isn't a thing we can point to and say how much is there—and so he's happy to pitch his tent "on a field of Nowhere":

> One day a Sufi sees an empty food-sack hanging on a nail.
> He begins to turn and tear his shirt, saying,

Food for what needs no food!
A cure for hunger!

His burning grows and others join him,
shouting and moaning in the love-fire.

An idle passerby-by comments, "It's only an empty sack."

The Sufi says, *Leave. You want what we do not want.*
You are not a lover.

A lover's food is the love of bread,
not the bread. No one who really loves,
loves existence.

Lovers have nothing to do with existence.
They collect the interest without the capital.

No wings, yet they fly all over the world. No hands,
but they carry the polo ball from the field.

That dervish got a sniff of reality.
Now he weaves baskets of pure vision.

Lovers pitch tents on a field of Nowhere.[6]

In *The Mysteries of Love*, Arthur Versluis describes how the mystic's love for the invisible infuses everything with meaning, throwing a mantle of significance over nature and human life:

> To love is always to long for that which is on the "other side of time"...
> For to live for the other world is not to desecrate or to deny this one—
> quite the reverse. No one can say that it is lovers who lay waste to our
> earth, who cut down forests, and into the oceans pour filth. No, lovers
> celebrate in this fleeting world. The Celtic, the Hindu, the Christian,
> the Islamic cultures, all of whom bear within them the worlds of
> lovers—they create things of beauty, whitewashed monuments and
> carven implements of infinity woven of this place's very fabric.... To
> live for the other world is, then, to invest this world with untold and
> untellable significances.[7]

By focusing on the invisible dance rather than paraphernalia that decorate it, our mystic Lovers focus on love's essential dynamics, its roots in reality. Our inner mystics want to square our concepts with reality first. If, for instance, reality isn't made up of things but of processes, love can't be about things either. Or, if we think love is about being permanently attached to forms, we're in for a surprise if reality's love is about a dance going on within the whole—a dance "we're all dancing to"—that takes us both into forms and out of them again:

> Reality is a rapture
> that takes you out of form,
> not a feeling that makes you
> more fascinated with forms.[8]

A Union That Already Exists

Because love has its roots in reality—and is the power behind the cosmic dance—love pervades everything. Love is the stuff of life, which is a Sufi way of talking about what's meant with "God is Love." Assuming this, our inner mystics also assume that we don't one day find love as if it wasn't there before. Mystic Lovers draw on the invisible-visible unity that exists "on the other side of time," eternally, and doesn't need to be created by putting two visibles together:

> The minute I heard my first love story
> I started looking for you, not knowing
> how blind that was.
>
> Lovers don't finally meet somewhere.
> They're in each other all along.[9]

When we come together in meaningful ways, therefore, we're not creating unions as much as celebrating the unity that's there, even if we weren't aware of it. For mystics, the unity exists long before anything appears visibly. That's why when love strikes, we know it. Something rings true from our invisible side—"This feels right, as if I've known you forever!" "Here's where I belong!"

The idea of soulmates probably started with this feeling of rightness, though mystic Lovers push the notion further: since we're connected with all that is, the entire universe is our soulmate. That's why we can feel an out-of-time rightness not only with people but also with activities, places, groups, ideas, or callings. For the Lovers in us, nothing less than this love-strike makes us happy:

> What was in that candle's light
> that opened and consumed me so quickly?
>
> Come back, my Friend! The form of our love
> is not a created form.
>
> Nothing can help me but that Beauty.[10]

Even in simple ways, we experience a pre-existing love at work. We may not realize it, but we share worlds long before we meet—"You loved that book too?" An unseen unity of spirit lays the ground for a visible union:

> . . . Anyone that feels drawn,
> for however short a time, to anyone else,
> those two share a common consciousness.[11]

The notion of looking for love "out there" in the form of Mr. or Ms. Right is, from our mystic Lovers' point of view, ill-conceived. Love isn't something we get from visibles but something we are as we move with the dance. True, thanks to traumas or years of bargaining, we may have lost our link to love's presence, but even so love doesn't stop dancing in us.

If we feel cut off from love, there's a reason. Reward-driven social systems thrive on our feeling cut off. Social and economic mechanisms of control depend on our believing that we must do something external to get love. That's the lie that sends us down the road of soul bargaining: "You lack love, and only I can give it to you. Since who you are is unacceptable, unlovable, you must do what I, the authority or social system over you, tell you to do. Then you'll be accepted."

From a lie, though, nothing works. If it's false that we're lacking love, then it's false that we need to bargain our souls to get it. As long as we're unaware of love moving within us, we'll bargain, but it won't do any good. Outward bonds won't make us more aware of what's within. We won't feel loved no matter what we do or who loves us.

Not that we don't experience love with others. But we're able to experience it only insofar as we feel love's dance within us first. The love we seek is there in us all along—"How can a lover be anything but the Beloved?":

> . . . Did you hear that?
> It's the man who was looking for treasure.
> He wants me to finish his story.
>   You didn't hear him?
> Then he must be inside me yelling, "Over here!
> Come over here!"
>   Don't think of him as a seeker, though.
> Whatever he's looking for, he is that himself.
> How can a lover be anything but the Beloved?[12]

Conscious of love as our core being, our inner Lovers are moved by the invisible dance, not by externals. Lovers "listen to different drummers" and follow "roads less traveled." Because they don't feel separated from love in the first place, they don't run after socially expected objects of love and then feel shame for not getting them. How can we be driven to want what we already have? How can we regret what we haven't lost? Because love never leaves Lovers, for them there's no waiting patiently or fearing love won't come:

> Dear soul, when the condition comes
> that we call being a lover,
> there's no patience, and no repenting.
>
> Both become huge absurdities. See regret
> as a worm and love as a dragon.

Shame, changeable weather. Love,
a quality which wants nothing.

For this kind of lover love
of anything or anyone is unreal.

Here, the source
and object are one.[13]

The Soul:
A Place of Emptiness Where Love Comes Through

Slowly, almost imperceptibly, our mystic Lovers redefine who we are. If love is the core of our being, and love is a dance, then we're a dance too. We're the place where love's dance goes on, and our feelings track the steps. The more we're aware of our experiences in this light, the more we feel the holomovement operating in us—"a growing consciousness" of the invisible at work:

What is the soul? A joy
when kindness comes, a weeping
at injury, a growing consciousness.

The more awareness one has
the closer to God he or she is.[14]

This redefinition of self is why the Lover comes up in this chapter, which, in the soul-love-freedom layout of the book, accentuates soul. Being a Lover makes us think differently about who we are in the grand scheme of things. Conventional self-definitions as egos or even souls don't fit our inner Lovers. Egos are taken to be fixed composites of opinions, beliefs, attitudes, expectations, habits, desires, and experiences. And souls are viewed roughly the same: as separate entities with fixed character traits, not to mention fixed karma.

The Buddha rejected these notions of ego and soul. If reality is a dynamic process, then fixed, isolated, and self-existent don't accurately describe anything. Mystic Lovers agree with the Buddha. Our essential being isn't a separate thing but an integral process moving with larger processes. We're where the invisible dance becomes visible, where the holomovement unfolds meaning.

Not that our forms aren't important. Personalities, egos, bodies, roles, relationships, even souls: they all function like the banks of a river. As the river moves through, the banks shift in response, creating better channels for what's unfolding. Our form-side becomes "a pen in the Friend's hand":

> I become a pen in the Friend's hand,
> tonight writing *say*, tomorrow *ray*.
> He trims the pen for fine calligraphy.
> The pen says, *I am here, but who am I?*[15]

Just as the pen is a tool for writing thoughts, so too our egos and souls are tools for focusing higher meanings. Rumi likens them to musical instruments. Our egos serve as instruments for the music our souls want to play, just as on another level, our souls are instruments for the music of the cosmic dance. As tools, neither egos nor souls are self-existent things. They take form to bring invisible processes into focus, to let music come through:

> Don't worry about saving these songs!
> And if one of our instruments breaks,
> it doesn't matter.
>
> We have fallen into the place
> where everything is music. . . .
>
> Poems reach up like spindrift
> and driftwood along the beach, wanting.
>
> They derive
> from a slow and powerful root
> that we can't see.
>
> Stop the words now.
> Open the window in the center of your chest,
> and let the spirits fly in and out.[16]

Lovers want their instruments to play as beautifully and clearly as possible, and mystics worldwide agree on how: be empty. The best lute is the one that's most hollow, for then the sound can resonate in it and flow out:

> We are lutes, no more, no less. If the soundbox
> is stuffed full of anything, no music.[17]

>   *

>   . . . The Prophet has said
> that a true seeker must be completely empty like a lute
> to make the sweet music of *Lord, Lord*.

> When the emptiness starts to get filled with something,
> the One who plays the lute puts it down
> and picks up another.

> There is nothing more subtle and delightful
> than to make that music.
>   Stay empty and held
> between those fingers, where *where*
> gets drunk with Nowhere.[18]

The more we're empty of opinions, expectations, fixed self-definitions—all the things that keep us dancing to externals and clog our channels to the unseen—the more we're open to our essence, and the more clearly our essence comes through. Being Lovers of essence, that's "what our souls want":

> Essence is emptiness.
> Everything else, accidental.

> Emptiness brings peace to your loving.
> Everything else, disease.

> In this world of trickery emptiness
> is what your soul wants.[19]

Spiritual exemplars aren't therefore people stuffed with spiritual truths, insights, powers, or even goodness. They're regular folks who, as Lovers of the invisible, allow themselves to be empty places for the invisible to move through. According to Rumi, that's how Muhammed was on the famous Night Journey when he ascended the seven heavens to commune with God:

> Muhammed was completely empty
> when he rose that Night
> through a hundred thousand years.
>
> Let wind blow through us.
> Let Shams cover
> our shadows
> like snow.[20]

Emptiness: Both Reality and the Way to It

Not only Rumi but mystics across cultures take emptiness as both a characterization of reality and the way to it. The late Frank Fools Crow, the wise medicine man of the Lakota, described his role in healing as that of a "hollow bone," an open channel for Spirit to come through. Shamans typically take this approach. The power to heal soul or body isn't theirs; they simply create the open space in consciousness where the healing spirits can come in.

The Mahayana, Vajrayana, and Chan or Zen schools of Buddhism take emptiness to be among the highest teachings of the Buddha, expressed most clearly in the famous *Heart Sutra*, which states: "Form is no other than emptiness, and emptiness no other than form." In these traditions, emptiness expresses an insight into reality, a sense that everything is shot through with the invisible. Nothing exists as a thing on its own, a self-existent form. Everything depends on what's invisible—on consciousness, meaning, love's unseen attraction, and the interconnectedness within the whole. What we call "existence" is a time-space manifestation of something that's essentially beyond time and space:

> Praise to the emptiness that blanks out existence. Existence:
> This place made from our love for that emptiness!

Yet somehow comes emptiness,
this existence goes.
Praise to that happening, over and over![21]

Taoist mystics love emptiness, and they express this love in their art. Taoist paintings are mostly space. Emptiness—described as the Void or Nonbeing—is the pregnant source from which all beings come. If we adopt emptiness as a way of life, we become flexible, spontaneous, and open to new forms. Consider a room, a cup, or a doorway, Taoists argue: their value lies in their ability to hold a space open. If they were chockful of stuff, they'd be of no use. We're like those places of emptiness relative to the holomovement, the Tao. The more empty we are, the more it flows through us. Rumi says:

I saw You and became empty.
This Emptiness, more beautiful than existence,
it obliterates existence, and yet when It comes,
existence thrives and creates more existence![22]

Confucian philosophy has a similar notion. In *Confucius—The Secular as Sacred*, Herbert Fingarette explains that in Confucian ceremonies, empty vessels are used to symbolize the emptiness of human beings in society: we take on meaning from what's going on around us. Instead of following this argument to relativism or situational ethics, Confucius used it to affirm the importance of grounding society on good principles, ones that bring us into harmony with heaven, T'ien. Then, when we move in society, we're filled with values that nourish the good in human life and bring the promise of heaven on earth.

In these traditions as well as in Western spirituality, prayer creates an open channel for the unseen, and that's all prayer has to do. In *Healing Words*, Larry Dossey reviews studies on prayer suggesting that praying for "x" to happen isn't nearly as beneficial as entering into a prayerful openness. Empty prayer brings greater healing benefits than prayer that specifies an outcome. For mystics, this makes sense. Prayer's value lies in its power to empty us of preconceptions. The best prayer clears the inward decks, creating a space for something beyond our concepts to unfold.

Settling into emptiness, which Taoists and Buddhists believe is our natural mode anyway, we move through life "with most joy":

> The planter works with most joy
> whose barn is completely empty,
> the planter who works for that
> which has not appeared.[23]

Emptiness lets us relax into who we are, so we don't have to be "on." Instead of figuring out how things should be and then moving mountains to make them happen, our inner mystics let go of "mountainous wanting":

> For years I pulled my own existence out of emptiness.
> Then one swoop, one swing of the arm,
> that work is over.
> Free of who I was, free of presence, free of
> dangerous fear, hope,
> free of mountainous wanting.
> The here-and-now mountain is a tiny piece of a piece
> of straw
> blown off into emptiness.[24]

Becoming Emptiness, Not Being Stuffed

We're not raised on emptiness, though, and our inner Lovers' devotion to it can be mystifying. We know what emptiness is, and we'd rather avoid it. If our stomachs are empty, we starve. If our bank accounts are empty, we're homeless. If our minds are empty, we fail tests. If our output is empty, we're fired. If our personalities are empty, we're boring and dull and no one will love us.

Stuffing ourselves with the right stuff, the culture tells us, is the way to happiness. In Shakespeare's *Much Ado about Nothing*, a messenger thinks to compliment Benedick by describing him as a man "stuffed with all honorable virtues," whereupon the clever Beatrice replies, "It is so indeed; he is no less than a stuffed man. But for the stuffing—well, we are all mortal."[25]

Notwithstanding Beatrice's mystic leanings, stuffing ourselves is what we've learned to do, using opinions, facts, beliefs, degrees, stratagems, and attitudes as soul-stuffers. Once filled, we defend our composite, as if we cram a house full of furniture and then sit at the door with a gun ready to shoot whoever says our collection isn't the best.

Mystic Lovers aren't keen on starvation or homelessness either. They eat and pay their bills like everyone else, but they do it by a different method. Whereas the stuffing way focuses on visibles, Lovers want invisibles in their lives even more, in fact, than visibles. But for that, Lovers must be empty. The emptier the Lover, the more the invisible can come through—the serendipitous, unimagined, and meaningful. "A new song comes out of the fire":

> There's hidden sweetness in the stomach's emptiness. . . .
> If the brain and the belly are burning clean
> with fasting, every moment a new song comes out of the fire.
> The fog clears, and new energy makes you
> run up the steps in front of you.
> Be emptier and cry like reed instruments cry.[26]

As hard as we work to get stuffed, our mystic Lovers work to unstuff us. Starting with our inner lives, getting unstuffed means questioning our mental and emotional content. To clear out old stuff and make room for what's coming through, we go "around and around all night in the house of the Friend," soul-searching, releasing, and healing, so we can be empty enough for the "Beloved":

> Around and around all night
> in the house of the Friend,
>
> this is how it must be,
> because the Beloved needs
> the cup empty, again empty.[27]

As to our outer lives, emptiness works there too, and our inner Lovers can make it happen. They're fully capable of emptying our lives of any job, marriage, relationship, schedule, or activity that crowds out the invisible, our true Beloved. How can we be empty inwardly, they reason, if we're swallowed up in outward pursuits? The trend toward a simpler life expressed, for instance, by Vicki Robin and the late Joe Dominguez in *Your Money or Your Life* or by Duane Elgin in *Voluntary Simplicity*, not to mention by the monastic vows of simplicity East and West, is a statement not only for social good but for inner quietude as well:

> I went to the Doctor. "I feel lost,
> blind with love. What should I do?"
>
> *Give up owning things and being*
> *somebody. Quit existing.*[28]

Even so, becoming empty represents a major paradigm shift in how we conceive of ourselves, and it's easy to slip back into "hunting" habits: hunting for new things to make ourselves seem more worthy. With the culture's idea of society as a predatory jungle, hunting is ingrained in us, which is why, as Rumi says, "there is that in me that has to be told fifty times a day" to let it go:

> You can open the wide door of the sky.
> Surely you will open me. All I have
> is this emptiness. Give it a nickname.
> Breaker and healer, break and heal this head.
> Don't press your seal to that pistachio nut.
> Put it here. There is that in me
> that has to be told fifty times a day:
> *Stop hunting. Step on this net.*[29]

The more we relax into emptiness, though, the easier it is to do so. If we've been carrying around fifty-pound weights, once we put them down, it's easier not to pick them up again. "Days full of wanting," we can "let them go by":

Days full of wanting, let them go by
without worrying that they do.

Stay where you are, inside
such a pure, hollow note.[30]

*

What a relief to be empty!
Then God can live your life.

When you stay tied to mind and desire, you stumble
in the mud like a nearsighted donkey.[31]

Emptying Ourselves of Ego-Separateness

One thing we stumble over is egos, the side of us that's most "tied to
mind and desire" and therefore most likely to behave, as Rumi so deli-
cately puts it, like "a nearsighted donkey." Not that egos are bad. We
need them for coming into form. Well-formed egos provide reliable
channels for soul energies to flow. They know how to protect soul energies and to keep a space open for our souls' expression. Good egos
don't get in the way. They make wonderful stagehands, but lead characters, no, that's not their job.

In the mystical scheme of things, egos and all the stuff that goes
with them have the same status as trinkets we buy on vacations. They
remind us of meaning, but they're not meaningful in themselves. If we
define our life's meaning through ego collections, we'll get trapped inside conglomerates of likes and dislikes, habits, images, histories, and
opinions. Neither the invisible nor even the true value of the visible
will be clear:

> While still yourself, you're shut off
> from the two worlds. Ego-drunken-
> ness cannot recognize either.[32]

Love is the remedy for stuffed egos. When we feel the pull of an invisible unity—love—we may at first think that means putting two egos

together. But if we do, the joining doesn't wear well. It comes to feel less like love and more like litigation—fighting over our egos' different stuff, jockeying for position as to whose stuff comes first, or declaring a truce by marking boundaries so our piles don't mix. Mystic Lovers see relationships differently. The unity doesn't come from the level of egos but of souls and of the invisible dance going on behind them. As the deeper unity comes through, it clears the channels—"dissolving and draining away the ego-life":

> Your love is a sweet poison we eat from your hand
> to dissolve and drain away the ego-life
> now spraying this fountain from us.[33]

When love strikes, even the best ego-containers get restructured. The new meaning changes our personal riverbanks, adapted as they are to past currents. Nor do we miss the old containers, since what's unfolding is "like the sun coming up":

> You are granite.
> I am an empty wine glass.
>
> You know what happens when we touch!
> You laugh like the sun coming up laughs
> at a star that disappears into it.[34]

Instead of trying to preserve ego forms, Rumi suggests we toss them in the air and let them break apart. That way, we stay open to "all we could become" and don't settle for "a love that turns us yellow":

> A chunk of dirt thrown in the air breaks to pieces.
> If you don't try to fly,
> and so break yourself apart,
> you will be broken open by death,
> when it's too late for all you could become.
>
> Leaves get yellow. The tree puts out fresh roots
> and makes them green.
> Why are you so content with a love that turns you yellow?[35]

If real union already exists on unseen levels, parcelling up the Ocean into egos and then hauling pieces of it around, saying how wonderful and heroic those pieces are, seems odd and unnecessary. True, our Lovers express meaning in specific, visible ways that we then associate with egos, but our Lovers do this not to ballyhoo the visible but to celebrate the invisible:

> Break your pitcher against a rock.
> We don't need any longer
> to haul pieces of the Ocean around.
>
> We must drown, away from heroism,
> and descriptions of heroism.
>
> Like a pure spirit lying down, pulling
> its body over it, like a bride her husband
> for a cover to keep her warm.[36]

With this perspective, why favor the ego-facsimile when we have the soul-original? Our original is a "True Human Being"—the "choice wine" that comes in exchange for the "sour buttermilk" of the ego:

> No one objects to exchanging
> sour buttermilk for choice wine.
>
> The illuminated life can happen now,
> in the moments left. Die to your ego,
> and become a True Human Being.[37]

In the following poem, "Hu" is the pronoun Sufis use to indicate our unseen presence and its power to "breathe" us beyond a narrow sense of "who":

> Muhammed is said to have said,
> "Whoever belongs to God, God belongs to."
>
> Our weak, uneven breathings,
> these dissolving personalities,

were breathed out by the eternal
Huuuuuuu, that never changes!

A drop of water constantly fears
that it may evaporate into air,
or be absorbed by the ground.

It doesn't want to be used up
in those ways, but when it lets go
and falls into the ocean it came from,
it finds protection from the other deaths.

Its droplet form is gone,
but its watery essence has become
vast and inviolable.

Listen to me, friends, because *you*
are a drop, and you can honor yourselves
in this way. What could be luckier

than to have the ocean come
to court the drop?

For God's sake, don't postpone your *yes!*
Give up and become the giver.[38]

Ego Distinctions: Not Root Categories

For mystics, letting go of the ego opens us to one of the most basic mystical truths, namely, that we're not separate beings at all. The appearance of separateness is an illusion—a function of the time-space-mass language we use in the world of forms but not a function of our beyond-forms reality:

I, you, he, she, we.
In the garden of mystic lovers,
these are not true distinctions.[39]

*

Sometimes afraid of reunion, sometimes
of separation: You and I, so fond of the notion
of a *you* and an *I*, should live
as though we'd never heard those pronouns.[40]

Not that this is an easy step to take when forms are constantly in front of us. Plus, as Rumi says, we're nervous about giving up separateness, fearing that we'll lose individuality. That's a thingish way to think, though, as if our individuality comes from keeping our piles of stuff separate.

In integral systems, individuality means expressing the whole in individualized ways. For mystics, being an individual doesn't mean being alone or isolated, a separate single. It means being so connected to the holomovement that life and meaning emerge from this whole-connectedness. Our hands don't lose individuality, for instance, because they're hooked to our bodies. If they were to separate themselves, act separately, or not allow the body's blood to flow through them, we and they would be in a fix.

It's not individuality, then, but the separateness notion of it that causes problems. When, for instance, corporations act as separate entities—huge egos—seeing themselves as having no relation to anything but profits, they take no responsibility for the social and environmental costs of how they do business. The hand goes off on its own at the expense of the body that sustains it. Like all mystics, Rumi is hard on this separateness concept of identity and individuality. Whatever form it takes, it "blocks us." To the invisible-visible dance, ego-separateness poses "a *No,* harder than stone":

You tighten your two hands together,
determined not to give up saying "I" and "we."
This tightening blocks you.[41]

       *

            . . . Mountains move, but sometimes
nothing affects an unbeliever. He keeps saying *I,*

or *we*, for the center of his being, which is,
as the *Qur'an* says, a *No*, harder than stone.[42]

Our mystic Lovers lure us away from the hard stones of egos with a gentle alternative: living from the inside out, from meaning to form, from invisible to visible. Ego exteriors divide us, whereas the world of inner meanings offers common ground. In dealing with others, our Lovers stick to the mystic premise: a unity, however hidden, already exists and is emerging because it has some new meaning or story to tell. If we focus on the meaning and not on ego divisions, we'll find the unity appearing.

Rumi pushes the premise further. Since we're all coming from the holomovement, the different stories about meaning belong to each of us. Everyone's life experience is part of us; just as in a hologram, each part contains the whole image. Their good is, in this light, our good too, their learning our learning, and their suffering our suffering. From the inner-seeing of mystics, we *are* everyone. When someone asked the Buddha why we should be kind to everyone, that was his answer—"Because you are everyone":

> When you are with everyone but me,
>   you're with no one.
> When you are with no one but me, you're with everyone.
>
> Instead of being so bound up *with* everyone, *be* everyone.
> When you become that many, you're nothing. Empty.[43]

Marrying the Beloved

Of course, that last poem can be read as the most dysfunctional, co-dependent, unhealthy, and ungrounded (we'll skip the *DSM*'s clinical epithets) poem ever written. Rumi doesn't mind, because that's not what he's talking about. For one thing, mystic Lovers come after the first six stages—after our Soul Searchers, Releasers, and Healers have alerted us to soul sickness and are helping us heal from it.

For another, whether the poem says something healthy or not depends on who "me" is. If it's a person, it's not healthy. But for Rumi, the "me" is our Beloved, which is shorthand for "our link to the unseen"—our own unseen essence as well as the essence of everyone else. If we're moving at-one with the holomovement, we're with everyone and indeed are everyone, since the invisible doesn't draw lines as we do.

But just in case we're a bit wobbly on what our mystic Lovers are doing with all this unity—being empty and nothing and everyone and what not—the mystic journey grounds us with the image of a ritual: the sacred marriage. In the sacred marriage, what scholars call the *hieros gamos*, we're not marrying a person but cementing our link to the invisible. The marriage is vertical, so to speak, a covenant that protects our bond with the higher source of meaning in our lives. We're marrying our more visible sides to our roots in the holomovement. Through the sacred marriage, we align all levels of our being with our source:

> The inner soul, that presence of which most know nothing,
> about which poets are so ambiguous,
> he married that one to the Beloved.[44]

Like all marriages, the sacred marriage establishes this as our primary relationship. Grounding our link to the whole through the image of a sacred marriage says no one *but no one* is allowed to mess with it. Our marriage to the Beloved is off-limits to anyone's meddlings because it's sacred and it makes our lives sacred, for from this relation, we draw our life and reasons for being.

In a way, it seems odd to talk about marrying the holomovement, as if our hands had to marry our bodies. But then our hands never had the notion that they were separate. We, however, do have that notion of separateness and, insofar as we do, marrying the whole is an offer we should jump at:

> When the ocean comes to you as a lover,
> marry, at once, quickly,
> for God's sake!

Don't postpone it!
Existence has no better gift.

No amount of searching
will find this.

A perfect falcon, for no reason,
has landed on your shoulder,
and become yours.[45]

Relating only ego to ego, stuff to stuff—horizontally—doesn't respect the sacred marriage. It doesn't honor the vertical dimension of meaning at the core of each partner. Horizontally, the puzzle pieces may fit—a match may be socially correct or personally convenient—but vertically, they may not form a picture that makes sense. If the union doesn't come from higher levels, horizontal concerns squeeze out our inner Lovers.

Once we make the sacred marriage—the vertical one—all other relationships become possible, make sense, and thrive. By honoring our sacred marriages above all else, mystic Lovers propose a new foundation for society. To have any relationship, we must each "marry our Beloved" and "let the thorn of the ego slide from our feet." Then, when we come together, we won't be toasting our unions with "embalming fluid." We'll each be drinking "from this other fountain," our individual weddedness to the whole:

You must marry your soul.
That wedding is the way.
Union with the world is sickness.

But it's *hard* to be separated from these forms!
You don't have enough patience to give this up?
But how do you have enough patience
to do without God?

You can't quit drinking the earth's dark drink?
But how can you *not* drink from this other fountain?

You get restless, you say, when you don't sip
the world's fermentation. But if for one second
you saw the beauty of the clear water of God,
you'd think this other was embalming fluid.

Nearness to the Beloved is the splendor
of your life. Marry the Beloved.
Let the thorn of the ego slide from your foot.[46]

8

Passionate Seeing

ARCHETYPE   *Visionary*

MYSTIC JOURNEY   *Dying as a Method of Regeneration*

Where There Is No Vision . . .

Mystic Lovers bank everything on what's unseen. For them, that's the stuff of life, giving our lives order and, above all, meaning. But not everyone feels that way, or more precisely, not every paradigm shares this priority. The visible-only value system—the one that grants holders of things (corporations) more rights than individuals, that says money talks (a perverse sort of mysticism), that destroys the planet's life-support systems with abandon, and that justifies wage slavery by the "right" of a few to accumulate huge sums—this value system has no time for invisibles, no time for justice, compassion, integrity, and the like.

That's ironic, not to mention self-deceived, since every value system, including this one, depends on an invisible assessment of worth. To some cultures, for instance, gold has no special value; good topsoil and a healthy nanny goat are worth far more. Shamans, astrologers, philosophers, and seers were once treated with the deference that businessmen, politicians, and actors now enjoy. Worth is inescapably intangible and exists in the eye of the beholder.

But the visible-only value system glosses over this point, claiming instead that granting visibles maximum worth isn't an intangible assessment but simply the way things are. By declaring quantifiables the only things of value (money, stocks, options, futures, options on futures, futures on options—how visible are these?), this paradigm ignores its own invisible logic: "We're not talking paradigms or choices here, we're talking reality, and that's the end of it!"

Rumi can debate with the best of them, but he's not inclined. Just because a paradigm dismisses the invisible doesn't mean the invisible goes away, and whether or not people value intangibles depends on where they are inwardly. Unless the Friend intervenes, debating doesn't make a dent:

> These matters are as real as the infinite is real,
> but they seem religious fantasies to some,
> to those who believe only in the reality
> of the sexual organs and the digestive tract.
>
> Don't mention the Friend to those.
> To others, sex and hunger are fading images,
> and the Friend is more constantly, solidly here.
> Let the former go to their church, and we'll go to ours.[1]

Rumi does, however, agree with Solomon: "Where there is no vision, the people perish."[2] Our Lovers' marriage to what's emerging from the unseen gives us "the energy of a whirlpool," connecting us with life's source. Without this vision, we're lost—"frantic fish at the bottom":

> Love is moonlight on your bedroom wall,
> the energy of a whirlpool.
>
> When it's not there,
> a human being becomes a frantic
> fish at the bottom of the place
> where the whirlpool was,
>
> or just a blank barrier between sleepers.[3]

On one hand, the visible-only, forget-vision paradigm doesn't fool us. We know that invisibles matter most in life: love, self-worth, happiness, friendship, fun, fulfillment, compassion, as well as hope, trust, and faith. Nor can such invisibles be bought. When they move through our lives, it's "like Christ coming through Mary," a gift from the unseen. On the other hand, the visible-only paradigm bites our heels. We get scared, then confused, then depressed, then resigned. Though we know invisibles count, we "run away" from them:

You and I have worked in the same shop for years.
Our loves are great fellow-workers.
Friends cluster there and every moment we notice
a new light coming out in the sky.
Invisible, yet taking form, like Christ coming through
Mary. In the cradle, God.

Shams, why this inconsistency?
That we live within love
and yet we run away?[4]

Mystics know the value of visibles as much as anyone. Without vision, though, visibles become a meaningless jumble and "a source of heartburn":

The visible bowl of form contains food
that is both nourishing and a source of heartburn.[5]

Instead of debating the no-vision paradigm, Rumi offers stories and images that suggest what it's like to live inside it. Without vision, for instance, there's no joy or aliveness, as if we're living in a tomb:

A child was crying with his head against
his father's coffin. "Why are they taking you
to such a terrible house? There's no carpet,
no lamp, no bread, no smell of cooking.

There's no door! No ladder leading up to the roof,
no neighbors to help out in difficulties.

We used to love to kiss you!
Why are you going where we can't?"

Juhi and his father were passing by.
Young Juhi said, "It sounds like they're taking
the corpse over to our house."

                                    "What do you mean?"
"All those things he said are true of our place."

Like that, sometimes people don't see the signs
that are so close, even how their homes
are unlit! The way you're living now is like
living in a tomb! There's none of God's light,
and no openness.
              Remember that you're alive!
Don't stay in a narrow, choked place.[6]

What puts us in a tomb is the fear that there won't be enough visibles to go around—Malthusian scarcity. Mystics don't worry about this,
though, because they figure survival doesn't depend on visibles in the
first place. With the contents of a kitchen, for instance, we can concoct
either a nourishing meal or a lethal poison. Not things but our vision
for arranging them makes the difference. The more our vision is in-
formed by knowledge, creativity, and above all wisdom, the more possibilities we enjoy for managing visibles well and the more we trust
unseen systems, like the ecosystem, to create food from dirt. A visible-
only perspective, however, isn't convinced. Its vision can't see that far:

There is a small green island
where one white cow lives alone,
a meadow of an island.

The cow grazes till nightfall, full and fat,
but during the night she panics
and grows thin as a single hair. "What shall I eat
tomorrow? There's nothing left!"

By dawn, the grass has grown up again, waist-high.
The cow starts eating and by dark
the meadow is clipped short.

She's full of strength and energy, but she panics
in the dark as before, and grows
abnormally thin overnight.

The cow does this over and over,
and this is all she does.

She never thinks, "This meadow has never failed
to grow back. Why should I be afraid
every night that it won't?"

The cow is the bodily soul.
The island field is this world
that grows lean with fear and fat with blessing,

lean and fat. White cow,
don't make yourself miserable
with what's to come, or not to come.[7]

When the cow "grows lean" with survival fears, she forgets the invisible qualities—the "strength and energy"—that she herself embodies. Living inside this tomb makes us feel inadequate, unaware that the riches we seek, we are:

. . . How long will you complain
about money and our prospects for money? The torrent
of our life has mostly gone by. Don't worry about
transient things. Think how the animals live.

The dove on the branch giving thanks.
The glorious singing of the nightingale.
The gnat. The elephant. Every living thing
trusts in God for its nourishment.

These pains that you feel are Messengers.
Listen to them. Turn them to sweetness. The night
is almost over. You were young once, and content.
Now you think about money all the time.

You used to *be* that money. You were a healthy vine.
Now you're a rotten fruit. You ought to be growing
sweeter and sweeter, but you've gone bad.[8]

What's Born from the Invisible

We "go bad" because a visible-only paradigm lacks the power of regeneration. Closed by nature, it runs down; its philosophical entropy becomes personally and culturally entropic as well. We get our vision

powers back, mystics say, by breaking with the closed model and returning to the big picture—how everything has its roots in the holomovement, which "fashions things before they come into being." By
expanding our perspective, we invite "the Lord of Beauty" back into
our souls, and it's springtime all over again:

> The Lord of Beauty enters the soul
> as a man walks into an orchard
> in Spring.
> > Come into me
> that way again! . . .
>
> Like a fresh idea in an artist's mind,
> you fashion things before they come into being.[9]

That everything "comes into being" from the holomovement is a
fundamental premise of mysticism. What's going on isn't what it seems
but is really "God's creative action." Mystics are the ultimate system
thinkers, assuming that everything emerges from one integral process.
Because we're accustomed to a visible-only, piece-by-piece view of
things, it's hard to imagine how this works. Yet even the most beautiful painting looks nonsensical if we view it through a microscope. How
easy would it be for an ant crawling over the *Mona Lisa* to see
Leonardo's vision for the painting?

> Consider the difference
> in our actions and God's actions.
>
> We often ask, "Why did you do that?"
> or "Why did I act like that?"
>
> We *do* act, and yet everything we do
> is God's creative action.
>
> We look back and analyze the events
> of our lives, but there is another way
> of seeing, a backward-and-forward-at-once
> vision, that is not rationally understandable.
>
> Only God can understand it.[10]

Big-picture vision isn't up in the clouds, though, but has practical value. If, for example, our vision says rewards come from "God's creative action," then it doesn't make sense to hold on to the good received as our exclusive possession. If rewards come our way, we should feed them back into the whole-systems that sustain us. What seems like visionary talk informs how we do business:

> In the village of Zarwan near the border of Yemen
> there was a good man, who took care of the poor
> and the troubled. They came to him, and he gave
> without calling attention to his giving, a tenth
> of his harvest of corn and wheat, and a tenth
> after the threshing. When it was ground into flour,
> he gave a tenth of that, and also a tenth of the bread.
> Anything that grew on his land he tithed four times.
> He instructed his sons, "After I am gone, continue
> to do the same. This produce is not our doing.
> We must give to what gave." A good farmer
> sows back the major part of his seed.
> He has no doubt that it will grow again.
> He generously moves his hand back and forth.[11]

The farmer's attitude reflects what mystic Visionaries assume to be true about everything, namely, that what emerges on the visible stage comes from a deeper, prior "Union" with invisible systems. By tuning in to the invisible-visible dance, we "become pregnant" with ideas, and "children are born." We receive "a new understanding," and we're off and running with a new vision:

> Those who live in Union
> become pregnant with the feelings and words
> of invisible forms!
>   Their amazed mouths
> open. Their eyes withdraw.
>
> Children are born of that illumination.
> We say "born," but that's not right.
> It only points to a new understanding.[12]

The Visionary archetype focuses on this generative process. It urges us to reach as far as we can into the invisible to see what's coming before it takes outward form. By exploring our unseen side, we have a chance to sort out "noble" from "vile," and the visible forms that follow reflect our choices:

> There are many wonders in the hiding place. The nights are pregnant until their results appear in the day-world. There is aching and wanting, and then what is hidden in the invisible world takes shape, and God brings the visible form together with its thinker. If the thought was noble, you will be ennobled. If it was vile, you will be vicious.[13]

Open to What's Coming Through

If vile is what we find, our Visionaries deal with it. Vileness manifests in our psyches because a no-vision paradigm threw us into some sort of visible-only feedback loop, trapping us there. Our inner Visionaries break the closed loop by "opening completely" and listening to the "passionate murmur" of the larger dance going on. With our Visionaries' broken-openness and "spirit-ear," we leave vile and vicious patterns behind, and our "dead body" revives:

> I see how love has "thoughts,"
> and that these thoughts are circling
> in conversation with majesty.
> Let me keep opening this moment
> like a dead body reviving.[14]

> *

> Don't put blankets over the drum!
> Open completely. Let your spirit-ear
> listen to the green dome's passionate murmur.[15]

Openness is our Visionaries' forté, since that's what allows visions to come through. For mystic Visionaries, though, openness is more than just considering new ideas. Their brand of openness is awe before the holomovement's workings and how thoroughly it infuses our lives with meaning. Being intellectually open doesn't touch this. The intellectual version has a "correct" flavor, techniques for appearing to be open that mask hidden agendas. Awe has none of that. Awe-openness lets thoughts and desires go the instant "Your Presence" becomes clear:

> In Your Presence I don't want what I thought
> I wanted, those three little hanging lamps.
>
> Inside Your Face the ancient manuscripts
> seem like rusty mirrors.
>
> You breathe; new shapes appear,
> and the music of a Desire as widespread
> as Spring begins to move
> like a great wagon.[16]

Awe is humility before the bigness of what's going on, though we only catch glimpses of it. What "heals our eyes" isn't what we see but the awe attitude that opens us to seeing. Whereas arguing over insights snares us in "mouse-holes" and "doctrinal labyrinths," awe gives us "keen, constant listening":

> Awe is the salve
> that will heal our eyes.
>
> And keen, constant listening.
> Stay out in the open like a date palm
> lifting its arms. Don't bore mouse-holes
> in the ground, arguing inside some
> doctrinal labyrinth.[17]

With awe, our whole being expands to accept what's emerging from the unseen, whether it's our personal unseen side or something more. Awe says, "Pour more on me of that power I was fashioned from":

> Rain fell on one man,
> he ran into his house.

But the swan spread its wings and said,
"Pour more on me of that power
I was fashioned from."[18]

Our Visionaries open so unconditionally because they assume that what's coming through is brought by the Friend. If vileness comes, we assume the Friend wants us to look at it for a reason. Instead of censoring vileness, our inner Visionaries listen to what the Friend has to say about it. The vision that we have a Friend, that the Friend is guiding us, that there's a meaning emerging: this vision opens us to feelings that may otherwise seem overwhelming. With the Friend at hand, we can "catch what sifts down" from whatever level:

> Spread your love-robe out to catch
> what sifts down from the ninth level.
>
> You strange, exiled bird with clipped wings,
> now you have four full-feathered pinions.
>
> You heart closed up in a chest, open,
> for the Friend is entering you.[19]

Noble or vile, "well-meaning or mean," these currents pass through us but don't belong to us. We choose which to ride, but the currents aren't ours to possess. If we're places of emptiness for the holomovement to move through, what would do the possessing? Living from the Lover's ego-emptiness, Visionaries let things not only come but also go, which is how they stay open:

> Poem, song, and story,
> the stream sweeps by, moving along
> what was never mine anyway.
>
> What I've done through an act of will,
> well-meaning or mean, these are brought in
> briefly by moonlight and carried obscurely off.[20]

*

> Observe the wonders as they occur around you.
> Don't claim them. Feel the artistry
> moving through, and be silent.[21]

How Vision Works: Focusing Energies

Don Quixote is the quintessential mystic Visionary—one who lives between the invisible and the visible and follows the vision wherever it leads. He doesn't have to be right about his vision or successful in defending it. He just has to stay engaged in the invisible-visible dance. If Cervantes read Rumi, he'd have found support for Don Quixote's method: vision keeps us going. When we're lost or disillusioned, it's our inner Visionaries that "buy us back into being":

> I hear you and I'm everywhere, a spreading music.
> You've done this many times.
> You already own me, but once more
> you buy me back into being.[22]

Our Visionaries bring us to life by reviving qualities latent in us: insight, imagination, creativity, hope, and courage. Through vision, these qualities converge. Whereas filters screen the holomovement, vision inspires us to be creative with it. With vision, "a thousand new roads come clear":

> . . . The mind, this globe
> of awareness, is a starry universe that when
> you push off from it with your foot,
>
> a thousand new roads come clear, as you yourself
> do at dawn, sailing through the light.[23]

To explore "a thousand new roads," we need vision to mediate between what we know and what's uncertain, the concrete and the elusive. Vision "takes messages" back and forth: "This road leads to these issues. Is that where you want to go?" "Maybe, but where might the other road take me?" As the invisible and visible talk back and forth, vision tells us what they're saying and, as it does, qualities come together with experiences. Meaning comes into focus:

A story is like the water
you heat for your bath.

It takes messages between the fire
and your skin. It lets them meet,
and it cleans you!

Very few can sit down
in the middle of the fire itself
like a salamander or Abraham.
We need intermediaries.

A feeling of fullness comes,
but usually it takes some bread
to bring it.

Beauty surrounds us,
but usually we need to be walking
in a garden to know it.[24]

As our vision goes, so go our energies and creativity. If we can't envision a new world, we can't create it. That's a rule, for instance, in hypnotherapy: you must visualize yourself thin before you can lose weight or imagine yourself not smoking before you can stop. Whatever vision we have channels our energies. Rumi, who uses astrological symbols in his poetry, shows how different signs, which pose different visions of life, focus our energies differently:

Whatever that Presence gives us
we take in. Earth signs feed.
Water signs wash and freshen.
Air signs clear the atmosphere.
Fire signs jiggle the skillet,
so we cook without getting burnt.[25]

Wherever our vision takes us, that's who we become. We create ourselves according to the molds our visions give us. If we're the invisible holomovement coming into focus, vision directs that focus, making us into who we are:

> Look at Saturn, lame ant. Look at
> Solomon! You become what you behold.
>
> A human being is essentially a spiritual eye.
> The skin and bones fall away.
> Whatever you really see, you are that.[26]

If our vision focuses us on money or food, for instance, our characters reflect this priority—"whatever you love, you are":

> If you want money more than anything,
> you'll be bought and sold.
>
> If you have a greed for food,
> you'll be a loaf of bread.
>
> This is a subtle truth:
> whatever you love, you are.[27]

Passionate Connecting

Moving at the center of vision is passion, the engine of our inner Visionaries. Passion is what keeps us going on a vision when we'd otherwise give up. Granted, our Visionaries' passions may have been messed with. The passion to be who we are seems threatening to those who want us to become someone else. But even though we may be confused about our passions, they persist. They outlast efforts to suppress them, because they're inspired from beyond:

> God picks up the reed-flute world and blows.
> Each note is a need coming through one of us,

a passion, a longing-pain.

> Remember the Lips
where the wind-breath originated,
and let your note be clear.
Don't try to end it.
Be your note.

> I'll show you how it's enough.[28]

"*Be* your note" sounds simple enough, but given the cultural paradigm, it's anything but. Who are we to have such a passion? Tilting at windmills doesn't pay. Visible-only lives don't leave much room for visions, and yet the passion to live them—to "*be* your note"—is there. Caught in the middle, we grow numb, not because we don't care about vision but because we care "*so much*":

> Sometimes a lover of God may faint
in the presence. Then the Beloved bends
and whispers in his ear, "Beggar, spread out
your robe. I'll fill it with gold.

> I've come to protect your consciousness.
Where has it gone? Come back into awareness!"

> This fainting is because
lovers want *so much*.[29]

If we don't "come back into awareness," life drags. No passion means no vision, and no vision means no reason to be alive, as if we're just doing time. Half despairing, half bored, we wonder, "How long do we have to *do* this"?

> Life freezes if it doesn't get a taste
of this almond cake.

> The stars come up spinning
every night, bewildered in love.

> They'd grow tired
with that revolving, if they weren't.

They'd say,
"How long do we have to *do* this!"[30]

Our Visionaries realize that with vision, something central to being human is at stake, and without it, our humanity slips away. Without a vision, a journey that starts with divine passion gets lost in visiting "meanspirited roadhouses." That's why Visionaries "gamble everything for love." What are pensions, benefits, or reputations compared to living who we are as "true human beings":

> Gamble everything for love,
> if you're a true human being.
>
> If not, leave
> this gathering.
>
> Half-heartedness doesn't reach
> into majesty. You set out
> to find God, but then you keep
>
> stopping for long periods
> at meanspirited roadhouses.[31]

Living from our passions, we shift to a different way of knowing, one that sees through events to the inner meaning. The daily news records the comings and goings of visibles, but inner seeing perceives "life as it's being lived":

> To your minds there is such a thing as *news*,
> whereas to the inner knowing, it's all
> in the middle of its happening.
>
> To doubters, this is a pain.
> To believers, it's gospel.
> To the lover and the visionary,
> it's life as it's being lived![32]

"Inner knowing" is put to the test when we're confronted with something low or base. What meaning can there be in someone being a jerk or worse—all the awful things that go on? Rumi relishes the challenge, for he often uses despicable behavior to illustrate some spiritual insight. His mystic knowing cares about the inner meaning, and he seems to relish using outrageous images to propel us past surface forms. As far as he's concerned, any behavior can be an opportunity for seeing the invisible-visible dance.

That's the Visionary archetype par excellence: only the vision matters; circumstances aren't the issue. Whatever the experience, if we follow it through, we'll find the holomovement and our own essence behind it.

Addictions are a good example. They're our souls' way of alerting us to pain that wants healing, and addictions see to it that things go from bad to worse until healing begins. Behind addictions, therefore, not something evil but something sacred is going on—if we have the vision to see it. Because our Visionaries do see it, they use that vision to lead us "from wanting to longing":

> Be fair. Admit that love has in it
> all the righteousness we need.
>
> Confess that you're willing to forget
> and be numb enough to call some
> low desire a holy name.
>
> Live as evidence
> that there is a way
> from wanting to longing.[33]

Vision connects us with our life's passion, and our passion connects us with our origins. As a result, we can't afford to dismiss either of them just because they don't fit our existing forms. In the ongoing dialogue between the part of us that's coming into being and the part that's here, why should only the "here" part get a hearing? Once we cultivate an ear for our unseen side—"the Beloved all around us"—we want to listen to that "Conversation" and stay awake to it:

> Lovers can't sleep when they feel the privacy
> of the Beloved all around them. Someone

who's thirsty may sleep for a little while,
but he or she will dream of water, a full jar
beside a creek, or the spiritual water you get
from another person. All night, listen
to the Conversation.[34]

Failure Angels

Staying awake to our Beloved, though, brings with it another night on the path: the night of failures. With dreams and aspirations comes the risk of their not working. Outwardly, hopes are dashed, plans fall through, people don't understand, and we wonder why we ever believed in a vision. Inwardly, it's just as up and down, full of doubts, uncertainties, and inner crises. We're tempted to fall asleep to being Visionaries, to lose hope.

Here again, we face a question of priorities and choice of worth. The visible-only paradigm equates doubts and mistakes with failure, and failure with death: if we're uncertain in school, we fail tests, and if we fail, we won't get a job, no one will love us, and we'll starve and die. This isn't reality, though, but a ruse of control: if we're afraid of failing, we won't step out of line. Fear of failing overrides vision every time—and makes us toe the line in control systems.

Our mystic Visionaries aren't fooled. They create and fail and keep creating, wiser for the failings. Living by vision is the priority; mistakes are just a phase of the process. In fact, what counts as a failure, if the passion for it comes from beyond and the experience supports our inner process? But even if we use the mistake/failure language, the Visionary priority is clear—making mistakes in following a vision is far better than playing it safe and having no vision at all:

Be a lover . . . that you come to know
your Beloved. Be faithful that you may know
Faith. The other parts of the universe did not accept
the next responsibility of love as you can.
They were afraid they might make a mistake
with it, the inspired knowing
that springs from being in love.[35]

Self-doubt serves our inner Visionaries well. As we listen to the invisible-visible "Conversation," we wonder if we've heard it rightly. Mindful of human fallibility, mystic Visionaries are passionate about questioning visions: "I think that's what's coming through, but let's see. . . ." This aura of uncertainty is found in virtually every mystic tradition, and for good reason. Whether we heard the Conversation rightly or not, it's always changing. The message of two days ago may not be what's coming through today. Self-doubt keeps us open to that:

> Your spirit needs to follow the changes happening
> in the spacious place it knows about.
>
> *There*, the scene is always new,
> a clairvoyant river of picturing,
> more beautiful than any on earth.
>
> This is where the sufis wash.[36]

Given this inner skepticism and openness, Visionaries don't make good dogmatists. They're not ones to say categorically, "And that's the way it is." Instead of responding to the Conversation with either "Yes, I knew" or "No, I didn't hear anything," our inner Visionaries say, "Lead me":

> Let the stretcher come and take you wherever
> that mercy knows you should go.
>
> If you say *Yes, I knew*, you'll be pretending,
> somewhat. And if you say *No*, that blade of No
> will slam shut your window into God and behead you.
>
> Be quiet in your confusion, and bewildered.
> When you're completely empty, within
> that silence, you'll be saying,
>
> > > *Lead me.*
> When you become that helpless,
> God's kindness will act through you.[37]

But we can be as open as the great wide sky and still get mightily confused. There's nothing about infinite, multidimensional reality that says it has to conform to our abilities to understand it. Utter bafflement is not an uncommon place for our Visionaries to be:

> I wish I knew what You wanted.
> You block the road and won't give me rest.
> You pull my lead-rope one way, then the other.[38]

Having intentions thwarted and hopes disappointed are part of this archetype's dynamics. What feels like failure sharpens our longings for what works, and we explore visions we'd otherwise ignore. The challenge is to give up not our capacity to be Visionaries but only this or that vision. That's how we hang in there long enough to see a breakthrough—how failure becomes "the key to the kingdom within":

> You know how it is. Sometimes
> we plan a trip to one place,
> but something takes us to another. . . .
>
> God fixes a passionate desire in you,
> and then disappoints you.
> God does that a hundred times!
>
> God breaks the wings of one intention
> and then gives you another,
> cuts the rope of contriving,
> so you'll remember your dependence.
>
> But sometimes your plans work out!
> You feel fulfilled and in control.
>
> That's because, if you were always failing,
> you might give up. But remember,
> it is by *failures* that lovers
> stay aware of how they're loved.
>
> Failure is the key
> to the kingdom within.[39]

Dying to Regenerate

Failure may be the key to the kingdom within, but we need methods to keep going in the face of it. Rumi offers at least two: first, dying to failures, so that second, we're sufficiently unencumbered to see with the Friend's eyes.

Dying is a universal symbol for what happens on the mystic journey. Ancient mystery schools simulated death experiences—ritual (not real) crucifixion or lying in a coffin—as major rites in the initiate's journey. Tibetans make bowls from skulls and put skulls in their iconography to remind them of impermanence and the importance of inner dying as a skill on the path. This symbolic use, as when the apostle Paul says, "I die daily,"[40] by no means recommends suicide, as cult members have tragi-cally interpreted.

We've already encountered a version of dying in the fifth stage with the archetype of the Releaser and the art of letting go. The Lover archetype also has us die for love, in the sense of becoming empty so that the Friend can reveal our essence beyond ego forms. Dying recurs on the mystic path, because its meaning is so basic: to go with the new, we must die to the old—not a revolutionary concept until we start doing it. To "develop the skill of dying," we must die to visible-only concepts of what both life and death are:

> . . . Here is the mystery
> of *Die before you die.* Favors come
> only after you develop the skill of dying,
> and even that capacity is a mystical favor.[41]

From a visible-only paradigm, life is about making ourselves into some visible ideal and then maintaining that image as long as we can. Death is the enemy, for it robs us of our achievement. From a mystic perspective, that way of living is death, because it traps us inside a coffin of our own making. For mystics, life is a continual "dying to how you are," so that our yet-unformed being has a chance to emerge.

In indigenous cultures, for instance, every major life change warrants a new name, signifying the death of one phase to make way for another. Traveling in Tibet in the 1940s, Heinrich Harrer discovered that even after illnesses people got new names: "One of my grown-up friends once changed his name after an attack of dysentery, to my perpetual confusion."[42] These cultures learn the natural efficacy of dying from the seasons. Winter's death isn't annihilation but a time of regeneration, of paring down to make room for new growth.

Nor is this a foreign concept. We can't evolve a work life that makes us happy until we die to a job concept that's unsatisfying. So, too, if we're unhappy in a relationship, something must die for things to improve. Either we die to the beliefs, expectations, and emotional habits that cause the misery, or we let the relationship itself die, so new ones can evolve:

> Die to how you are.
> Childhood dies and becomes maturity.
> Some of the ground dies and turns to gold. Sadness
> changes into joy.[43]

Our inner Visionaries depend on "the skill of dying" to keep their visionary capacities fresh. Without that skill, the long history of confusions, mistakes, and failures becomes overwhelming. Unless we know how to die to visions that have served their purpose, we die instead to our inner Visionaries.

That won't do for our mystics, who depend on our Visionaries to see "hundreds of thousands of impressions from the invisible world." By dying to ourselves as fixed entities whose happiness depends on making a personal vision a success, we allow ourselves to become "plural, no longer single," and our pluralness "gets dizzy with the abundance" that then pours through:

> There is a way of passing away
> from the personal, a dying
> that makes one plural,
> no longer single.
>
> A gnat lights in buttermilk
> to become nourishment for many.

Your soul is like that, Husam.
Hundreds of thousands of impressions
from the invisible world are eagerly wanting
to come through you! I get dizzy with the abundance.

When life is this dear, it means the source
is pulling us. Freshness comes from there.[44]

From a passion for vision, our Visionaries readily die to "a thousand half-loves," so we can "take one whole heart home." That's the priority. If the price of living from our Friend is dying to Friend-less ways of living, we're not negotiating annihilation; we're getting the best deal around:

Lovers in their brief delight
gamble both worlds away,
a century's worth of work
for one chance to surrender.

Many slow growth-stages build
to quick bursts of blossom.

A thousand half-loves
must be forsaken to take
one whole heart home.[45]

       *

I would love to kiss you.
The price of kissing is your life.

Now my loving is running toward my life shouting,
What a bargain, let's buy it.[46]

For our Visionaries, dying is as natural as breathing. We get excited about plans, and then we die to them. We observe events, and we die to them too. We experience profound upheavals of mind, soul, and body, and we die to them as well. Dying keeps us fresh and flexible. It's how our Visionaries live our Lovers' emptiness, with visions coming and going in an unconstricted flow:

I say what I think I should do.
     You say *Die*.
I say my lamp's oil has turned to water.
     You say *Die*.
I say I burn like a moth in the candle
     of your face. You say *Die*.[47]

With the skill of dying comes inner quietude, a "resting in peace" from the "old life" of "frantic running." Dying cuts the thread that ties having a vision to wanting it to work out as we plan. Visionaries are passionate about visions, but they hold them in a quiet, open, non-pushy way. When the holomovement introduces new currents, our role is simply to provide the space for their emergence, like the "speechless full moon" provides space for the sun's light to be reflected. Dying gives us the inner quietness to be that open space:

Inside this new love, die.
Your way begins on the other side.
Become the sky.
Take an axe to the prison wall.
Escape.
Walk out like someone suddenly born into color.
Do it now.
You're covered with thick cloud.
Slide out the side. Die,
and be quiet. Quietness is the surest sign
that you've died.
Your old life was a frantic running
from silence.

The speechless full moon
comes out now.[48]

Seeing with the Friend's Eyes

Once we're skilled at dying, we're open to "borrowing the Beloved's eye" and "looking through them." This is our Visionaries' payoff. By seeing with vision—using the lens of the invisible and visible working together—everything is transformed, and "things you have hated will become helpers":

> Eyesight becomes vision
> after a meeting with the Friend.
>
> Another seeing rises behind the eyes
> and looks out *through* the eyes.[49]
>
> ＊
>
> Borrow the Beloved's eyes.
> Look through them and you'll see the Beloved's face
> everywhere. No tiredness, no jaded boredom.
> "I shall be your eye and your hand and your loving."
> Let that happen, and things
> you have hated will become helpers.[50]

Seeing has to do with how we receive and process information. We're used to doing that according to visibles—for example, this job offers more money than that one, so it must be better—but that's seeing like the ant on the *Mona Lisa*. Rumi borrows the Indian image of people feeling an elephant in the dark. One palm can't convey the total picture. Reading only from visibles is like that:

> Sense-knowledge is the way the palm knows the elephant
> in the total pitchdark. A palm can't know the whole animal
> at once. The Ocean has an eye. The foam-bubbles of phenomena
> see differently. We bump against each other,
> asleep in the bottom of our bodies' boats.
>
> We should try to wake up and look with the clear Eye
> of the water we float upon.[51]

To see with the Beloved's eyes, though, we have to "purify our eyes" of the "foam-bubble" way of seeing. The Visionary archetype does that for us. Awe-openness, passionate seeing, willingness to make mistakes and to die to existing forms—all the elements that go into being Visionaries purify our way of seeing. Our perspective shifts, and seeing "with the clear Eye of the water we float upon," we find meaning emerging beyond our concepts—our lives "fill with radiant forms":

> Purify your eyes, and see the pure world.
> Your life will fill with radiant forms.
>
> It's a question of cleaning
> and then developing the spiritual senses.[52]

Through visions, we connect with each other. But sharing a vision isn't enough. Nazis shared a vision, as did Jim Jones's followers. Some corporations ask that we share their vision of maximizing profits, while some churches ask that we share a vision of a chosen few going to heaven and everyone else going to hell. Sharing a vision can be fascist, oppressive, and exploitive.

Our mystic Visionaries join "a community of the Spirit" not on the basis of sharing this or that vision but on the basis of sharing the method of being Visionaries. Not a particular vision but the Visionary method, that's what draws our inner mystics together. Someone whose vision for life is quite different from ours may nonetheless evoke a kindred feeling, for we sense an inner Visionary at work. The outer dressings can be completely unfamiliar—different beliefs, religions, faces, customs, or political affiliations—but if the inner dynamics are those of the Visionary, we sense "Home":

> There is a community of the Spirit.
> Join it, and feel the delight
> of walking in the noisy street,
> and *being* the noise.
>
> Drink *all* your passion,
> and be a disgrace.
>
> Close both eyes
> to see with the Other Eye.

Open your hands,
if you want to be held.

Consider what you've been doing!
Why do you stay with such a mean-spirited
and dangerous partner?

For the security of having food, admit it!
Here's the better arrangement: Give up this life,
and get a hundred new lives.[53]

9

Creating No Place

ARCHETYPE *Wanderer*

MYSTIC JOURNEY *Traveling in the World as Lovers and Visionaries*

No Place for a True Person

Living as mystic Lovers and Visionaries does something to us, something that flips a switch in our core operating systems and puts us on another track. Competitive, predatory, or otherwise invasive ways of connecting fade, as completely different notions of society take root in us. If life isn't about running after visibles—defending what we've got and fighting to get more—then society can't be about that either, not if it's to serve as a home for True Human Beings.

Of course, society as it is and was eight centuries ago is anything but such a home. Owning visibles and having visible power outrank being "a True Person." Respect, security, power, truth, freedom: they all come from hoarding visibles, or so we're to believe, and if we fail to squirrel away an impressive pile of our own, we become wage slaves to those more adept at squirrelling.

Our inner mystics don't fare well in this social climate. If we play the game, we lose touch with our mystical side. Yet if we don't play, we're likely to end up "sick and exhausted." In "Sabzawar," a True Person is hard to find, even though when it comes to life-and-death issues, that's all that really matters:[1]

> Once the great King Muhammed Khwarizm
> besieged Sabzawar. They gave up easily.
> "Whatever you require as tribute we will give."
>
> "Bring me a holy person, someone who lives
> united with God, or I will harvest
> your inhabitants like corn."

They brought sacks of gold. They knew that
no one in Sabzawar lived in that state.
"Do you think I am still a child
that I should be fascinated with coins?"

For three days and nights
they called through the town
looking for an Abu Bakr.

Finally, they saw a traveler
lying in a ruined corner of a wall,
sick and exhausted.

Immediately, they recognized a True Person.
"Get up! The king wants to see you.
You can save our lives!"

"I'm not supposed to be here.
If I could walk, I would already have arrived
in the city where my friends are."

They lifted him above their heads on a board
like corpses are carried on
and bore him to the king.

Sabzawar is this world,
where a True Person wastes away,
apparently worthless,

yet all the king wants from Sabzawar
is such a one. Nothing else will do.[2]

Fortunately, mystics have more options than "lying in a ruined corner of a wall," and this stage on the mystic path explores what those
options are. Mystics may look weak and worthless—how else would
they appear to a paradigm that values visibles more than anything?—
yet they're lions in disguise. Our mystics' leonine powers aren't no-
ticed only because they're invisible. To mystics, invisible doesn't mean
ineffective but the opposite: ultimately effective.

Consciousness and Its Shadow

The greatest invisible power that our mystics possess is consciousness. According to David Bohm, everything in the visible world has its origin in the holomovement, which is a dynamic energy-consciousness unity. Consciousness is the underlying reality, which unfolds its order through meaning. Ideas stir within us. We sense something cooking in the unseen, and we catch the scent of it through feelings, intuitions, and dropped hints from synchronous experiences.

So what's this have to do with finding options other than "lying in a ruined corner"? Everything. When it comes to social action, our mystics use consciousness as their frontline force for change. Instead of trying to push the visible with another visible (preferably a bigger one), they leapfrog over the visible to its source in consciousness and make changes from there.

Change consciousness, and the visible can't help but shift. Whatever consciousness does, the visible reflects it. Outward forms are like shadows of consciousness, to use Plato's analogy, casting images that go wherever consciousness leads. Sometimes it looks as if the shadow is running ahead of consciousness, sometimes behind, and sometimes as if there's no shadow at all. Yet no matter what the shadow does, it's consciousness that casts it.

Gandhi used this philosophy to create a strategy for social change. He designed his *Satyagraha*—nonviolent noncooperation—campaigns to focus consciousness on injustice, assuming that the greater awareness would bring consciousness shifts, which in turn would cast new shadows.

In this endeavor, Gandhi sought not to create power struggles but to change the consciousness of everyone involved. Naturally, he wanted to change the dominator consciousness of the British. But far more than that, he wanted to change the consciousness of the Indians themselves: to reject British materialist values, to rebuild self-respect and self-government, and to return to the spiritual roots of Indian philosophy. To support his cause, he appealed to the conscience of the world. When world opinion, from schoolchildren to foreign leaders, as well as several hundred million Indians, recognized the injustice of

British colonial rule and the wisdom of Gandhi's alternative, the British had to leave.

In India today, Gandhi's strategy continues in the work of Pandurang Shastri Athavale, who in 1997 received the Templeton Prize for Progress in Religion.[3] Since the 1950s, Athavale has combined spiritual self-knowledge and selfless devotion to create a "silent" revolution— one that's transformed 100,000 of India's poorest villages and improved the lives of an estimated twenty million people. He calls the inner work that's the foundation of it all *Swadhyaha*, which means "self-study" with a spiritual twist, namely, that every self carries the presence of God within. Respect, dignity, and self-worth arise from this spiritual truth rather than from outward appearances. Acknowledging the divine presence within makes it easier to perceive that presence in everyone else.

The visible shadow cast by this consciousness has created amazing reforms through self-supporting, self-managed community projects: village temples where people of all creeds, castes, and colors worship together and discuss ways to improve village life; "farms for God" where villagers share their time and produce with the needy; community fishing boats, "floating temples of God," managed by villagers and shared with the needy; "orchards for God" and dairies operated the same way; community trusts that provide short- and long-term grants for villagers, who, when they're on their feet and generating excess capital, contribute to the fund; youth centers, cultural activity centers, "divine brain trusts" for young people to discuss ideas—the list goes on and on.

Observing this grassroots movement firsthand, British green economist Paul Ekins—not one to look outside the discipline of economics for solving economic problems—commented to us, "This is the first time I've seen that when there's a genuine spiritual transformation, economic and social problems take care of themselves."

Creating No Place

With consciousness, we create our worlds. If what's going on inside are cravings for power and money, then the shadows cast by this consciousness will be of like nature. Outer forms neither cause greed nor have the power to prevent it. Only consciousness does.

If we ignore consciousness and assume that the visible is all there is, then we look to external forms for security and happiness. Historically, we've experimented with outward mechanisms for imposing social order: political forms (kingship, republic, democracy, plutocracy), economic forms (communism and capitalism), as well as blendings of the two (state and corporate socialism). When we make a "social contract" with these systems, as John Locke put it, we bargain away a chunk of our freedom for a promise of security.

But as Plato predicted, when consciousness is pushed to the background, outward forms degenerate to some guise of dictatorship—as now exists with the supra-governmental rule of global corporate powers. No visible form can protect us if consciousness is bent on domination, since any social form can be corrupted. Neither communism nor capitalism nor democracy nor republics have been immune; none proved the ideal systems their adherents hoped.

For Rumi, that's no surprise. Forms aren't ideal; neither do they have power in and of themselves. They house consciousness, but it's the consciousness living there that determines how the house is maintained: whether it grows more beautiful or degenerates, whether it's oppressive or a joy. Consciousness and the values that guide us are the only guarantees:

> At night, when [Ibrahim, the king] slept, guards
> were patroling the roof, protecting him,
> they thought. But his real security
> was the justice of his decisions.[4]

That's why for mystics, home is no place; it's not found in outward forms. Sixteenth-century statesman and writer Thomas More coined the term *utopia*, literally "no place." For mystics, utopia exists not as a place but as a consciousness—one whose shadow offers a sheltering shade rather than a disagreeable darkness. Our mystics' home has "no form and no location":

Noah's ark is the symbol of our species,
a boat wandering the ocean.

A plant grows deep in the center of that water.
It has no form and no location.[5]

When mystics think about creating communities, it's the no place of consciousness that they think about first. By-laws, policies, chains of command, buildings, teams: none of these are either good or bad, to paraphrase Hamlet, until consciousness makes them so. Whether or not these forms approximate the ideals set for them depends on consciousness. To start with the form is to start with the shadow, as if to draw a shadowy shape on the ground when nothing's there to cast it. If we want utopia, Rumi's advice is simple—"Move within":

Keep walking, though there's no place to get to.
Don't try to see through the distances.
That's not for human beings. Move within,
but don't move the way fear makes you move.[6]

How Love and Vision Make Us Wanderers

Within lie vast worlds, which our inner Wanderers want to explore. When our Lovers fire in us a love for the unseen, running after forms loses its charm. Our hearts aren't in it anymore. Like the kings in the following stories, we "abandon kingdoms, because we want more than kingdoms":

Imra'u 'l-Qays, King of the Arabs,
was very handsome, and a poet, full of love-songs.

Women loved him desperately.
Everyone loved him, but there came one night
an experience that changed him completely.
He left his kingdom and his family.
He put on dervish robes and wandered
from one weather, one landscape, to another.

Love dissolved his king-self
and led him to Tabuk, where he worked for a time
making bricks. Someone told the King of Tabuk
about Imra'u 'l-Qays, and that king went to visit him
at night.

       "King of the Arabs, handsome Joseph of this age,
ruler of two empires, one composed of territories,
and the other of the beauty of women,
if you would consent to stay with me,
I would be honored. You abandon kingdoms,
because you want more
than kingdoms."

The King of Tabuk went on like this,
praising Imra'u 'l-Qays, and talking theology
and philosophy. Imra'u 'l-Qays kept silent.
Then suddenly he leaned and whispered something
in the second king's ear, and that second, that
second king became a wanderer too.

They walked out of town hand in hand.
No royal belts, no thrones.

This is what love does and continues to do. . . .

All that world-power wants, really,
is this weakness.[7]

    In spite of its posturings, "all that world-power wants, really, is this weakness," the intangibles of soul, love, and freedom "flowing through all human beings." If we have these, fame, wealth, and power don't matter:

    I have nothing to do with being famous,
    or making grand judgments,
    or feeling full of shame.

    I borrow nothing.
    I don't want anything from anybody.

I flow through all human beings.
Love is my only companion.[8]

Not that our inner mystics are immune to discouragement or despair. Our Lover Wanderers see disturbing shadows as much as anyone and find them just as confusing—where's the justice or the peace? Sabzawar isn't home to our inner mystics; we're just visiting, and sometimes we get lost:

> Will I get to the moonshaped threshing floor
> before I die? I feel blessed with this wandering
> in the love-sun, but I do not see the road.
> I know it's here somewhere,
> but I don't see its justice, or its peace.[9]

That's why our Wanderers draw on our Visionaries as well. Whereas our Lovers lift our hearts out of bargaining ways, our Visionaries lift our heads. We see through Sabzawar, that it's just "a big game of king of the mountain":

> . . . Ibrahim was resting at night,
> and he heard footsteps on the roof.
>
> "Who could this be? Spirits?"
>
> A marvelous group of beings
> put their heads down over the roof-edge,
> "We're looking for camels!"
>
> "Whoever heard of camels on a roof?"
>
> "Yes. And whoever heard of trying
> to be in union with God while
> acting as a head of state?"
>
> That's all it took for Ibrahim.
> He was gone, vanished.
>
> His beard and his robe were there,
> but his real self was on an ecstatic
> dervish retreat on Mt. Qaf.

Everyone still brags of what he did.
This world is proud of those
who suddenly change. . . .

Ibrahim was one of these who dreamed
of the true reality and freed himself.

Muhammed said that the sign of this happening
is that one loses interest in illusory happiness.

This was how it was once for a young prince.
Age has no bearing on this transformation.

He saw, suddenly, that the world was a big game
of king of the mountain: boys scrambling
on a pile of sand. One gets to the top
and calls out, "I am the king!"
Then another throws him off
and makes his momentary claim,
and then another, and so on.

These world-complications can become
very simple, very quickly.

No words are necessary
to see into reality.

Just *be*,
and It is.[10]

What the Lover did to Imra'u 'l-Qays and the Visionary to Ibrahim, they do to us and the world. Shadow houses are too small for our Friend, which is why our Wanderers introduce us to more spacious accommodations in no place:

Start the drumbeat. Everything we've said
about the Friend is true. The beauty of that
peacefulness makes the whole world restless.[11]

Wanderer: Being a Lover in Society

What does it mean, though, to be a Wanderer? The Wanderer archetype sounds the least practical, yet it may well be the most, for our Wanderers carry the mystic archetypes into society. Like Taoist sages, Wanderers move through society almost invisibly, everywhere introducing a different consciousness.

Whereas the Seeker leads us away from the visible to explore the invisible, the Wanderer brings us back to it. Not the visible per se but the visible-only paradigm creates Sabzawars. To reconnect with the visible, we simply need to bring the invisible along, and our inner Lovers show us how. To be a Wanderer is to be a Lover not only in our inner journeyings but in society as well.

Lover Wanderers love how the invisible permeates the visible. When we love people, animals, and things, we love the ideas, qualities, and values they express. We love how each being embodies something intangible, something that's the holomovement coming through or, in Swadhyaha terms, that's of the divine presence. In other words, we love neither the invisible alone nor the visible alone but how the two merge in "love's confusing joy":

> If you want what visible reality
> can give, you're an employee.
>
> If you want the unseen world,
> you're not living your truth.
>
> Both wishes are foolish,
> but you'll be forgiven for forgetting
> that what you really want is
> love's confusing joy.[12]

When our Lover Wanderers lead us back to the visible, we reconnect on a new basis. Instead of going to the visible for external rewards, we're looking for "one whiff of the wine-musk"—the scent of meaning unfolding. When our Lovers catch that scent, our Wanderers follow it wherever it leads:

Someone in charge would give up all his power,
if he caught one whiff of the wine-musk
from the room where the Lovers
are doing who-knows-what!

One of them tries to dig a hole through a mountain.
One flees from academic honors.
One laughs at famous mustaches![13]

Compared to following what's meaningful, going along conven-
tionally accepted paths seems hollow, peopled with "grief-armies":

A fire has risen above my tombstone hat.
I don't want learning, or dignity,
or respectability.

I want this music and this dawn
and the warmth of your cheek against mine.

The grief-armies assemble,
but I'm not going with them.[14]

Our Lover Wanderers pursue the quest for meaning, even if we live
apparently ordinary lives. Being a Wanderer doesn't mean living on the
street or that we can't work in established institutions. Being a Wanderer is a mind-set, one that doesn't care to be "a picture on a bathhouse wall"—the Fortune 500 list of Rumi's day—but instead accepts
that we're "the King's son," the holomovement unfolding, and lives
from a passion to find out what this means:

You are the King's son.
Why do you close yourself up?
Become a Lover.

Don't aspire to be a General
or a Minister of State.

One is a boredom for you,
the other a disgrace.

You've been a picture on a bathhouse wall
long enough. No one recognizes you here, do they?[15]

Guided by meaning, our Lover Wanderers can wander and not be led astray. The two things that confuse us most have already been addressed. First, the Healer has made us aware of soul sickness and the way to heal it. If soul sickness tugs at us, we know what that feels like, and, though the quest for meaning is behind it, we know a less painful route. Second, visible-only thinking is a classic derailer, but our Lovers are wise to that as well. Visibles are "surface flames," whereas our Lovers live in "the center." From that center, our wanderings move with a "dance" that's "the joy of existence":

My love wanders the rooms, melodious,
flute-notes, plucked wires,
full of a wine the Magi drank
on the way to Bethlehem.

We are three. The moon comes
from its quiet corner, puts a pitcher of water
down in the center. The circle
of surface flames.

One of us kneels to kiss the threshold.

One drinks, with wine-flames playing over his face.

One watches the gathering,

and says to any cold onlookers,

This dance is the joy of existence.[16]

Lover Wanderers: Free Spirits Not Driven by Wants

Dancing "the joy of existence," our Lover Wanderers bring a free and open spirit to community. We enter communities to participate in a flow of meaning, trusting that whatever shadow this activity casts will include the means to meet our needs.

By contrast, visible-only thinking defines community as the place where we negotiate wants, and whether or not we get ours satisfied defines our standing. The more wants we can finagle the community to satisfy, the more important we are. Who gets what is the focus. The daily news, business dealings, as well as private interactions revolve around the question Who gets whose way? But want-driven communities aren't much fun. For one thing, they spawn insatiability: if having more makes us seem more worthy, then we always want more to feel good about ourselves. For another, they make us defensive of what we have, fueling turf wars over possessions and positions. But worst, they put the greediest at the top, where Plato thought the least want-driven should be.

Our Lover Wanderers have no interest in want-based communities. Like Imra'u 'l-Qays, we walk away from them, preferring to be led "by the guide" to the no place where real security lies:

> Don't worry about forms.
> If someone wants your horse,
> let him have it. Horses are for
> hurrying ahead of the others.[17]

> *

> We don't have to follow
> the pressure-flow of wanting.
> We can be led by the guide.

> Wishes may or may not come true
> in this house of disappointment.

> Let's push the door open
> together and leave.[18]
> Give up wanting what other people have.

> *

> That way you're safe.
> "Where, where can I be safe?" you ask.[19]

Yet "giving up wanting what other people have" isn't easy, not when the want-driven model is constantly in our faces. Rumi tells a story of a preacher who deals with this issue by praying "long and with enthusiasm for thieves and muggers." When his congregation asks why, he explains:

> "Because they have done me such generous favors.
> Every time I turn back toward the things they want,
> I run into them. They beat me and leave me nearly dead
> in the road, and I understand, again, that what they want
> is not what I want. They keep me on the spiritual path.
> That's why I honor them and pray for them."[20]

Fortunately, Rumi offers another method, a mystical one, for finding peace about our wants. Ultimately, what we all want are the invisibles that come from reality's self-dynamics—dynamics that are our dynamics too. If we're grounded in "This Moment," we're connected to these dynamics, to how the holomovement unfolds as something that's uniquely us. Since the holomovement includes all that is, everything is present, embedded in each moment, and that's adequate to "bring what we need":

> This Silence. This Moment.
> Every *moment*,
>
> if it's genuinely inside you,
> brings what you need.[21]

On this premise, our Lover Wanderers wear wants lightly. We have them, but we also let them go. In Hawaiian kahuna philosophy, this is the method of prayer: pray, and then "release the wish." Only by releasing the desire, so that it's "completely free of the personal," do we allow it to travel from the visible realm to the yet-forming levels that generate change. By sending our wants into "nothing, nothing," we don't push for specific outcomes—perhaps disastrous were they actually to occur—but allow what works within the whole to emerge:

You're not a slave.
You're a king.

If you *want* something,
release the wish and let it light
on its desire, completely free of the personal.

Then sit and sound the drum
of nothing, nothing.[22]

Wanderer: Being a Visionary in Society

Whereas our Lovers free us to be Wanderers by quieting the "pressure-flow of wanting," our Visionaries guide our wanderings with a shift in perspective—outer to inner, king-of-the-mountain to "the King's son" (or Queen's daughter). Besides being a Lover in society, being a mystic Wanderer means living the Visionary method. Rather than imposing visions, we simply see inside what's going on: see inside people to their mystic yearnings and see inside events to the unfolding meaning. What appears on the surface—"dust hanging in the air"—isn't where the action is:

The rider has passed, but his
dust hangs in the air.

Don't stare at these particles!
The rider's direction is *there*.[23]

By listening for the inner meaning, our Visionary Wanderers "hear the source," "even if what is being said is trivial and wrong." We say things we don't mean, nor do we realize how others hear us. Knowing this about ourselves and others, we look past surface confusions to the deep motivation. Long explanations may not communicate as much as looks or gestures. It's those hints of the "rider's direction" that our Visionary Wanderers notice:

Every spoken word is a covering for the inner self.
A little curtain-flick no wider than a slice

of roast meat can reveal hundreds of exploding suns.
Even if what is being said is trivial and wrong,
the listener hears the source. One breeze comes
from across a garden. Another from across the ash-heap.
Think how different the voices of the fox
and the lion, and what they tell you!

Hearing someone is lifting the lid off the cooking pot.
You learn what's for supper. Though some people
can know just by the smell, a sweet stew
from a sour soup cooked with vinegar.[24]

Inside-seeing drives home the Platonic truth that appearances aren't the reality: "Eye-sight is in conflict with inner knowing." Things that seem pleasant may be "a viper and a cause of panic" for our Visionary Wanderers, while things that seem unpleasant may be "a source of light." Nothing is what it seems, nor does anything have just one meaning:

Joseph's brothers did not see Joseph's beauty,
but Jacob never lost sight of it. Moses at first
saw only a wooden staff, but to his other seeing
it was a viper and a cause of panic.
Eye-sight is in conflict with inner knowing.
Moses' hand is a hand and a source of light.[25]

The inner is the real story, appearances the shadow of it. The more we hear the "tambourine inside," the less we're confused by shadows—"lies and cynical jokes." We see what's really going on—"a brilliant city inside the Soul":

Struck, the dancers hear a tambourine inside them,
as a wave turns to foam on its very top, begin.

Maybe you don't hear that tambourine,
or the tree leaves clapping time.

Close the ears on your head
that listen mostly to lies and cynical jokes.

> There are other things to hear and see:
> dance-music and a brilliant city
> inside the Soul.[26]

Not Judging from Externals

Our Visionary Wanderers bring a shift in perspective for communities as well: What does a community see of us? Are we judged by externals or valued for our qualities? How communities answer this affects how we answer the questions: Which side do we put forward when we interact? What do we present to others, and what do we connect with in them? For Visionary Wanderers, not outward but inward factors lead: "World-power means nothing. Only the unsayable, jeweled inner life matters."[27] On the mystic scale of happiness, we "don't win here with loud publicity." The more we let externals drift into the background—"lose our feathers"—the more we connect with meaning:

> You don't win here with loud publicity.
> Union comes of not being.
> These birds do not learn to fly,
> until they lose all their feathers.[28]

Yet in cultures dominated by the visible-only paradigm, externals come first, and we're judged accordingly—from body, possessions, race, sex, and family status to credentials, positions, sexual orientations, and religious, ethnic, and political affiliations. Whereas our Visionaries use an open, self-questioning method, judging from externals does the opposite. From externals alone, we can be labeled "success" or "loser," "good" or "bad," dismissing who we are beyond these or any other labels. In Al Pacino's film *Looking for Richard*, a toothless, African American beggar on the streets of New York speaks about Shakespeare with greater insight and passion than any of the scholars interviewed, fine as they were. Judging from externals inspires no humility, no awe before the bigness of what's going on with us as the holomovement unfolds, especially if we're toothless beggars:

The soul must suffer secrets
that can't be said, public humiliation,
people pointing in contempt.[29]

In communities that judge from externals, we internalize the habit and forget we're doing it. Naturally, we need to make judgments as we go through life, but we need to make wise judgments—ones that give due weight to the inner. When we forget the inner, we lose compassion for ourselves and others:

Solomon was busy judging others,
when it was his personal thoughts
that were disrupting the community.

His crown slid crooked on his head.
He put it straight, but the crown went
awry again. Eight times this happened.

Finally he began to talk to his headpiece.
"Why do you keep tilting over my eyes?"

"I have to. When your power loses compassion,
I have to show what such a condition looks like."

Immediately Solomon recognized the truth.
He knelt and asked forgiveness.
The crown centered itself on his crown.[30]

Solomon "recognized the truth," because judging from externals doesn't fit human experience. Externals count only as long as we don't know someone. The better we know a person or group, the less externals matter. What flows between us is meaning, an exchange of inner knowing:

Everything that gets exchanged between people, whether it's spoken or not, is a form of thought. Human beings are discourse. The rest is blood and bones and nerves. Call it speech, that flowing. Compare it to the sun, which is always warming us, even when we can't see it. . . . Every-

thing that happens is filled with pleasure and warmth because of the delight of the discourse that's always going on, and if it weren't, nothing
would have any meaning.[31]

Biology agrees with this definition. Our species is called *Homo sapi-
ens*—humans as knowers, discerners of meaning—rather than *Homo
acquisitivus* or *Homo competitio*. Why not base communities on our nature as beings who thrive on exchanging meaning—"discourse"? Why
tolerate in communities a standard that has so little to do with what
we're about as a species?

Our Visionary Wanderers know externals are unreliable. Shadows
distort, making things seem bigger or smaller than they are. That's why
our mystics are so dogged in following "the Presence" within, externals
be damned:

> Ask within, and when the Presence directs you,
> whatever you do will be right, even though
> externally it may seem wrong. Don't curse the oyster
> for having an ugly, encrusted shell. Inside,
> it's all pearl. There's no way to ever say
> how we are with phenomena.[32]

True, if we're inner-directed, it may look as if we're wandering
through life like some "lame and dreamy goat." Inner direction doesn't
put us on the fast track: tenure, promotions, political clout, prestigious
positions. Even if we're bringing up the rear, though, our Visionary
Wanderers can surprise us—something about the last being first. . . .

> You've seen a herd of goats
> going down to the water.
>
> The lame and dreamy goat
> brings up the rear.
>
> There are worried faces about that one,
> but now they're laughing,
>
> because look, as they return,
> that goat is leading!

There are many different kinds of knowing.
The lame goat's kind is a branch
that traces back to the roots of presence.

Learn from the lame goat,
and lead the herd home.[33]

Using the Inner to Resolve Conflicts

But what about a community's most common concern: conflicts? Can Visionary Wanderers deal with the clash of differences that can tear communities apart? Our mystics reply with another question: Which is a better basis for resolving conflicts, inner or outer?

From a mystic's reading of history, the outer gives rise to conflicts; the inner resolves them. The more externally oriented we are, the more we're likely to fight over externals, whether land and contracts or reputations and images. By contrast, the more inwardly oriented we are, the greater our resources for finding mutually beneficial solutions. Even if we fight over intangibles (religion, ideas, philosophies), external criteria—who gets whose way? which intangible is the right one?—trigger the conflict. Otherwise we'd adopt the Sufis' attitude of tolerance, which respects "every soul" as the holomovement unfolding:

'Every soul is born for a certain purpose, and the light of that purpose is kindled in his soul', says Sa'di. This explains why the Sufi in his tolerance allows every one to have his own path, and does not compare the principles of others with his own, but allows freedom of thought to everyone, since he himself is a freethinker.[34]

Working from the inner inspires this mutual respect by shifting the focus back to what counts. At the end of the day, we all want peace, happiness, security, respect, beauty, and fulfillment, all of which flow from our roots in soul, love, and freedom. Only when we try to get these values through external means do we "begin pushing each other about." It's the names we use, how we think these values translate into external forms, that cause trouble. We want "one wine," but we place our orders differently:

A man gives one coin to be spent among four people.

The Persian says, "I want *angur*."
The Arab says, "*Inab*, you rascal."
The Turk says, "*Uzum!*"
The Greek says, "Shut up all of you.
We'll have *istafil*."

They begin pushing each other about,
then hitting each other with their fists, no stopping it.

If a many-languaged master had been there,
He could have made peace and told them:
I can give each of you what you want
with this one coin. Trust me, keep quiet,
and you four enemies will agree.

I know a silent, inner meaning
that makes of your four words one wine.[35]

Educator Win Wenger's work in conflict resolution offers compelling support for the mystic method. Experimenting with the imagery that our minds generate in the alpha brain state, Wenger discovered that opposing factions often share common images about how disputes can be resolved. In the meditative mode, both sides envision mutually acceptable solutions. Wenger's challenge is to help disputants carry that vision over to the beta brain state—normal consciousness, swayed as it is by externals. The unifying vision is there, yet we stumble over "names":

Every war, and every conflict between human beings,
has happened because of this disagreement
about *names*. It's such an unnecessary foolishness,
because just beyond the arguing,
there's a long table of companionship, set,
and waiting for us to sit down.[36]

With inside-seeing, what appears as conflict dissolves into a deeper unity of purpose. We need more than one approach, talent, or activity to get a complex job done. That's why we have communities, which thrive on differences, from divisions of labor in businesses to diverse personalities in families. If we focus on the visible differences and forget the invisible purposes that unite us, we'll think we're "thwarting each other," when in fact there's a harmony we don't see:

> . . . Watch two men washing clothes.
> One makes dry clothes wet. The other makes
> wet clothes dry. They seem to be thwarting each other,
> but their work is a perfect harmony.[37]

The more we rely on inside-seeing, the more we sense the hidden harmony. Even if we can't see it, though, our Visionary Wanderers assume it's somehow there. At the least, we're working together in the unseen dynamics of consciousness evolution. Throughout his decades of nonviolent resistance to China's brutal invasion of Tibet, for instance, the Dalai Lama has always maintained that he learns most from his enemies. He's "washing clothes" with the Chinese—purifying consciousness, his own first. Inside-seeing deepens us that way. From "jostling competitively" over externals, we "mature and soften." We listen for the harmony through the differences and "become one juice":

> You know the way it is
> with grapes, and with human beings!
>
> When we're immature, we jostle competitively
> in the bunch. Then we mature and soften.
> Our skins rip open, and we become one juice!
>
> We grow in that way through
> the breath of a heart-master.[38]

For our Visionary Wanderers, invisibles unite us. Ethics, integrity, and justice, for instance, form the real order and security of society. Instead of "looking for bits of grain," profits at the expense of harmony, our "Solomon" honors the unseen unity that's already there among us and makes it visible. Guided by this "intelligence," our "soul-birds sing unanimously":

Under the aegis of Solomon
the deer and the leopard were friends.

The dove rode safely in the hawk's talons.
Sheep did not panic when a wolf came near.

Solomon is the intelligence
that connects former enemies.

Don't look for bits of grain like an ant.
Look for the granary master,
and you'll have grain and the Presence
as well. Solomon lives now!

God has said there will never be a time
without a Solomon. In that consciousness
there is no guile, and inside it
your soul-birds sing unanimously.[39]

Free to Be Creative with Harmony

Our Lovers' free spirit combined with our Visionaries' inside-seeing creates the radical freedom that characterizes Wanderers. There's no external that our inner Wanderers want so much that they're willing to sacrifice our souls' freedom to get it. Even life in a visible form isn't worth that much. In his letters, Seneca, who was commanded to commit suicide by the emperor Nero, wrote, "'Rehearse death.' To say this is to tell a person to rehearse his freedom. A person who has learned how to die has unlearned how to be a slave. He is above—or at any rate beyond the reach of—all political coercion."[40]

Fortunately, standing against mad tyrants isn't the main occupation of our Wanderers. We can do it in a pinch, but we'd rather be creative with our unseen unity. Looking past outward forms, our Wanderers flex our invisible powers by "noticing" the harmonies around us. If we're not judging from externals, we're free to see "streams streaming toward the ocean" where otherwise we'd see just beggars, kids, animals, workers, prisoners, or dumb masses. For Wanderers, no form is "just" anything; every being is the holomovement expressed, a "cup that can hold the Ocean":

Notice how each particle moves.
Notice how everyone has just arrived here
          from a journey.
Notice how each wants a different food.
Notice how the stars vanish as the sun comes up,
          and how all streams stream toward the ocean.

Look at the chefs preparing special plates
          for everyone, according to what they need.
Look at this cup that can hold the Ocean.[41]

That being so, who we are flows from the same source as everyone else, and there's more where that came from. Our Wanderers don't feel a need to bottle up goodness, wisdom, knowledge, or power and then slap on labels according to who has how much. Instead, "they swim the huge fluid freedom":

Are you jealous of the ocean's generosity?
Why would you refuse to give
this joy to anyone?

Fish don't hold the sacred liquid in cups.
They swim the huge fluid freedom.[42]

"Swimming the huge fluid freedom," our inner Wanderers are free to "receive nourishment from everyone we meet." Whereas judging from externals shuts off this access—what would a beggar know about Shakespeare?—seeing beyond them frees us to be creative, to "make good and generous things begin":

. . . We receive nourishment
from everyone we meet. Any association
is food. Planet comes near planet,
and both are affected.

Man comes together with woman,
and there's a new baby! Iron meets stone,
sparks. Rain enters the ground, and sweet herbs appear.

When green things and people converge,
there'll be laughter and dancing,
and that makes good and generous things begin.[43]

The more we're creative with the harmony underlying relationships, the more communities function like a chorus. We all sing our
own individual notes, which are not only different but also change
constantly. Instead of noise, though, our Wanderers create music:

Go up on the roof at night
in this city of the Soul.

Let *everyone* climb on their roofs
and sing their notes!
Sing loud![44]

A Wanderer's Freedom to Wander the Universe

In esoteric circles, "Wanderers" are beings who travel the universe en-
lightening consciousness, incarnating wherever they feel drawn. They
take the form of humans or animals, depending on what they want to
do. Being cosmic explorers of consciousness and its changes, their
home is no place. Our inner Wanderers carry that free explorer-spirit
into everyday life.

Our Wanderers' spirit is free, because exploring isn't about outcomes or achievements. If it were, we'd always have to be right and
take the most direct route there—no wrong turns. That's a heavy way
to live, though. If we're here to engage in a process, we find what's ours
to do as we journey along. Not the outcome but being on the path—
that's what draws our inner Wanderers to the journey. The "twists and
turns," side roads, and detours all have a place in creating meaning, in
bringing "knowing" to light:

Either this deep desire of mine
will be found on this journey,
or when I get back home!

It may be that the satisfaction I need
depends on my going away, so that when I've gone
and come back, I'll find it at home.

I will search for the Friend with all my passion
and all my energy, until I learn
that I don't need to search.

The real truth of existence is sealed,
until after many twists and turns of the road.

As in the algebraical method of "the two errors,"
the correct answer comes only after two substitutions,
after two mistakes. Then the seeker says,

"If I had known the real way it was,
I would have stopped all the looking around."

But that knowing depends
on the time spent looking![45]

"Twists and turns of the road" may be euphemisms for mistakes, hurts felt and inflicted, or years lost in numbed-out craziness. None of that fazes our Wanderers, though, since all those terms reflect external evaluations of an inner process. Of course we get lost on journeys. It's confusing. Whatever directions we may have remembered in coming here got garbled on arrival:

Your eyes are the mystery, with thousands
of lives living in the edges.

Your hair full of forgetfulness,
your face pure praise.

So clarity is decorated
with mistakes![46]

Plus we're not sure where we really are. We "live in the nowhere," but we also "have an address here." We have "eyes that see from that nowhere," as well as "eyes that judge distances." We "own two shops." Coming from the invisible and reconnecting with the visible, we end up "running back and forth."

The reason for making the commute, though, is important. Going from invisible to visible and back again changes consciousness, which in turn changes the shadows. Through back-and-forthing, we come to see both the invisible and the visible in new lights. Even someone who's a "cynical snake" has a holomovement side, as the Dalai Lama suggests. Journeying back and forth and shifting consciousness as we go, we gradually close the shops built on wants and fears—selling bait and fish-hooks—and keep open the shops where together we can be "the free-swimming fish":

> Live in the nowhere that you came from,
> even though you have an address here.
>
> That's why you see things in two ways.
> Sometimes you look at a person
> and see a cynical snake.
>
> Someone else sees a joyful lover,
> and you're both right!
>
> Everyone is half and half,
> like the black and white ox.
>
> Joseph looked ugly to his brothers,
> and most handsome to his father.
>
> You have eyes that see from that nowhere,
> and eyes that judge distances,
> how high and how low.
>
> You own two shops,
> and you run back and forth.
>
> Try to close the one that's a fearful trap,
> getting always smaller. Checkmate,
> this way. Checkmate, that.

Keep open the shop
where you're not selling fish-hooks anymore.
You *are* the free-swimming fish.[47]

Not bothered by the ups and downs, our Wanderers' path is unconditioned by expectations and preconceptions—it's free. As many
thinkers have observed, not outer space but inner space is the new
frontier, Hamlet's "undiscovered country," which Indian philosopher
and teacher Jiddu Krishnamurti described as a pathless land. Our Wanderers put us on this frontier, finding whatever paths are right for us,
until we forget the paths for the meaning and consciousness that's
emerging:

There's a way of going that's like the stars.
                                        No,
even freer than they are, completely unconditioned,
unlocated, unpathed. A journey without a sky![48]

10

Cooking Up
True Human Beings

ARCHETYPE   *Alchemist*
MYSTIC JOURNEY   *Going through the Refining Fire*

Mysticism for Mystics

The last three stages of the mystic path explore the classic mystic: mystics as Alchemists, Contemplatives, and Wise Fools. Having broken away from the visible-only paradigm (chapters 1–3), gone within to heal soul sickness (chapters 4–6), and evolved a new basis for reconnecting with the visible (chapters 7–9), our inner mystics are now free to wander the invisible universe—the ideas and principles that underlie everything.

Classic mystics are free beings, as free as humans can be. Whereas stages four to six focus on reclaiming soul, and seven to nine on reclaiming love, these last three stages focus on reclaiming freedom. Small, meanly negotiated freedom won't do. It wasn't enough for the Buddha, the writers of the Upanishads, Socrates, or Lao Tzu. And it's not enough for us. Being at liberty to vote for one of two partisan politicians, to buy one of ten brands of soap, or to watch one of a hundred television channels isn't the freedom mystics have in mind. Our inner mystics want cosmic freedom—the freedom to evolve consciousness— and the ball's in our court for getting it. How else could it be? Freedom contingent on external authorities or conditions doesn't satisfy mystics, because it's not real freedom. Gandhi was more free in jail than the British viceroy in his palace.

Though freedom is the minimum we need to explore reality, our inner mystics need something else too. No matter what the discipline— math, music, chemistry, art—a few core principles orient us to the field, otherwise we get lost in infinity. So, too, for our mystics. In the last three stages, mystics seek universal principles appropriate to their field, which is nothing less than all of reality.

With this quest for ultimate principles, the focus shifts from the unfolding to the enfolding side of the holomovement. When we ask about principles, we're really asking: How does everything hang together—fit—within the whole? To recall David Bohm's theory, the holomovement has two phases: unfolding from the whole-order, then enfolding back into it, both of which go on simultaneously. On the unfolding side, the unseen order of the whole spreads out as the order of nature and consciousness. But because the holomovement is all-inclusive, orders don't unfold and then get lost. They're constantly being reintegrated. Something is created, and then something is learned and changed as a result. The process is two-way: generative then integrative, creating then seeing the meaning of it all.

To illustrate the two sides, Bohm used the analogy of the snowflakes that children make by folding paper and then cutting intricate patterns. To see the full snowflake, we have to unfold the folded original. If we want to develop the spread-out order further, however, we have to re-fold it—enfold it—to make new cuts. Trying to make the cuts in the spread-out form is the hard way. It doesn't have the same power, nor does it produce the same order and symmetry.

In other words, if we want to change the visible, we must first enfold it back into its invisible origins. If, for example, we're not happy with our families, schools, society, or our own personalities, we need to see them in light of the unseen consciousness that's creating them, which in turn is created by ideas and paradigms. By enfolding experiences back into their invisible origins and refining the order there, we're able to unfold something new—new forms of personalities, families, schools, businesses, and culture. Hence Rumi's advice:

> Work in the invisible world
> at least as hard
> as you do in the visible.[1]

Everyone does this forth-and-backing all the time; our inner mystics just itch to go back farther. They want to enfold experience back into its primal order, and there's nothing more primal than the whole,

God, or the holomovement. With the holomovement as the ground of everything—expressed by Islam in its core teaching, "There is no Reality but God; there is only God"—our inner mystics seek universal principles to guide our explorations.

That's what these last three stages do. The Alchemist works with the universal principle of transmutation, the Contemplative reflects on the universal principle of attraction, while the Wise Fool steps off the cliff of conventional wisdom into the universal principle of cosmic freedom. These core principles of mystic philosophy serve as touchstones or guiding stars. Following them, we reintegrate our lives with the whole-order—we find our way home.

The Alchemist:
Working with Universal Transmutation

The universal principle of change—that everything is in flux (Heraclitus), that all is impermanent (the Buddha), or that everything is constantly transmuting into something else (alchemy)—grows naturally from our journeys as Wanderers. Journeys are transforming experiences, so much so that we're willing to endure any expense and discomfort to go on vacations that often leave us exhausted. What we really want from a vacation is to be changed by it, to come back somehow different. Understanding this deep desire, indigenous cultures send people on vision or hero quests. They realize that transformation is compelling, because it's liberating. It proves we're not boxed in fixed forms. We can change, and journeys give us firsthand experiences of this:

> Journeys bring power and love
> back into you. If you can't go somewhere,
> move in the passageways of the self.
> They are like shafts of light,
> always changing, and you change
> when you explore them.[2]

For Alchemists, the inner changes we experience point to a universal process. Change becomes our Alchemists' guiding star, the challenge being to explore where it leads. One thing for sure, it doesn't lead to the concept of change as random or entropic motion. Nor is the Alchemists' concept of growth quantitative increase—higher profits or bigger land development projects.

For alchemists, change is ordered growth that comes from the whole and enfolds back into it—whole-guided change. The body, for instance, regularly gives us new stomachs, livers, hearts, and even bones. That's a case of integrated growth, growth that enfolds with the whole system. Cancerous growth, by contrast, doesn't enfold. Industries that pollute don't either, nor does the concentration of wealth by the few impoverishing the many. Blind growth that's destructive to whole systems isn't the growth alchemists seek; it's what they seek to remedy.

Historically, alchemists are famous for their quest to change lead, copper, mercury, or some other metal into gold. Their theory was that everything in the universe is growing toward its ideal form, gold being the perfect form toward which all metals grow. If base metals stayed in the ground long enough, they'd turn to gold on their own. By understanding how transmutation works, alchemists learn how to facilitate the process.

Though Isaac Newton was himself a closet alchemist—writing extensively on it and even suffering a bad case of mercury poisoning from it—alchemy fell into disrepute with the rise of modern science. Psychologist Carl Jung revived it with his discovery that his clients' dream symbols mirrored the complex imagery of alchemy. He concluded that alchemy's teachings provide metaphors for the soul's growth, which in turn reflect cosmic processes of transformation. Apparently, alchemists' understanding of enfolding growth is embedded in our psyches. Whether we've ever studied alchemy or not, its wisdom guides us.

Yet alchemy is neither all outer (changing metals) nor all inner (changing us); it's both. We and nature grow from the most fundamental process of unfolding-enfolding change: the ongoing transmutation from the invisible to the visible back into the invisible. Nature and matter represent one way of telling this story, consciousness another. How each fares affects the other's telling of the story they share—transformation that doesn't quit:

Think of the phoenix coming up out of ashes,
but not flying off.
For a moment we have form.
We can't see.
How can we be conscious and you be conscious
at the same time and separate?
Copper when an alchemist works on it loses its copper
qualities. Seeds in Spring
begin to be trees, no longer seed. Brushwood
put in the fire changes. The snow-world melts.
You step in my footprint and it's gone.[3]

Caterpillars turn into butterflies and acorns into oaks. Our bodies transmute food into chemicals, while our minds transmute experiences into knowledge. Reality is one enormous transmutation going on—often into more complex orders—suggesting one heck of a force behind it. According to alchemy, behind all change lies the "transformative power" of the whole. We experience this power in ourselves through our souls, which spur us to change. Our souls, in turn, are spurred by a higher change power, "the Soul within that soul":

A loaf of bread wrapped in a cloth for the table
is just an object, but inside a human body
it becomes a gladness for being alive!
The animal-soul transmutes it. Think
what must be the transformative power
of the true soul, and the Soul
within that soul.[4]

To what end? Where are changes heading? These questions are taboo for most modern scientists—naive attempts to project purpose onto a purposeless universe. Alchemists aren't so dismissive. Like David Bohm, who conceived of meaning as intrinsic to the holomovement, alchemists view meaning as central to the transformation going on both in us and in nature. Mind and matter aren't split; they come from the same source in holomovement meaning. We change *because* of that whole-meaning. Indeed, we come into form at all because some invisible meaning had and has a purpose to unfold.

Though the meanings that call us into form are infinitely diverse, alchemists nonetheless describe an end toward which everything is changing: "perfection." This perfection grows from the "love," the unique connectedness with the invisible-visible dance, that brought us here in the first place. We're growing toward the perfect realization of our origin in wholeness:

> Objects move from inorganic to vegetation
> to selves endowed with spirit through the urgency
> of every love that wants to come to perfection.[5]

We don't talk about perfection these days. The mere mention of it throws our neuroses into overdrive. If we're moving toward perfection, then we're not perfect now, and if we're not, then we must be inadequate, flawed, unacceptable, unlovable—we all know where that leads. Our Alchemists think differently. For them, perfection operates on many levels. If perfection unites meaning with form, then we experience perfection every time we have a new insight. To feel life's meaning in any way, great or small, is to experience perfection.

But even if we think about perfection as the end toward which all things are changing, our Alchemists don't use it as a judgment about where we are but rather as a guiding star that steers us through the upheavals of change. Perfection doesn't characterize specific forms anyway but the whole and how everything fits into it. The invisible-visible dance is perfect, not this or that step. Freeze-framed and out of context, a dance step might look awkward or wrong, whereas in the fluid dance, it's beautiful and right. The whole-perfection guides the steps.

Yet the whole-view is precisely what we don't have, making it hard if not impossible for us to judge what's perfect or not step-wise. Alchemists deal with this problem by focusing on the enfolding process. The purpose of forms isn't to be perfect in and of themselves but to reintegrate with the whole. What alchemists seek—and what they believe humanity and nature seek through ongoing transmutations—isn't perfection but perfectibility, the enfolding side. Alchemists see forms in the context that reveals their perfect meaning, that shows how forms fit within a larger process.

The criterion of perfectibility, therefore, is "union with you"—moving with the holomovement's workings—and that guides us through change. Far from judgmental perfectionism, the Alchemists' notion that all forms integrate with the holomovement inspires us to value forms all the more. Whatever the form, whether it's coming or going, it has a role in the total transformation. We need both "boats" and "water" to sail them on:

> Only union with you gives joy.
> The rest is tearing down one building
> to put up another.
>   But don't break
> with forms!
>
> Boats cannot move without water.[6]

Even things we'd call evil have a holomovement meaning. That sounds terrible—how about Hitler or Stalin, for heaven's sake?—but if change is what's going on, even evil can spur it. Things that aren't good in themselves can nonetheless serve the good, if they bump us in that direction. For our Alchemists, the more we use every occasion for transformation, the more we see how "everything blooms from one natural stem," including what we call "good and evil." The essential meaning and "the evolving forms" meet:

> The essence and the evolving forms
> run to meet each other like children
> to their father and mother.
> Good and evil, dead and alive, everything blooms
> from one natural stem.[7]

Faced with a spur-to-change as sharp as evil, the question always is How bad do things have to get before we hear the essence message, fold up the snowflake, and make new cuts?

Connecting with the Source of Change

For our inner Alchemists, suffering evils is bad enough, but ignoring their spur-to-change messages is worse. Fortunately, we can avoid the evil of stalled growth by going back to the "Source." That way, we don't get lost in "the Fantasies of Phenomena" that come "trooping" through our lives. Using experiences to point us in the enfolding direction, we go from phenomena to meanings, and from there to the "Source they come from." We respond to change by refolding the snowflake:

> Think of how PHENOMENA come trooping
> out of the Desert of Non-existence
> into this materiality.
>> Morning and night,
> they arrive in a long line and take over
> from each other, "It's my turn now. Get out!"
>
> A son comes of age, and the father packs up.
> This place of phenomena is a wide exchange
> of highways, with everything going all sorts
> of different ways.
>> We seem to be sitting still,
> but we're actually moving, and the Fantasies
> of Phenomena are sliding through us
> like ideas through curtains.
>> They go to the well
> of deep love inside each of us.
> They fill their jars there, and they leave.
>
> There is a Source they come from,
> and a fountain inside here.[8]

As we go to the Source to gain a perspective on what's going on, we learn to move with the unfolding-enfolding process. We look to what's unfolding from "non-time, non-space," which is where the "real work begins." Our job as Alchemists isn't to force the unfolding—to push the river—but to "learn" from what unfolds, integrating it with a larger meaning. That's what makes "a Master" artist or craftsman. Apprentices see only this or that job to be done, whereas the Master sees the whole work and how everything fits into it:

> Your personal intelligence is not capable of doing
> work. It can learn, but it cannot create.
>
> That must come from non-time, non-space.
> Real work begins there.
>
> Mind does its fine-tuning hair-splitting,
> but no craft or art begins
> or can continue without a Master
> giving wisdom into it.[9]

Understanding how change comes from the Source and then re-integrates with it, we do what we can to move with the process. We make "ointments" that "honor [the] soul" and nudge us in an enfolding direction: poetry, therapy, nutrition, exercise, vacations, time to read and meditate. Our inner Alchemists put all sorts of soul-nurturing potions together for us, realizing that the power to help, guide, and transmute isn't in the potions or even in us but in the enfolding momentum that "ignites" our "embers" into an alchemical fire:

> I was a thorn rushing to be
> with a rose, vinegar blending
> with honey, a pot of poison turning
> to healing salve, the pasty
> wine-dregs thrown into whitewater.
>
> I was a diseased eye reaching
> for Jesus' robe, raw meat
> cooking in the flame.
>
> Then I found some dust
> to make an ointment of
> that would honor my soul,

and in mixing that,
I found poetry.

Love says, "You are right,
but don't claim those changes.

Remember, I am the wind.
You are an ember
I ignite."[10]

Controlling Change
or Moving with Its Uncertainties?

Even our best efforts to move with change, though, can leave us at sea. We sense things shifting, yet we're not sure where they're headed. What comes from the Source can leave us feeling like "bats swung by powerful arms," while alchemical fires can transmute "all stability" into "smoke":

The whole place goes up, all stability gone to smoke.
Sometimes high, sometimes low, we begin anywhere,
we have no method.
We're the bat swung by powerful arms.
Balls keep rolling from us, thousands of them underfoot.[11]

Since change is the only true certainty in life, how do we deal with the uncertainties that go with it? One response is to try to control change and bend it to our advantage. Those who take this route become sorcerers, whether they conjure in medieval huts or corporate boardrooms, family gatherings or church pews. After a visit to various Buddhist groups in America, a Tibetan-Bhutanese Buddhist monk commented, "Some were good and some not so good. Some seem to be looking for something for themselves, not for mankind":[12]

In sorcery there are demonic helpers
who find ways to make you successful.

You have been doing such things
with the name of God.[13]

Sorcery isn't the way of the mystic, because it attempts to enfold forms not into the holomovement but into a personal, selfish-interests agenda. As an integrating context, that's too small. The transmutations going on in and around us are bigger than that, involving meanings and purposes—perfectibilities—beyond our imaginings. The fortunes the robber barons amassed from controlling changes in industry didn't bring the happiness that might have been theirs had they abandoned their sorcery and followed a less controlling path.

Trying to harness the holomovement's change powers for personal ends is as absurd as having a mouse lead a camel. Mouse-sorcery hasn't the resources to guide us when we come to the "great river"—the currents of meaning and fulfillment. With mouse-sorcerer methods, we're in over our heads:

> A mouse caught hold of a camel's leading-rope
> in his two forelegs and walked off with it,
> imitating the camel-drivers.
>   The camel went along,
> letting the mouse feel heroic.
>   "Enjoy yourself,"
> he thought. "I have something to teach you, presently."
>
> They came to the edge of a great river.
> The mouse was dumbfounded.
>   "What are you waiting for?
> Step forward into the river. You are my leader.
> Don't stop here."
>   "I am afraid of being drowned."
>
> The camel walked into the water. "It's only
> just above the knee."
>   "*Your* knee! Your knee
> is a hundred times over my head!"
>   "Well, maybe you shouldn't
> be leading a camel. Stay with those like yourself.
> A mouse has nothing really to say to a camel."
>
> "Would you help me get across?"
>
> "Get up on my hump. I am made
> to take hundreds like you across."[14]

Engaging in change doesn't mean controlling it—leading the camel. Genuine change grows from who we are, since that's what is most real. When we go to the depths of our being, we feel the pulse of change and how it draws us perfectly along an enfolding path. Only when we feel cut off from who we are do we feel alienated from change, afraid of it, and therefore driven to control it. That's when we behave like the mouse and create worlds of manipulation, a pretense of control, having "no idea what we are":

> In complete control, pretending control,
> with dignified authority, we are charlatans.
> Or maybe just a goat's hair brush in a painter's hand.
> We have no idea what we are.[15]

Whereas the mouse method "distorts Universal Intelligence" with "particular intelligences," working from who we are opens us to "the Mind of the Whole." According to that Mind, we don't hunt the whole; it hunts us. There's something that the whole wants with us—our lives being, after all, the whole expressed. Based on his experiences in Nazi concentration camps, psychiatrist Viktor Frankl wrote, "*It did not really matter what we expected from life, but rather what life expected from us. . . . Life ultimately means taking the responsibility . . . to fulfill the tasks which it constantly sets for each individual.*"[16] From the whole we have a purpose, a meaning and destiny, that the Mind of the Whole "sees" and wants to bring out in our lives:

> There's not one mind-form everywhere equal, as some have said,
> but it is particular intelligences that distort Universal
> Intelligence, the ones that use light to hunt with.
> The Mind of the Whole does otherwise. It gets a glimpse
> of a lovely hunt going on, where God
> is Hunter and everything else the hunted. That Mind
> sees and tries to quit hunting and completely
> be prey. That's the difference.[17]

Does this make Rumi a determinist? Are we automatons before God, at the mercy of divine forces? Should we be passive before change? Not likely given someone as freedom-loving as Rumi, who also rode off to join a three-day battle defending the city of Damascus against the Mongols.[18] Passive before change wasn't his style. Instead, Rumi is expressing our Alchemists' quest to be guided by holomovement currents. He wants us actively working with the Mind of the Whole, rather than conjuring inside small-minded interests:

> The saying, *Whatever God wills, will happen,*
> does not end, "Therefore be passive."
>
> Rather, it means, *Forget yourself,*
> *and get ready to help.* . . .
>
> Stay alert then, and close by,
> like a worker waiting to perform
> whatever needs to be done. . . .
>
> The way you distinguish a true commentary
> from a false is this:
>   Whichever explication
> makes you feel fiery and hopeful, humble
> and *active*, that's the true one.
>
> If it makes you lazy, it's not right.[19]

Muslims say "if God wills" whenever they talk about doing something. Thomas à Kempis had a Christian version: "Man proposes, but God disposes."[20] Our inner Alchemists want change that enfolds with the whole-order, because if it doesn't, it won't bring the intangible qualities— fulfillment, satisfaction, joy—that make change worthwhile. Since ultimate fittings-in are beyond our capacity to calculate, we simply say to ourselves, "We'll do this, *if God wills*." That way, we go ahead and act, but if things don't work out as we hoped, we're not devastated. We wanted them to work only on the condition that they were enfoldable:

> Some people work and become wealthy.
> Others do the same and remain poor.
>
> Marriage fills one with energy.
> Another it drains.

Don't trust ways. They change.
A means flails about like a donkey's tail.

Always add the gratitude clause
to any sentence, *if God wills*,
then go.[21]

Living as mystic Alchemists means, therefore, living with uncertainty. Not only do we allow for it, but we trust that things *not* working out may be for the best. There's a purpose to our plans failing, even if we don't see it. Uncertainty about "ways" and "means" is inevitable, but it's also the best approach. What we want most from change isn't this or that result but the perfecting that goes on in us. Through our "bewilderments and wonderings," our "trust in the Unseen grows." On the deepest levels, we already have "Union"—that's our bottom-line reality. Whether this unseen union works itself out in our lives through "effort" or "giving up effort," "tailoring" or "goldsmithing," is incidental:

You fear losing a certain eminent position.
You hope to gain something from that, but it comes
from elsewhere. Existence does this switching trick,
giving you hope from one source, then satisfaction
from another.
        It keeps you bewildered and wondering,
and lets your trust in the Unseen grow.

You think to make your living from tailoring,
but then somehow money comes in
through goldsmithing,
which had never entered your mind.

I don't know whether the Union I want will come
through my effort, or my giving up effort,
or from something completely separate
from anything I do or don't do.[22]

Accepting uncertainties is liberating. We're free to be "straw in a strong wind." If transmutation is what's going on, if that's the principle guiding us, then we need to be free to follow where it leads. Not expecting ourselves to be certain gives us the inward space to do this, to move with change:

> Sometimes it's freezing, sometimes honey-warm.
> Sometimes we're separate, sometimes together.
>
> Everything keeps changing. How could we not?[23]

> *

> I'm straw in a strong wind.
> How could I possibly know where I'll end up?
> New moon, full moon, half moon,
> I'm just following the sun. The moon
> doesn't care about being fat or thin!
>
> All it cares about is the sun![24]

Going through the Refining Fire

Following the sun, though, takes us through heat and fire. We find our true mettle—who we are without the props of certainty around us. For our inner Alchemists, changes in our bodies, emotions, relationships, professions, and philosophies serve as the alchemical crucible, the refining fire, through which we pass to become in form what we are in essence. We're gold hidden under dross, and our lives are an alchemical process—soul-cooking—to reveal who we truly are:

> A chickpea leaps almost over the rim of the pot
> where it's being boiled.
>
> "Why are you doing this to me?"
>
> The cook knocks him down with the ladle.
>
> "Don't you try to jump out.
> You think I'm torturing you.
> I'm giving you flavor,
> so you can mix with spices and rice
> and be the lovely vitality of a human being.

Remember when you drank rain in the garden.
That was for this.". . .

Eventually the chickpea
will say to the cook,
         "Boil me some more.
Hit me with the skimming spoon.
I can't do this by myself.

I'm like an elephant that dreams of gardens
back in Hindustan and doesn't pay attention
to his driver. You're my Cook, my Driver,
my Way into Existence. I love your cooking."[25]

Neither Rumi nor our Alchemists suggest that life as alchemy isn't painful. Life is painful, alchemy or not. Indeed, the Buddha's first noble truth says that life is *dukkha*, which means "suffering" arising from the impermanence of things. Not being certain, not having plans work out, not having desires fulfilled, being cooked and pounded: it all hurts. Our Alchemists advise us to "stand the pain" and "melt in the healing elixir." What's burning up isn't who we are but who we're not, "poisonous impulses" that don't match our essence. Through the burning, something beautiful emerges, one of "God's Lions," an image Rumi uses for a True Human Being. But lions aren't made without pain along the way:

In Qazwin, they have a custom of tattooing themselves
for good luck, with blue ink, on the back
of the hand, the shoulder, wherever.

A certain man there goes to his barber
and asks to be given a powerful, heroic, Blue Lion
on his shoulder blade. "And do it with flair!
I've got Leo Ascending. I want plenty of blue!"

But as soon as the needle starts pricking,
he howls,
         "What are you doing?"
                  "The lion."

"Which limb did you start with?"
                              "I began with the tail."
"Well, leave out the tail. That lion's rump
is in a bad place for me. It cuts off my wind."

The barber continues, and immediately
the man yells out,
                    "Oooooooo! Which part now?"
                                        "The ear."
"Doc, let's do a lion with no ears this time."
                                        The barber
shakes his head, and once more the needle,
and once more the wailing,
                         "Where are you now?"
                                        "The belly."
"I like a lion without a belly."
                         The Master Lion-Maker
stands for a long time with his fingers in his teeth.
Finally, he throws the needle down.
                    "No one has ever been asked
to do such a thing! To create a lion
without a tail or a head or a stomach.
God himself could not do it!"

Brother, stand the pain.
Escape the poison of your impulses.
The sky will bow to your beauty, if you do.
Learn to light the candle. Rise with the sun.
Turn away from the cave of your sleeping.
That way a thorn expands to a Rose.
A particular glows with the Universal.

What is it to praise?
Make yourself particles.

What is it to know something of God?
Burn inside that Presence. Burn up.

Copper melts in the healing elixir.

So melt your self in the Mixture
that Sustains Existence.[26]

What hurts isn't what's happening but our fears about what's to
come. We cling to how things are and feel pain when they shift. According to the Buddha's second noble truth, this clinging attachment—
tanha—is the cause of all suffering. Change *is*; it neither hurts nor
doesn't hurt. We hurt, though, when we hold on to things that are impermanent, whether they're people, jobs, self-images, or belief systems. For the Buddha, that's good news, because we can do something
about it. We can cease clinging and so find an end to suffering (the third
noble truth).

Rumi, in true alchemical form, says that's bound to happen anyway.
Clinging is a "sign of unripeness." With maturing, we automatically let
go. Showing the way of transformation in his fourth noble truth, the
eightfold path, the Buddha simply acted as an alchemist in speeding up
the process:

> . . . You're still in early Spring.
> July hasn't happened yet in you.
>   This world is a tree,
> and we are green, half-ripe fruit on it.
> We hold tight to the limbs, because we know
> we're not ready to be taken into the palace.
>
> When we mature and sweeten,
>   we'll feel ashamed
> at having clung so clingingly.
>   To hold fast
> is a sure sign of unripeness.[27]

Alchemists assume that everything is growing into what it truly is,
and there's no better example of this than agriculture. Plants are constantly growing "perfect" forms: leaves, fruit, trees, and seeds. From the
seeds, we know the genus of the plants, but we don't know their
unique forms until they ripen. Inner alchemy is how we make our own
unique "globe of soul-fruit":

These leaves, our bodily personalities, seem identical,
but the globe of soul-fruit
we make,
each is elaborately
unique.[28]

That's where our gardener-Alchemists come in. How we tend the
seeds affects what sort of plants they become. In mystic alchemy, we're
the seeds and the gardeners of them too:

> ... Water the fruit trees,
> and don't water the thorns. Be generous
> to what nurtures the Spirit and God's luminous
> Reason-Light. Don't honor what causes
> dysentery and knotted-up tumors.[29]

We have, as Rumi says, a choice about which plants to water. The
clinging, the mouse control, the soul-disconnectedness: those plants
give us "dysentery and knotted-up tumors." No sense in watering
them, in "feeding our diseases"—diseases that manifest as rigid, not-us
identities, as envy and possessiveness, or as the insecurities that lead to
domination, grandiosity, lying, greed, and manipulation—some of the
first-rate tumors and trots that make life nasty.

Instead of feeding those, our mystic Alchemists "feed our real nature" with our "original food," food that isn't merely "dust kicked up
from the carpet." What "Sustains Existence" is a bigger sense of who
we are and what's going on with our lives. In *Man's Search for Meaning*,
Viktor Frankl quotes Nietzsche, "He who has a *why* to live for can
bear with almost any *how*."[30] Those who survived Nazi death camps
weren't the physically strongest but those who were sustained by
inner meaning:

> Every soul needs different nourishment,
> but be aware if your food is accidental
> and habitual, or if it's something
> that feeds your real nature.

It may be, like those who eat clay, that human beings
have forgotten what their original food is.
They may be feeding their diseases.

Our true food is God's light. . . .

Tasting that is done without silverware,
and without a throat. It comes down
from the throne of God. This other
is just dust kicked up from the carpet.[31]

Embracing the Full Dimensions of Who We Are

From ancient times, alchemists put themselves through the refining
fire from a deep conviction that human beings—indeed all beings—are
more than we appear. *Beauty and the Beast* is an alchemical story, with
the Beast-form concealing a prince and Beauty's love serving as the alchemical elixir that catalyzes the prince's transformation back into his
original form. What we see of each other is like "a play put on in the
courtyard," but our essence is "the theatre of God":

There are definite levels of soul.
The first is phenomenal, a play put on
in the courtyard, mingling human and divine.

What happens in the inner essence
of soul is the theatre of God![32]

Sogyal Rinpoche describes Buddhist meditation as focusing on this
inner essence: "The purpose of meditation is to awaken in us the sky-
like nature of mind, and to introduce us to that which we really are,
our unchanging pure awareness, which underlies the whole of life and
death."[33] Through meditation and alchemy, we discover the vastness of
our nature as "a True Person":

I need a mouth as wide as the sky
to say the nature of a True Person, language
as large as longing.[34]

Judged by appearances—one among six billion, by day a wage slave, by night a couch potato, our heads caught up in trying to get by—we think we're small and insignificant, yet the "True Person" we are is anything but. There's a "beauty and elegance and clarity and love" at our core that surpasses anything we can imagine and is worth more than anything outward:

> Some human beings no bigger than a water trough
> scooped out of a log are greater glories
> than the universe full of stars.
>
> *We have honored you,* says the *Qur'an.*
> A grieving human being heard that from God!
>
> The beauty and elegance and clarity and love
> that we have deserve to be offered into
> regions higher than this visible one.[35]

Because this "secret core in everyone" is as ineffable as the holomovement itself, it's absurd to pass judgment on where we are spiritually—or on where anyone else is either. "Not even Gabriel can know" it:

> This piece of food cannot be eaten,
> nor this bit of wisdom found by looking.
> There is a secret core in everyone
> not even Gabriel can know by trying to know.[36]

All this is present in us, yet we don't feel it. We look at our lives, relationships, and moods, and think, "You must be joking!" According to our Alchemists, this reaction stems from a narrow concept of great beings, as if great beings smile all the time, behave like saints and celibates, and live in a moral straitjacket. Any genuine emotion counts as evidence that, whoever we are, we're not spiritual, not someone Gabriel would want to know.

That's not thinking alchemically. Alchemists focus on change and development, on dynamics rather than static outcomes. For them, states don't matter as much as processes, and processes take many forms. Transmutation turns us "upsidedown," just as cooking dinner messes up the kitchen. Rumi suggests we let the messiness, the "restlessness," of our lives "be the moisture in an oyster that helps to form one pearl":

> Yesterday at dawn, my Friend said, *How long*
> *will this unconsciousness go on?*
>
> You fill yourself with the sharp pain of Love,
> rather than its fulfillment.
>
> I said, "But I can't get to You!
> You are the whole dark night,
> and I am a single candle.
>
> My life is upsidedown
> because of You!"
>
> The Friend replied, *I am your deepest being.*
> *Quit talking about* wanting *Me!*
>
> I said, "Then what is this
> restlessness?"
>
> The Friend, *Does a drop*
> *stay still in the Ocean?*
>
> *Move with the Entirety,*
> *and with the tiniest particular.*
>
> *Be the moisture in an oyster*
> *that helps to form one pearl.*[37]

Alchemy at Work in Our Lives

Our inner Alchemists see beyond "restlessness," because they assume there's an in-built principle of enfolding growth guiding each of us. Because transmutation is a universal principle, enfolding with the whole is our destiny. We enfold with the whole not because we're good or not good, messy or not messy, but because that's reality and we're part of

it. Every experience, every phase of our lives plays a role in our alchemical process. Growth that's whole-guided is embedded in us—
"There is an inner wakefulness that directs the dream":

> Humankind is being led along an evolving course,
> through this migration of intelligences,
> and though we seem to be sleeping,
> there is an inner wakefulness
> that directs the dream,
>
> and that will eventually startle us back
> to the truth of who we are.[38]

This is what Carl Jung discovered with his patients. Their dream images led them through alchemical transmutations—inner shifts—that
brought healing changes no therapist could have imposed. The healing
work that went on daily was processed at night in their inner laboratories, guided by their own alchemical wisdom. According to both Jung
and Rumi, we have "spiritual alchemists . . . all around us," touching us in
our dreams and causing "new plants [to] spring up in our awarenesses":

> There are these people who remember,
> who return in sleep to Hindustan.
>
> If you're not one of those elephants,
> let the spiritual alchemists,
> who are all around us, change you
> into one. Every night they touch us
> in different ways. New plants
> spring up in our awarenesses![39]

Indeed, "the Presence of our Self" is the presence of a Master Alchemist. "That One," our own soul, knows where we are in transformation and what catalyzes it. In the thick of everyday life—with its
trials and tribulations, decisions big and small, even daily hassles,
stresses, and apparent trivialities—we don't sense the changes going on
in us or where they're leading. But our "Self" does. Our deepest being

sees the big picture of enfolding growth working itself out in our lives—how we're growing into "the truth of who we are." Our inner Alchemists open us to this level of knowing. As they do, we find we don't need external authorities to tell us about everyday alchemy; we tell ourselves:

> More needs to be said on this, but the Holy Spirit
> will tell it to you when I'm not here.
>   *You'll* tell it
> to *yourself*. Not I, or some other "I," You
> who are Me!
>   As when you fall asleep and go
> from the presence of your self to the Presence
> of your Self. You hear That One and you think,
> "Someone must have communicated telepathically
> in my sleep."[40]

Because of this in-built principle, alchemists are struck by how individual the alchemical process is: "Each lion is his own path." Where we are in transformation isn't where anyone else is, and what catalyzes our change is our secret. No one else knows. On conscious levels, not even we know. That's why, historically, alchemists worked alone in their laboratories. They were evolving their own being according to a life path that was theirs alone. Though they compared notes and supported each other, alchemy is an individualized work, time reflecting on our souls and where they're taking us. In alchemy, each person's life—whatever its course—is the laboratory from which amazing transmutations come.

As a result, our inner Alchemists respect how we're each guided from within. No matter how old or young a person, how messy or ontrack, there's timeless wisdom at work. That's a mettle our Alchemists don't meddle with. In his introduction to *Feeling the Shoulder of the Lion*, Coleman Barks writes:

> In alchemy the lion is an intermediate transformational symbol. . . .
> Shams was associated with [the lion], and he was completely his own

man. Whenever students would begin to gather around him in a dependent relationship, he would excuse himself and vanish. . . . Lions
carry no baggage. Each lion is his own path, and he wants everyone to
take total responsibility for himself or herself. . . . The lion is a knight out
in the wilderness by himself. . . .

    . . . The chief lion attribute is his authority. It is an authority over
himself, and it is also an authority that comes from living close to a deep
sense of self that he will not betray. . . . Being a lion is not *fitting in*. He
does not refer to group behavior, only to that which he generates and
validates from within.[41]

By submitting ourselves to the alchemical fire of our own experiences and trusting our in-built Alchemists to see us through, we "unfold our own myth." Transformation accelerates: beasts emerge as
princes, ruins as wealth, and moisture as pearls. *That* this happens is the
universal principle of enfolding growth, but *how* it happens is our own
story. It's our seed growing, our "soul's code" coming to light. True, because we haven't heard a story quite like it before, we can feel lost and
overwhelmed. We don't realize that through the fire and upheavals,
phoenix-like, we've been growing "wings":

> An oyster opens his mouth to swallow one drop.
> Now there's a pearl.
> A vagrant wanders empty ruins.
> Suddenly he's wealthy.
>
> But don't be satisfied with stories, how things
> have gone with others. Unfold
> your own myth, without complicated explanation,
> so everyone will understand the passage,
> *We have opened you.*
>
> Start walking toward Shams. Your legs will get heavy
> and tired. Then comes a moment
> of feeling the wings you've grown,
> lifting.[42]

Because the alchemical path is radically individual, it makes no
sense to compare our path to anyone else's. Did we meditate enough?
Did we follow the right techniques? Did we improve ourselves as much

as others have? Our inner Alchemists don't ask these questions, because alchemy is there in our lives all the time no matter what we're
doing. Our lives are alchemy, and the transformation we undergo
shows the meaning of the pain and the happiness we've experienced.
Knowing this—that wherever we are, inner alchemy is going on—we
embrace our inner Alchemists and move with them:

> You come to reading books late in life.
> Don't worry if you see the young ones
> ahead of you. Don't hurry.
> You're tired and ready to quit?
> Let your hands play music.[43]

If we can't compare our path to anyone else's, if our life experiences
are our best alchemical meditation, then we can't say whether we're
behind or ahead. Our lives unfold in step with our inner changes.
Granted, alchemy is a work of patience, of "gradualness and delibera-
tion." Acorns need time to grow into oaks. Lives spread out over time.
But by shifting our perspective from the view that events happen randomly, unrelated to our souls' purpose, to the alchemical view that it's
all of a piece with meaning at the center, we see what's going on and
what we can do to attend the process—to be good gardeners to our
"gradually growing wholeness":

> A new moon teaches gradualness
> and deliberation and how one gives birth
> to oneself slowly. Patience with small details
> makes perfect a large work, like the universe.
>
> What nine months of attention does for an embryo
> forty early mornings will do
> for your gradually growing wholeness.[44]

Growing a Huge Work:
Catalysts for Collective Transformation

Historically, alchemists believed that alchemy could grow not only individuals but also the world into its innate wholeness. Religion histo-
rian Mircea Eliade writes: "It is the alchemist's dream to heal the world

in its totality; the Philosopher's Stone is conceived as the *Filius Macro-cosmi* who heals the world. . . . The ultimate goal of the [great work] is Cosmic Salvation."[45] According to alchemists, the soul of the world is as much in need of transformation as we are, and given the state of things, who can argue with them?

But how can such a vast transformation occur? Through their medieval fiddlings with chemistry, alchemists showed that the hardest forms—metals—can change, and not only that, they can change into something beautiful and malleable. To go a step further, alchemists sought a universal solvent that could dissolve any substance, even gold, regardless of how hard it was. Behind these symbols is alchemy's message: no matter how fixed things seem, they can change, and no matter how resistant to change a form may be, it can dissolve:

> Don't say such changes cannot happen.
> A vast freedom could live inside you.[46]

With a subversive call to transformation like that, no wonder the Church outlawed alchemy. If we think things are set in stone—humans as selfish, greedy, violent creatures, for instance, or institutions that are just as bad—then we don't apply alchemy to them. We put up with abusive systems—we tolerate them believing we have no other choice—and then we wonder what sort of planet we landed on. By contrast, knowing the power of transformation serves as a catalyst for making change happen.

And it *is* happening. Because the principle of enfolding growth is universal, change goes on constantly. It's built into not only us but also the universe—into society and nature. Everything feels the pull to grow into its perfect form within the whole. Just because society looks like a bunch of people doing their own things, and some nasty things at that, doesn't mean it's outside the holomovement.

Yet what exactly are alchemists proposing? Growing our souls is no small work, but growing society and nature—that's huge. Sometimes we see society growing, and then we don't. Sometimes it seems as if we can make a difference, and then we think we're fooling ourselves. Rumi's been there:

Some huge work goes on growing,
or not growing.
How could one person's words matter?

Where you walk, heads pop from the ground.
What is one seed-head compared to you?

On my death-day I'll know the answer.[47]

Our Alchemists don't say we should run out and try to fix things.
Rather, they say that, in tending our own transformation, we tend
more than we realize. In the unbroken field of the holomovement,
consciousness is a catalyst. Every thought, every feeling, but especially
every transformation sends out ripples. Though we may not be able to
track the ripples, they nonetheless affect the field.

For our Alchemists, doing what's ours to do is the "Philosopher's
Stone," which, dropped into the pool of world consciousness, catalyzes
world-healing. It doesn't matter that no one knows what we're doing
or where the impulse to change is coming from. The real work of transformation is primarily unseen. Not just movers and shakers but everyone has a hand in it. Rumi tells a story about a man drumming the
"sahur" (the drum call to the predawn meal during Ramadan) by the
gate of an empty building. Someone asks, "Why beat this drum where
nobody is?" The man replies:

Inside any deep asking is the answering.
Like that, something lets me know
that I should be drumming
the *sahur* here.

Some people go to war.
Some endure painful difficulties.
Some wait patiently.

Everybody does service of some sort.
Mine is drumming at this gate
where the only listener is God,

the One who buys a dirty sack
and gives inner light in return,

who takes the dissolving ice of this body
and gives a vast countryside,
the One who receives our grief
and changes it to a lovely river.[48]

But when doing what's ours to do makes us run head-on into established institutions and ingrained paradigms, we wonder, "How *long* should we keep pounding this cold iron?" Is what we're doing making any difference besides wearing us out emotionally, if not physically and financially as well? Are the change prospects worth going into the fire for? To flee the fire, though, we'd have to flee our souls, and worse, to flee the "motion" behind them that "comes from the creator." Which is more costly?

The Prophets have wondered to themselves,
                     "How *long*
should we keep pounding this cold iron? How *long*
do we have to whisper into an empty cage?"

Every motion of created beings
comes from the creator.

The first soul pushes,
and your second soul responds.

So don't be timid.
Load the ship and set out.

No one knows for certain
whether the vessel will sink
or reach the harbor.

Just don't be one of those merchants
who won't risk the ocean!

This is much more important
than losing or making money!

This is your connection to God. . . .

Be companions with the prophets
even though no one here will know that you are,
not even the helpers of the Qutb, the abdals.

You can't imagine what *profit* will come!
When one of those generous ones
invites you into his fire,
go quickly!
                    Don't say,
"But will it burn me? Will it hurt?"[49]

Going into the alchemical fire burns up the notion that we're stones
that can't change and inspires instead the Alchemists' vision that
everything is enfolding toward its perfection. "The whole world is a
form for truth"—it's all the holomovement's activity. Seen alchemically,
the universe "turns to gold." A place of determined pain and darkness
becomes "every moment, a new beauty":

                    . . . The whole world
          is a form for truth.
                    When someone does not feel grateful
          to that, the forms appear to be *as he feels*.
          They mirror his anger, his greed, and his fear.
          Make peace with the universe. Take joy in it.

          It will turn to gold. Resurrection
          will be *now*. Every moment,
          a new beauty.[50]

11

Conversing Ocean to Ocean

ARCHETYPE *Contemplative*
MYSTIC JOURNEY *The Return: Coming Home to Our Origins*

The Contemplative: Living in Stillness

Through the torrents of change we arrive at the Contemplative. In so doing, we complete the holomovement's cycle—unfolding from wholeness and then enfolding back into it. Rumi likens the cycle to that of pearls driven by "the hurricane of experience" away from their quiet shells, only to be brought back, after much journeying, to "another stillness":

> I was happy enough to stay still
> inside the pearl inside the shell,
>
> but the hurricane of experience
> lashed me out of hiding and made me
>
> a wave moving into shore, saying loudly
> the ocean's secret as I went, and then
>
> spent there, I slept like fog against
> the cliff, another stillness.[1]

Stillness comes as we digest all that's unfolded through the mystic journey. Whereas our Alchemists—and all the mystic archetypes, for that matter—say we're treasures born of the whole, our Contemplatives accept this. Accepting, though, is an art. It's not something we can force. Siddhartha Gautama tried the "go get 'em" path to Buddhahood during his years of self-mortification, but it didn't bring the inner stillness he sought. So he changed his method. He sat down under the bodhi tree and let enlightenment come to him.

276

That's the Contemplative way. Our Contemplatives sit down under the truth of our being and let it enlighten consciousness, assuming that wisdom and knowing lie within. Because we each have "a channel into the Ocean," instead of "asking for water from a little pool," our inner Contemplatives simply hold the space of "spiritual emptiness" where "Light" can pour in:

> The mystery of spiritual emptiness may be living
> in a pilgrim's heart, and yet the knowing of it
> may not yet be his.
>
> Wait for the illuminating openness,
> as though your chest were filling with Light,
> as when God said,
>> *Did We not expand you?*
>>> (*Qur'an,* XCIV, 1)
> Don't look for it outside yourself.
> You are the source of milk. Don't milk others!
>
> There is a milk-fountain inside you.
> Don't walk around with an empty bucket.
> You have a channel into the Ocean, and yet
> you ask for water from a little pool.[2]

Whereas our Alchemists' freedom moves with the currents of transmutation, our Contemplatives' freedom lives in stillness. Though these two seem contradictory, both express our mystics' freedom to live from the invisible. One says we're free to shift forms all we want, that it's the nature of forms to shift in response to the unseen reality behind them. The other, the Contemplatives' freedom, says that, amid changes, we're free to stay rooted in the invisible, to live from the central stillness around which changes occur.

Living from our "channel into the Ocean," we're less caught up in "duality." Instead of seeing chaos, our Contemplatives see transforming energies—mystic archetypes—at work. Contemplatives look beneath the surface of things, "through the foam and broken sticks," to the "pearl on the bottom." Not that Contemplatives trash foam and sticks. Foam and sticks have their beauty, a "poignancy" that reflects the ocean's currents. But our Contemplatives want what's deeper. Why watch the mesmeric heavings of surface debris when treasures lie below?

> When you see a pearl on the bottom,
> you reach through the foam and broken sticks
> on the surface. When the sun comes up, you forget
> about locating the constellation of Scorpio.
>
> When you see the splendor of union,
> the attractions of duality seem poignant
> and lovely, but much less interesting.[3]

The Contemplative's Method

But how do our Contemplatives move past dualistic categories—the familiar ones we've internalized: me/not-me, us/them, spirit/matter—to experience reality's inside story? Every mystic tradition answers this question differently, from the vast complexity of Tibetan Buddhism to the stark simplicity of Zen. Sufism falls somewhere in between. Rumi, mindful of the diversity of methods, simply sketches the broad lines of how Contemplatives contemplate.

Naturally, Contemplatives go within—that's true for every mystic tradition. What's the point of having our own channels into the Ocean, or "baskets of fresh bread on our heads," and not dipping into them?

> There is a basket of fresh bread on your head, and yet
> you go door to door asking for crusts.
>
> Knock on your inner door. No other.[4]

When we go within, our inner Contemplatives don't give us a list of rules to follow, because contemplation isn't a do-it-right-or-fail proposition. It's simply inner listening—becoming quiet enough to hear "a voice within." Inner listening is a turn of mind that comes with practice, until it becomes second nature:

> . . . Sit quietly, and listen
> for a voice within that will say,
> > *Be more silent.*
> As that happens,
> > your soul starts to revive.
> Give up talking, and your positions of power.
> Give up the excessive money.
> > Turn toward the teachers
> and the prophets who don't live in Saba.
>
> They can help you grow sweet again
> and fragrant and wild and fresh
> and thankful for any small event.[5]

"Saba" was a city where everyone had everything, and no one cared about the unseen world. Saba's "over-richness is a subtle disease,"[6] Rumi says, for which "sitting quietly, and listening for a voice within" is the remedy. To do that, though, we have to expand contemplation to include a way of life that's conducive to it. If we're preoccupied with "excessive money" and "positions of power," inner quietude eludes us. "Small events" lose their magic, while we lose our freshness. To help us "grow sweet again," our Contemplatives clear away unnecessary distractions within *and* without.

Rumi often uses flowing water as a symbol of consciousness, like Tibetan Buddhists, who describe the essential mind as a stream of luminous knowing. The stream stays clear when it flows unhindered, but "when desire-weeds grow thick, the intelligence can't flow."

Unlike some mystical traditions that take a dim view of the intellect, though, Rumi regards the "reasonable mind" as an ally. When it runs strong, it can "clear the clogged stream." Because we can't hear the inner Ocean when outer distractions intrude, reason helps us design our lives to support our inner listening. It inspires us to pare down to what's essential. That's rational as well as mystically sound—it's how "you see in":

> The way the soul is
> with the senses and the intellect
> is like a creek.

When desire-weeds grow thick,
the intelligence can't flow,
and soul-creatures stay hidden.

But sometimes your reasonable mind
runs so strong it clears
the clogged stream
as though with God's hand.

No longer weeping and frustrated,
your being grows as powerful
as your wantings were before.

Laughing and satisfied, that masterful flowing
lets soul-creatures appear.

You look down,
and it's lucid dreaming.

The gates made of light
swing open. You see in.[7]

Clearing away outer distractions, our Contemplatives then clear away inner ones as well, especially "the elaborate language-dance of personality." "Desire-singing and rage-ranting," angling and manipulating, figuring who's got the upper hand—this dance leaves us out of sorts. Our inner mystics just don't have a constitution for it. It's a stream-clogger, as anyone who's sat down to contemplate when that's going on inside knows.

Not that we can't "study foam and flotsam near the edge" and "explain them at length." Rumi's letters reveal him to be fully aware of what goes on between people and tender in helping others deal with people-ish concerns.[8] As Contemplatives, though, we long to "see all the way to the ocean." We want the big picture not as an interesting theory but as our essential being—"those who look out to sea become the sea":

Don't be absorbed with the waterwheel's motion.
Turn your head and gaze at the river. You say,

"But I'm looking there already." There are several signs
in eyes that see all the way to the ocean. Bewilderment

is one. Those who study foam and flotsam near the edge
have purposes, and they'll explain them at length!

Those who look out to sea become the sea,
and they can't speak about that. On the beach

there's desire-singing and rage-ranting,
the elaborate language-dance of personality,

but in the waves and underneath there's no volition,
no hypocrisy, just love forming and unfolding.[9]

With the outer designed to support inner listening and the inner focused beyond personal "foam and flotsam," we can hear what's going
on in our souls—and in the Soul of the soul. Inner stillness reveals a
new under-the-waves world and a new way of being to go with it: "just
love forming and unfolding."

The old way—the way of the city of Saba—is, for our Contemplatives, like living "inside black water in a well." That's how dark and confining it is to be absorbed in externals. Born into that life, though, we
don't know much else. Inner listening takes us back to our souls' home,
to "an open field of sunlight" and to "a moving palace that floats
through the air." When we're quiet, we hear our souls, and when we
act from them, we "feel a river moving in us, a joy":

When you do things from your soul,
you feel a river moving in you, a joy.

When actions come from another section,
the feeling disappears. . . .

We are born and live inside black water in a well.
How could we know what an open field of sunlight is?

Don't insist on going where you think you want to go.
Ask the way to the Spring.

Your living pieces will form a harmony.

There is a moving palace that floats through the air,
with balconies and clear water running in every part of it,
infinity everywhere, yet contained under a single tent.[10]

Contemplation is essentially going home—a method that not only aligns us with our unseen reality but heals and regenerates our seen-side too. When we get stuck in deadening patterns—"habitual whirlpools"—mystic contemplation is the cure. It sends us back to the ocean, which renews us from our origin.

The going-home method even restores hope. We start off life hoping to achieve things. We entertain this hope on the larger hope that the human race won't do itself in. But as the years go by, many of our plans fall through, while the world seems bent on multiplying sorrows rather than mending them. After enough personal sorrows and exposure to enough collective ones, we "hurt so hard we can't hope" anymore. That's when we need a trip to the ocean. Our inner Contemplatives' "secret medicine" is to return us to the place where hope starts, more, to where our capacity to hope is born:

How to cure bad water? Send it back to the river.
How to cure bad habits? Send me back to you.

When water gets caught in habitual whirlpools,
dig a way out through the bottom
to the ocean. There is a secret medicine
given only to those who hurt so hard
they can't hope.

The hopers would feel slighted if they knew.[11]

The Return

The idea of returning to our origins—that "these time and place personalities" are borrowed clothes and that this money/power-driven world isn't our home—lies deep in all of us, or the return wouldn't be such a powerful theme, recurring not only in mystical writings but also in myths from ancient times to the present. We're on some sort of cosmic, soul-refining journey. What we do while we're here isn't the be-all and end-all of our existence but a step along the way. Doing it well means doing it in a way that points us homeward:

> We have borrowed these clothes,
> these time and place personalities,
> from a light, and when we praise,
> we're pouring them back in.[12]

Rumi likens our condition to that of a reed cut from the marshes and made into a flute. Behind the flute's music—its "crying sound"— is the reed's longing to return to the reedbed:

> Listen to the story told by the reed,
> of being separated.
>
> "Since I was cut from the reedbed,
> I have made this crying sound.
>
> Anyone apart from someone he loves
> understands what I say.
>
> Anyone pulled from a source
> longs to go back."[13]

For Rumi, every sound we make sends that same message: that we feel separated from the whole and want to be woven back into it. Naturally, we don't conceive of our communications that way. We think we're talking about bills, schedules, and who's picking up the groceries. Nonetheless, all the longing for the good, which we translate into wanting this or that good thing, as well as all the unhappiness we express at feeling separated from the good, boils down to the reed's cry. Coleman Barks writes:

> Rumi has what amounts to a theory of language associated with this instrument. The reed flute says one thing through its empty cane center:

I want to go back to the canebrake. No matter how intricate it gets, Rumi says, language underneath all its sounds is the one hollow resonance of separation, the wail of the human condition at being uprooted from the whole.[14]

Not only our words but everything about us—our desires, emotions, relationships, events, experiences, personalities—serve as an elaborate language, a "caravan bell," that one way or another calls us home. Thanks to constant proddings within and without, we "stay light-footed, and keep moving":

> We are all far from home.
> Language is our caravan bell.
>
> Don't stop anywhere.
> The moment you're attracted to a place,
> you grow bored with it.
>
> Think of the big moves you've already made,
> from a single cell to a human being!
>
> Stay light-footed, and keep moving.
> Turkish, Arabic, Greek, any tongue
> is a wind that was formerly water.
>
> As a breeze carries the ocean inside it,
> so underneath every sentence is,
> *Come back to the source.*[15]

The return isn't a linear process, though, as the image of going home at the end of a journey makes it seem. The return expresses the enfolding side of the holomovement, which operates all the time. Unfolding and enfolding work like the push-pull forces of magnetism. Push and pull happen so constantly that we don't feel them as distinct forces, yet both are present. They set up a rhythm that's like the turning of a waterwheel in a river, our souls being the waterwheels into which holomovement water flows and then returns to the holomovement river. Whichever way we turn, water keeps coming through:

In this river the soul is a waterwheel
that no matter how it's facing, water pours
through, turning, re-turning to the river.

Even if you put your side
or your back to the river,
water still comes through.

A shadow can't ignore the sun
that all day creates and moves it![16]

Coming home to our origins is something we do all the time—and must do to regenerate and evolve. As Rumi says, "conscious decisions and personal memory are much too small a place to live." Returning to the ocean gives us a vast home, and we expand just by going there, which is why our inner Contemplatives take us there regularly. Dreams, for instance, carry us nightly to worlds and ways of being that feel more like home. During the day, we renew ourselves with "the milk of millennia" through other means as well—"everyone does this in different ways"—often through "some absorbing work":

For hundreds of thousands of years I have been dust-grains
floating and flying in the will of the air,
often forgetting ever being
in that state, but in sleep
I migrate back. I spring loose
from the four-branched, time-and-space cross,
this waiting room.

I walk into a huge pasture.
I nurse the milk of millennia.

Everyone does this in different ways.
Knowing that conscious decisions
and personal memory
are much too small a place to live,
every human being streams at night

into the loving nowhere, or during the day,
in some absorbing work.[17]

Plato likens our time away from home to being chained in a cave, condemned to look at shadows. Rumi expresses the emotional side of this predicament. As beautiful as its gardens are, this world is like "a street where a funeral is passing," full of grief. But what makes the cave and the chains that hold us? What causes the funeral and grief? Not reality but a paradigm that multiplies suffering. Not forms but an attachment to them. Returning to our origins regenerates us because, in going back, we find the reality beyond the paradigm, and the source of forms beyond those we cling to.

The return, therefore, isn't literal. "Let us rise together and leave 'this world'" doesn't mean suicide. Rather, Rumi is suggesting that we give ourselves back to the holomovement by embracing its enfolding side. As we do, we'll leave the "black water in a well" and return to the "open field of sunlight." From silence and stillness, we "start out":

> This world of two gardens, and both so beautiful.
> This world, a street where a funeral is passing.
> Let us rise together and leave "this world,"
>
> as water goes bowing down itself to the ocean.
> From gardens to the gardener, from grieving
> to wedding feast. . . .
>
> So let's begin the journey home,
> with love and compassion for guides,
> and grace protecting. Let your soul turn
>
> into an empty mirror that passionately wants
> to reflect Joseph. Hand him your present.
>
> Now let silence speak, and as that
> gift begins, we'll start out.[18]

Love: The Universal Principle of Attraction That Draws Us

The return pulls us, because the holomovement embeds in us enfolding yearnings. We return because reality draws us; our origin calls us
back. Longing for home is a "thirst" we "can't help" having; it's put in
us from beyond:

> We can't help being thirsty,
> moving toward the voice
> of water.
> > Milk-drinkers draw close
> to the mother. Muslims, Christians, Jews,
> Buddhists, Hindus, shamans,
> everyone hears the intelligent sound
> and moves, with thirst, to meet it.[19]

This thirst for home, born as it is of reality's dynamics, points to a
deeper truth: the universal principle of attraction. According to this
principle, everything is not only interconnected but also engaged in a
mutual attraction, a sort of spiritual magnetism. We can be connected
to things without caring much about them, but to be attracted is to long
to actively participate in the life of that which is also attracted to us.
Suddenly, all the connections in the universe come alive, each part
wanting and needing every other to be what it is. For Rumi, that's the
nature of the reality—"Every bit of the universe is filled with wanting,
and whatever any bit wants, wants the wanter!":

> Remember what the soul wants,
> because in that, eternity
> is *wanting* our souls!

> Which is the meaning of the text,
> *They love That, and That loves them.*

> If I keep on explaining this,
> the *Mathnawi* will run to eighty volumes!

The gist is: whatever anyone seeks,
that is seeking the seeker.

No matter if it's animal,
or vegetable, or mineral.

Every bit of the universe
is filled with wanting,
and whatever any bit wants,
wants the wanter![20]

In everyday terms, if we feel drawn to something, we can bet that it's drawn to us too, indeed that it's drawing us to itself. Einstein wanted physics, but, in view of its evolution, physics also wanted him. Parents want their children, but perhaps they became parents because their children, existing on another level, wanted them too. Lovers want a Beloved who also loves them. Mutual attraction isn't unique to human affairs, though. It's a universal principle, since for Rumi, love applies to everything—"all the particles of the world are in love and looking for lovers." Water wants a "water-drinker." In the cosmic dance, the dancers want each other, or there'd be no dance:

The lamps of lovers connect,
not at their ceramic bases,
but in their lightedness.

No lover wants union with the Beloved
without the Beloved also wanting the lover. . . .

Lightning from here strikes *there*.
When you begin to love God, God
is loving *you*. A clapping sound
does not come from one hand.

A thirsty man calls out, "Delicious water,
where are you?" while the water moans,
"Where is the water-drinker?"

The thirst in our souls *is* the attraction
put out by the Water itself.

We belong to It,
and It to us.

God's wisdom made us lovers of one another.
In fact, all the particles of the world
are in love and looking for lovers.[21]

When we seek God, wisdom, health, or happiness, that very seeking is evidence of what we seek already present in us. It's love in us that makes us long for love. Love is both object and subject:

You have read in the text where *They love Him*
blends with *He loves them*.
Those joining Loves
are both Qualities of God.[22]

In other words, "the looking itself is a *trace* of what we're looking for."[23] It's our love of beauty, for instance, that makes us seek beauty in our lives—in which case, where's the beauty? Not out there, but in us as our longing for beauty and our ability to recognize it.

We all have longings, and if Rumi's right, they all boil down to the longing to return to who we are within the whole. If we let longings exist in their purest, most boiled-down form, they guide us, because they're the whole pulling us to itself. If, however, we try to quench their fire with external fulfillments, chances are we'll become addicts. We'll attempt to escape the very longings that are gifts to us, that draw us toward the good within. To have the good, we simply need to let our longings live in us. We don't have to gain the results we desire or get "return messages." Our longing "*is* the return message":

One night a man was crying,
                    Allah! Allah!
His lips grew sweet with the praising,
until a cynic said,
              "So! I've heard you
calling out, but have you ever
gotten any response?"

The man had no answer to that.
He quit praying and fell into a confused sleep.

He dreamed he saw Khidr, the guide of souls,
in a thick, green foliage.
                              "Why did you stop praising?"
"Because I've never heard anything back."
                                   "This longing
you express *is* the return message."

The grief you cry out from
draws you toward union.

Your pure sadness
that wants help
is the secret cup.

Listen to the moan of a dog for its master.
That whining is the connection.

There are love-dogs
no one knows the names of.

Give your life
to be one of them.[24]

Connected at the Roots

The universal principle of attraction presents reality as a dynamic unity, an interwoven whole, held by bonds of mutual attraction. Tales of Rumi's life include many teachings on connectedness, and he always presents it not as a dry abstraction but as a "sharing in the existence of one another":

> Once Moulana [Rumi] explained that all members of the entire creation share in the existence of one another—and nothing exists singly and unattached . . . all are interdependent.[25]

We're connected from our innermost being—a unity "inside us"—because we're all woven into the whole, and "no being is unconnected to that reality."[26] We think and act in our own ways, as branches move differently, yet like the branches, we don't bump into each other as we "sway," because we "connect at the roots":

> Spring overall. But inside us
> there's another unity.
>
> Behind each eye here,
> one glowing weather.
>
> Every forest branch moves differently
> in the breeze, but as they sway
> they connect at the roots.[27]

On the level of forms, we don't see this connectedness. Things appear to happen randomly and of themselves. The psychological, family, economic, political, and religious systems that give rise to actions aren't evident on the surface—much less is the whole system of reality evident. Rumi tells a story about ants trying to figure out the mysterious movements of a pen:

> Once, a tiny ant saw a pen moving on paper
> and tried to tell the mystery to another ant.
>
> "It was so amazing how that penpoint
> made beautiful pictures of basil leaves
> and beds of roses and lilies."
>
> Another ant suggested, "The real artist, though,
> is the finger. The pen itself is
> just an instrument."
> > A third ant said, "But,
> consider further. Notice there's an arm above
> whose strength controls the fingers. . . ."
>
> The argument went on, up and up, until the chief ant
> said,
> > "Do not regard any accomplishment as proceeding
> from any material form. All living forms become

unconscious in sleep and death. Form is
just the clothes of the spirit."

But even that wise ant neglected to say
what flowed inside *that*. He never mentioned
the existence of God, without which intelligence
and love and spirit would be inert.[28]

Forms hide our connectedness, especially since we look so different and so separate from each other. From "outward forms," we don't
see "the entire galactic whirling of the Universe," but it's there, even
in a gnat:

A tiny gnat's outward form flies around and around
in pain and wanting, while the gnat's inward nature
includes the entire galactic whirling of the Universe![29]

Listening to the Universe of Connectedness

Contemplatives get around this problem—that forms obscure essence—
by *sohbet*, the Sufi term for mystical conversation, a deep communing
that goes on between our own essence and the essence of others. If
forms don't reveal the universe in the outward gnat, then why not
commune with the inward gnat—or inward stone, tree, plant, baby, or
dog—to discover that hidden presence?

Though the black-water-in-a-well paradigm dismisses this as absurd, communing with this hidden presence is natural to Contemplatives—and has been from time immemorial. The universal principle of
attraction draws us together, making us long to engage in the inner life,
meaning, and awareness of the universe. What blocks us from doing
this is simply the assumption that we live in an unconscious universe—
that nothing has an inner life except humans, and even then, only if
they speak our language. Contemplatives assume instead that there's a
knowing embedded in everything. The ocean inside all forms gives us
the means to know each other, ocean to ocean:

Children love their seashell toys,
and with them they learn about the ocean,
because a little piece of ocean
inside the child, and inside the toy,
knows the whole ocean.[30]

Francis of Assisi, just twenty-five years Rumi's senior, reintro-
duced communion with nature in Europe, conversing with "Brother
Wolf," the birds, and all animals—a practice common in pre-Roman
wisdom traditions. On some level, mystics say, we're all communing
with the essence of everything, since "every particle is eloquently
alive," and our inner Contemplatives tune in to that reality. To seem
normal, of course, we've learned to shut out this knowing. Yet nar-
rowing ourselves to fit the un-"Hearing" norm is depressing, for it re-
duces a universe that's "eloquently alive" to "dead grass thrown out
for cattle":

> Some comment on the text, *The Spiritual World*
> *is speaking, if we could only hear it.*
>
> Every particle is eloquently alive. That Hearing
> makes the way we usually are seem like
> so much dead grass thrown out for cattle.[31]

How do we get our inner-knowing back? "Only with the help of the
One whose love opens into the spirit's telling." Our inner Contemplative is such a one. In contemplative stillness, we feel the attraction—
love—going on, and by following that attraction back to our origin, we
go to the place where we need no language to understand each other.
At the roots, we share the same being, and that common root opens a
channel between us:

> Everyone, and every thing, and every action, glorifies
> You, but sometimes the way one does it
> is not recognized by another.

Human beings rarely understand how inanimate objects
are doing it, the walls and the doors and the rocks,
those masters of glorification!

We squabble over the doctrines of the Sunnis
and the Jabris, and all their seventy-two
different interpretations. It never ends.

But we don't hear the inanimate objects
speaking to each other, and to us!

How can we understand the praising
of what doesn't speak?

Only with the help of the One whose love
opens into the spirit's telling.[32]

Rumi tells of a baby who used this method. Not being able to speak,
babies have been assumed to lack intelligent awareness, as if they're
undeveloped blobs of flesh. Fortunately, pioneers such as David
Chamberlain in *Babies Remember Birth* present a radically different
picture—one that Rumi agrees with:

A village woman once was walking by Muhammed.
She thought he was just an ordinary illiterate.
She didn't believe that he was a prophet.

She was carrying a two-months old baby.
As she came near Muhammed, the baby turned
and said, "Peace be with you, Messenger of God."

The mother cried out, surprised and angry,
"What are you saying,
and how can you suddenly talk!"

The child replied, "God taught me first,
and then Gabriel."
                    "Who is this Gabriel?
I don't see anyone."

"He is above your head,
mother. Turn around. He has been telling me
many things."
             "Do you really see him?"
                            "Yes.
He is continually delivering me from this
degraded state into sublimity." . . .

So the little one spoke, and the mother
took in a fragrance that let her surrender
to that state.
             When God gives this knowing,
inanimate stones, plants, animals, everything,
fills with unfolding significance.[33]

"Inanimate stones, plants, animals, everything, fills with unfolding significance": in affirming this, Rumi draws on the cross-cultural experience of shamans, who view nature as an equal partner in life. Eliot Cowan, the designated successor of a Huichol Indian shaman, writes in *Plant Spirit Medicine*:

To think that plants are mere dumb creatures that do not know ecstasy is ignorance or tragic arrogant folly. All things enjoy ecstatic union with nature. Life without ecstasy is not true life and not worth living. . . . The point is the joy of being in the dance of creation as an equal partner with everything.[34]

Rumi embraces this view. Plants and trees participate in a mystical awareness, a fellowship of creation:

The tree limbs will move like people dancing,
who suddenly know what the mystical life is.

The leaves snap their fingers like they're hearing music.
They are! A sliver of a mirror shines out
from under a felt covering. Think how it will be
when the whole thing is open to the air and the sunlight![35]

Cowan believes that pharmaceutical companies miss the true heal-ing power of plants, which lies not in plant biology or chemistry but in their spirit and their relationship with us. If we want the help of plants, we need only ask for it. That's what Solomon did, drawing on "the uni-versal intellect," our shared roots in the whole, as his means of com-municating:

> Every morning Solomon comes to the mosque
> not built by hands and sees a new plant
> growing there. He asks, "Are you a medicine?
> What is your name and your usefulness?"

> Each morning the new plant tells him
> its nature. "I am helpful to this condition
> and detrimental to that, and such is
> my name on the unseen tablets."

> Solomon relates the information
> to his physicians, and they write it down,
> so the body may be relieved of pain.

> Knowledge of medicine, and of astronomy, comes
> in this way from the universal intellect,
> not from the particular mind.

> All tools and crafts were given
> by that wider intelligence
> and then modified by the individual mind.

> Learn from Solomon.
> Be apprenticed to him.

> Master the craft he teaches,
> and then practice it.[36]

Listening to the universe of connectedness shifts our relationship to the earth and nature. Not only do plants and animals become equal partners, but more than that, we participate in their being by opening ourselves to their awareness. We learn from them, sense their needs, and help them as friends:

> One day Rumi asked one of his young disciples to bring him a great dish of rich and delicious food. The young man was alarmed because he thought that Rumi was living as an ascetic. Rumi used to pray all night and eat hardly anything. "What he really wants is to go off secretly and eat all this food!" The disciple secretly followed Rumi as he carried the food through the streets of Konya and out into the fields and into the ruins of a tomb. "Now I'll unmask his pretentions!" But what the young disciple found was an exhausted mother dog with six puppies. Rumi was feeding her by hand so that she could care for her children. "But how did you know that she was here, and hungry?" Rumi laughed, "When you have become awake, your ears are so sensitive they can hear the cries of a sparrow ten thousand miles away."[37]

"Not a Single You"

Listening to the universe of connectedness shifts our relationship to ourselves as well. What sense does it make for us to identify with one narrow slice of the holomovement's dynamics? Alchemists say everything is in flux, ourselves included. Why freeze-frame this flux and identify ourselves with static pictures of it? What do we gain by reducing ourselves to the time-and-space personalities we've borrowed? Of course we need to be functional within forms, but is it wise to build our entire life's philosophy around that convention? That would be like taking our separate street addresses as our core reality—and a separate and isolated reality at that—ignoring the larger network of streets.

In other words, when we divide reality into me and not-me, what real grounds do we have for making this division if reality is as an unbroken whole? Though human law divides land into ownerships, the earth remains undivided. As a convention, the notion of me and not-me is useful, just as street addresses are useful. But from the perspective of the roots, how separate are the branches?

Our inner Contemplatives wonder about these things. The Buddha wondered about them too, which is how he arrived at the notion of *anatta*, no-self. A separate self views reality through the lens of the apparent discontinuities among forms, whereas the Buddha and our inner Contemplatives see continuity as the larger reality. What appears to be not-us is, from the perspective of the unbroken whole, us as well. The writers of the *Upanishads* revolutionized Hindu philosophy with precisely this perception. There's one reality going on, and "you are that." Rumi expresses this same idea some two thousand years later:

> We take long trips.
> We puzzle over the meaning of a painting or a book,
> when what we're wanting to see and understand
> in this world, we *are* that.[38]

"We *are* that" is John Donne's point in his famous meditation, "No man is an island," only Rumi says we're not just every other human but the island too—"a Sky and an Ocean"—or, to give Donne his due, we're "a piece of the continent, a part of the main."[39] We're "not a single You" but "hundreds of you's":

> . . . You are not a single You,
> good Friend, you are a Sky and an Ocean,
> a tremendous YHUUUUUU, a nine hundred times huge
> drowning place for all your hundreds of you's.[40]

This suggests, among other things, that not only do we live in the unbroken field of consciousness, but that we *are* "the consciousness of the world." If we're intimately sharing in the existence of each other, envy and jealousy fall away. Instead of assuming that the purpose of life is to establish ourselves as separate entities, we tune in to the whole-dynamics moving in us and in everyone else as well, beyond "positive and negative," us and not-us dualities—"The true self is a no-self."

Immersed in the holomovement's unfoldings and enfoldings, we even drop the duality of surface debris versus pearls beneath. If it's all Ocean and all us, then what difference does it make whether we're moving at "the bottom, the surface, or some middle region"?

"You are the consciousness of the world, and I want
to tell you what I didn't tell Adam, or Abraham,

what Jesus held back from saying." Language has been
qualified up until now with signifiers denoting

positive and negative. No more of that. The true self
is a no-self. Fall in love with the lover who

disappears in a love for you. Be water searching
for thirst. Be silent and all ear. When Spring

ecstasy floods, build a dam or everything will wash
away. Oh let it go! Under the foundation's ruins

there's a treasure. Those drowned in God want to be
more drowned. They can't decide, being thrown

about, whether they love more the bottom,
the surface, or some middle region.[41]

People joke about "I am you," and "you are me," and "we are the world," and who's who, and what are we talking about? It's amusing, but it's also serious, because we spend considerable time and effort with ourselves and therapists sorting out what's "me" and what's not—no small consideration for having a healthy self in healthy relationships.

Yet these are issues of getting our street addresses clear, so we don't throw our stuff into someone else's house and others don't throw their stuff into ours. Contemplatives know the value of this, but that's not their focus. Our inner Contemplatives want meaning, and a well-defined street address can give only so much. For deeper meaning, we need the big picture. What's going on in the holomovement says something about what we're doing here, and it's more than staying in the house.

That's why we contemplate our address and our whole street, as well as our community, city, nation, earth, purpose, principles, souls, and on to the ultimate nature of things. Nor is it odd to move in this direction. From birth, we expand our frame of meaning all through life, finding meaning by identifying with families, friends, teams, religions, political groups, and causes. Our inner Contemplatives simply nudge us to keep expanding.

Expanding our frame of meaning, though, doesn't leave us unchanged. It redefines who we are. In mystical contemplation, the boundaries of skin, brain, personality, and memory have the cosmic status of street addresses—useful conventions but not reality dividers. If the Ocean is our deepest being, then from that level, we participate in all of it, no part being more or less "us" than any other: "I am all orders of being, the circling galaxy." The true self is, therefore, a no-self, and the true address everywhere—"mast, rudder, helmsman, and keel" and "also the coral reef they founder on"—in which case, to say who we truly are, we say "I am You":

> I am dust particles in sunlight.
> I am the round sun.
>
> To the bits of dust I say, *Stay*.
> To the sun, *Keep moving*.
>
> I am morning mist,
> and the breathing of evening.
>
> I am wind in the top of a grove,
> and surf on the cliff.
>
> Mast, rudder, helmsman, and keel,
> I am also the coral reef they founder on.
>
> I am a tree with a trained parrot in its branches.
> Silence, thought, and voice.
>
> The musical air coming through a flute,
> a spark off a stone, a flickering in metal.
>
> Both candle and the moth crazy around it.
> Rose and nightingale lost in the fragrance.
>
> I am all orders of being,
> the circling galaxy,

the evolutionary intelligence,
the lift and the falling away.

What is and what isn't. You
who know Jelaluddin, You

the One in all, say who
I am. Say I am You.[42]

12

Damn Fool Mystics

ARCHETYPE *Wise Fool*
MYSTIC JOURNEY *Rolling Around Anywhere*

Throwing Egos to the Wind

If we're "hundreds of you's," then one in particular isn't all there is
to us. The mystic way doesn't try to eradicate egos with denials and
humiliations but lets the poor things be—only lets them be in a context so wide that ego issues fall into their proper place. What's going
on in that "nine hundred times huge drowning place for all your
hundreds of you's" is so all-engaging that we forget about whose ego
is doing what. Even the sense of having a separate soul fades "in this
Ocean of pearling currents." The mystic world into which we're
emerging isn't built around a separate anything. It's a seamless fab-
ric, in which case, why latch on to one thread as if it's us and the rest
isn't?

> Day and night I guarded the pearl of my soul.
> Now in this Ocean of pearling currents,
> I've lost track of which was mine.[1]

"At the edge of the ocean," Rumi says, "footprints disappear."[2] Trying to make a footprint that lasts forever—the greatest book, the largest
fortune, the unforgettable celebrity, or the famous child—doesn't interest our inner mystics. Why should it? Egos aren't our bottom-line
reality any more than our toenails are. If our toenails start making
permanent marks, we cut them.

The endeavor to turn something impermanent into something permanent is foolish, because it's not doable. On one hand, we try to hold
the ocean back so it doesn't wash over our footprints, while on the
other, we try to separate ourselves from its currents. Seeing the futility

of both, our mystics throw egos to the wind—with "one swoop, one swing of the arm, that work is over."[3] From a perspective that's "free of who I was,"[4] it's folly to bother about ego images: what sort of impression we make, how long it lingers, or how many minds it lingers in. Our inner mystics would rather think of "roses and pomegranates, and of the ocean where pearls are made . . . ":

> There was once a man
> who rushed terrified into a house,
> his face yellow, his lips blue, and his hands
> trembling like an old man's.
> > "What's wrong?"
> "Outside! They're rounding up donkeys
> to do some labor!"
> > "Why are you upset?"
> "They are so fierce in their purpose
> that they might take me too!"
> Don't be like this man.
> Quit talking about your fears of work
> and of being uncomfortable.
>
> It's time to speak of roses and pomegranates,
> and of the ocean where pearls are made
> of language and vision, and of the invisible ladders,
> which are different for each person, that lead
> to the infinite place where trees
> murmur among themselves,
> > "What a fine stretch
> this is in the air today!"
> > And nightingales ask
> the just-beginning nubs of fruit that appear
> when the blossoms fall off,
> > "Give us some of what
> you're drinking!"
> > Join that endless joy-talking,
> and forget the other, the worrying that
> you might be taken for a jackass![5]

Our egos are to our souls—and our souls in turn are to the Soul of the soul, to holomovement meaning—as candles are to flames. The point isn't to be a candle forever but to "become entirely flame." Personal images have to do with virtues and vices, pride and shame, but these are shadows cast by the candle. In the candle's light, they disappear. The flame provides a refuge from our shadow images. In burning, our personal candles fulfill their purpose, and the shadows they cast in being that particular candle don't matter anymore:

> A candle is made to become entirely flame.
> In that annihilating moment
> it has no shadow.
>
> It is nothing but a tongue of light
> describing a refuge.
>
> Look at this
> just-finishing candle stub
> as someone who is finally safe
> from virtue and vice,
>
> the pride and the shame
> we claim from those.[6]

Wise Fools

Nothing exemplifies this free, larger-than-egos spirit more than the archetype of the Wise Fool. As far as Wise Fools are concerned, it's foolish to live in the service of egos. When this archetype kicks in, we don't care about "reasonableness," expectations, or images—all the narrow "definitions" of what it is to be us. Breaking "loose from definition," our Wise Fools "wriggle free":

> For forty years I made plans and worried about them.
> Now sixty-two, I've escaped reasonableness.
>
> By definition, human beings do not see or hear.
> I broke loose from definition.

Skin outside, seeds inside,
a fig lives caught between, and like that fig,
I wriggle free.[7]

Shakespeare presented the spectrum of fools in his plays, from the truly foolish to the Wise Fool. In *Twelfth Night*, for instance, Malvolio, who deemed himself righteous and wise, was shown to be the foolish fool, whereas Feste, the clown, was, as Viola said, "wise enough to play the fool."[8] Shakespeare was echoing the apostle Paul, who wrote: "Let no man deceive himself. If any man among you seems to be wise in this world, let him become a fool, that he may be wise. For the wisdom of this world is foolishness with God."[9]

Clearly, when it comes to wisdom and foolishness, things aren't what they seem. What seems wise according to the conventional paradigm (with egos seeking control at the center of it) is foolishness to mystics, whereas what seems foolish to conventional ways of thinking (you don't get ahead by being mystics) is wise in view of life's deeper meanings. As Wise Fools see it, nothing is entirely what it seems. When asked how he is, Feste the clown replies, "The better for my foes and the worse for my friends," explaining, "[My friends] praise me and make an ass of me; now my foes tell me plainly I am an ass; so that by my foes, sir, I profit in the knowledge of myself, and by my friends I am abused."[10]

The reality behind appearances continually plays tricks on us—the reliable sun appearing to move or simple sticks seeming to bend in water. We think in knowing the form, we know the reality, but that's not so. There's always a story, and a story behind the story, stories we then call "physics," "history," "psychology," and so on. But no story tells reality like it ultimately is, not even "religion" or "philosophy" stories. Mindful of the limits of human knowing, our Wise Fools keep pushing us to "see through the veils to how things really are":

. . . When you eventually see
through the veils to how things really are,
you will keep saying again
and again,

"This is certainly not like
we thought it was!"[11]

Seeing things differently from the officially veiled ways of seeing puts us at odds with the "crowd of thousands." We have to choose between the Wise Fool's freedom and the accepted paradigm, which has to do with gaining "power over an entire nation." This isn't a hard choice for our inner mystics:

> Which is worth more, a crowd of thousands,
> or your own genuine solitude?
> Freedom, or power over an entire nation?
>
> A little while alone in your room
> will prove more valuable than anything else
> that could ever be given you.[12]

The choice is easy because veiled reality isn't reality. The thicker the veil, the less it's a place where we can find truth, justice, freedom, or any other invisible basic that happiness requires. Seeing the folly of seeking life's staples in the wrong place, Wise Fools "burn inside union with one truth":

> You who long for powerful positions,
> keep worrying about that, and your land!
>
> We burn inside union
> with one truth,
>
>> *There is no reality but God.*
>> *There's only God.*[13]

Living inside reality's unfoldings and enfoldings, our Wise Fools are "experts in laziness." Sensing the big picture—"they continuously see God working all around them"—our inner mystics don't feel driven to make things happen by will, force of effort, or harried schedules. "Go with the flow" is definitely the Wise Fool mode. Instead of pushing the river, Wise Fools lie back and float on it—and reap full measure for doing so:

> Gnostics are experts in laziness. They rely on it,
> because they continuously see God working all around them.
> The harvest keeps coming in, yet they
> never even did the ploughing![14]

Not that our Wise Fools do nothing. They don't push the river, but they don't sit on the banks either. Our Wise Fools leap into "the exchanging flow"—not for gain or reputation but simply "to be part of" it:

> Even if you don't know what you want,
> buy *something*, to be part of the exchanging flow.
>
> Start a huge, foolish, project,
> like Noah.
>
> It makes absolutely no difference
> what people think of you.[15]

Our Wise Fools live with abandon, throwing appearances to the wind, because they never take their eyes off the invisible. The invisible is what matters, and everything is "a garden gate," a doorway, to it. Not all doorways to the unseen are framed by cathedral walls. Very few are, since gates to the invisible are everywhere. If a dog is the nearest gate, our Wise Fools go for it:

> Majnun saw Layla's dog and began kissing it,
> running around like a hajji circling the Kaaba,
> bowing to its paws, holding its head, scratching
> its stomach, giving it sweets and rosewater.
>
> "You idiot," said someone passing by.
> "Dogs lick their privates and sniff
> excrement on the road. This is *insane*,
> the intimate way you treat that dog."

"Look through my eyes," said the lover.
"See the loyalty, how he guards the house
of my Friend, how he's so glad to see us.

Whatever we feel, grief, the simple delight
of being out in the sun, he feels
that with us completely.

Don't look too much at surface actions.
Discover the lion, the rose of his real nature.
Friend, this dog is a garden gate into the invisible."

Anyone preoccupied with pointing out what's wrong
misses the unseen. Look at his face![16]

Escaping Conventions and Cleverness

In throwing egos and appearances to wind, our Wise Fools throw cleverness with them. "Clever figuring" is how we get ahead in the world, and our Wise Fools want none of it. If we're really clever about life, we'll give up cleverness, since all it's really doing is making Malvolio-fools of us:

No better love than love with no object,
no more satisfying work than work with no purpose.

If you could give up tricks and cleverness,
that would be the cleverest trick![17]

Being on the mystic path is what matters, and our Wise Fools live it without regard to external "objects" and "purposes." We're on the mystic path not to get something from it, not because we're bad and need fixing or because we want to become more spiritual, but simply because it's our being to do so. To be on the mystic path is to celebrate our freedom to live from our essence:

This has nothing to do with clever figuring.
It has to do with service to God.
Quit talking about it![18]

That's why when "Love enters, . . . the brilliant scholars get goofy." Inside the prestigious-and-scholarly Rumi was a Wise-Fool Rumi—the one who told outrageous stories, who sat up all night talking about nothing (emptiness), and who wanted only to dance, listen to music, and recite poems. Our Wise Fools precipitate such a shift. What once seemed all-consumingly important suddenly seems trivial, and what really matters suddenly defies being brushed aside:

> Love enters, and the brilliant scholars
> get goofy. The full moon becomes
> a simple dirt road.
> > Walk there
> with degenerates and saints, with
> children and old people.
>
> Be a slow pawn as well as
> the wide-ranging queen,
> then you'll be king.[19]

By prompting us to choose what ultimately matters, our Wise Fools make us more alive than we ever thought possible, though they put us through hoops to get there. Remnants of cleverness-thinking, of fearing that we'll be thought ridiculous, of comparing ourselves to others, of doing what we think we're supposed to do instead of what's core-us: all such layers of conventional foolery peel away, until we stay with our simple being—no pretenses, titles, or masks:

> I was dead, then alive.
> Weeping, then laughing.
>
> The power of Love came into me,
> and I became fierce like a lion,
> then tender like the evening star.

He said, "You're not mad enough.
You don't belong in this house."

I went wild and had to be tied up.
He said, "Still not wild enough
to stay with us!"

I broke through another layer
into joyfulness.

He said, "It's not enough."
I died.

He said, "You're a clever little man,
full of fantasy and doubting."

I plucked out my feathers and became a fool.
He said, "Now you're the candle
for this assembly."

But I'm no candle. Look!
I'm scattered smoke.

He said, "You are the Sheikh, the Guide."
But I'm not a Teacher. I have no power.

He said, "You already have wings.
I cannot give you wings."

But I wanted *His* wings.
I felt like some flightless chicken.

Then New Events said to me,
"Don't move. A sublime generosity
is coming toward you."

And Old Love said, "Stay with me."
I said, "I will."[20]

Wise Fools as Mirrors

Staying with our core being, our Wise Fools become empty mirrors that
reflect the shape of human character. "When you look in a mirror, you
see yourself, not the state of the mirror."[21] Emptied of egos, cleverness,
and conventions, our inner Wise Fools "cannot help reflecting," which
is why we can see ourselves and others most clearly in them:

> There's no hiding the fragrance that comes
> from an ecstatic. A polished mirror
> cannot help reflecting.[22]

In courts from ancient times to the Renaissance, Wise Fools served
as mirrors for rulers, so royal heads wouldn't be turned by adulation
and power. In Shakespeare's *King Lear*, for instance, only the Fool could
mirror to the King the truth of his folly—that he would be guided by his
daughters' words rather than by their characters, that he would be old
before he would be wise. None but Fools could speak so openly; anyone else would be killed for it. As much as rulers tried to control
"truth"—and ignore what truths they couldn't control—they knew
they ignored their Fools' mirrorings at their peril:

> You may have heard, it's the custom for Kings
> to let warriors stand on the left, the side of the heart,
> and courage. On the right, they put the Chancellor,
> and various secretaries, because the practice
> of bookkeeping and writing usually belongs
> to the right hand. In the center,
> > the Sufis,
> because in meditation they become mirrors.
> The King can look at their faces
> and see his original state.[23]

Being a mirror for human character isn't an easy job, though. The
easier Wise Fools make it seem, the more mastery it requires—the mystic mastery of inner stillness. Otherwise all we see is the mirror's cloudy

surface. Rumi tells about "a great-hearted ruler who loved wine" and sent a servant to get some. On the way back, the servant ran into an old ascetic who railed against drinking and broke the wine jar. When the servant told the ruler, he was furious: "Where is this ascetic who thinks he can tell everyone what to do?"

> But the ascetic heard him coming and hid
> beneath a pile of ropemaker's wool.
>
> From under there one could hear muttering,
> "Only a perfect steel mirror
> can reflect a man's face and tell
> its faults, not someone scared
> and unhappy, like me."[24]

Mindful that our mirrors, having been through the trenches, are mud-caked and clouded, Seneca advised that we compare notes on cleaning rather than presume to be mirrors for each other:

> "So you're giving me advice, are you?" you say. "Have you already given yourself advice, then? Have you already put yourself straight? Is that how you have time for reforming other people?" No, I'm not so shameless as to set about treating people when I'm sick myself. I'm talking to you as if I were lying in the same hospital ward, about the illness we're both suffering from, and passing on some remedies.[25]

Having received offers to mirror to him his defects for loving Shams, Rumi knows the problem. His solution is self-reflection, that we be our own students and polish our own mirrors. By self-cultivation, we stay "in union," and that union tells us when to *"speak"* and when to *"Be silent."* Then, it's not the mirror that does the talking but what's beyond it—"the ocean moving through":

> You are the only faithful student you have.
> All the others leave eventually.
>
> Have you been making yourself shallow
> with making others eminent?

Just remember, when you're in union,
you don't have to fear
that you'll be drained.

The command comes to *speak*,
and you feel the ocean
moving through you.
Then comes, *Be silent*,
as when the rain stops,
and the trees in the orchard
begin to draw moisture
up into themselves.[26]

To self-work, our Wise Fools' ego-emptiness brings a free and un-attached spirit. If we're more than ego images, then we're not bound to what we see in the mirror. From our "non-being" or not-yet-formed side, we can shift forms all we want. When "an empty mirror and our worst destructive habits" come together, the real "art and crafting" of our souls, lives, and characters begin:

. . . What is the mirror of being?
Non-being. Always bring a mirror of non-existence
as a gift. Any other present is foolish.

Let the poor man look deep into generosity.
Let bread see a hungry man.
Let kindling behold a spark from the flint.

An empty mirror and your worst destructive habits,
when they are held up to each other,
that's when the real making begins.
That's what art and crafting are.[27]

But more than scars of trench life appear on our Wise Fools' mirrors; we also see our essence. In the faces of meditative Sufis, the King could "see his original state." Gazing in the mystic mirror all along the mystic path "kindles remembering" of who we are and gives us a chance to "fall in love" with ourselves, to love ourselves as we are in our origin and essence:

> Give the beautiful ones mirrors,
> and let them fall in love with themselves.
>
> That way they polish their souls
> and kindle remembering in others.[28]

With a love for who we are, we can look at all the different mind-sets, roles, and behaviors we've explored and laugh at them. This laughter isn't nasty or humiliating, though. Wise Fools laugh from a liberating joy that we can be all these things and not be imprisoned by any of them. It's a happy joke, this joke on us, that what we took to be our all isn't a fraction of our being:

> The world is an open green
> in the middle of a garden.
>
> Beings in various forms
> see their reflections and laugh,
> love-messages flashing from every eye.[29]

Beyond Forms and Language

The Wise Fool comes last on the mystic path because, more than any other archetype, it represents a freedom from forms, a seeing beyond them, which is the essence of mysticism. No matter what the form, reality is more.

Language being the form of thought, Wise Fools look beyond that too. To use an Oriental analogy, language serves us well when it's used like a finger pointing to the moon. So, too, language helps us understand reality, but it's not reality. It has limits, especially when it comes to intangibles. If words can't even capture what of our loved ones remain in us—what they've meant to us—how can words express "the One who lives in each of us"?

Oneness,
which is the reality, cannot be understood
with lamp and sun images. The blurring
of a plural into a unity is wrong.

No image can describe
what of our fathers and mothers,
our grandfathers and grandmothers, remains.

Language does not touch the One
who lives in each of us.[30]

Geared to forms, we're not in a good position to talk about formless realities—"How can our bald heads explain hair?" That being so, we're easily deceived by language, if we don't stay grounded in our own experiences:

A man was describing a large fish. "Wait a minute," said another. "How do you know anything about fish?" "I have taken many boatrides," said the first. "Say something *specific* about fish." "They have horns like a camel." The other responded, "Well, I knew you didn't know anything about fish. Now I see you can't tell a camel from a cow."[31]

The statements that religion and science make about reality—for example, that it's only physical or only mental, that empirical reasoning is the only way to know it, that survival of the fittest is the ultimate law, that God smiles on this group but frowns on that one, that God is a being who smiles and frowns, or also that "there is no reality but God" and that the holomovement concept describes it—any or all of these statements may turn out to be fish stories. We don't know.

Socrates, coming straight from the Wise Fool archetype, said that this is the beginning of wisdom—knowing that we don't know. As precise as we try to make our language, our stories about reality may nonetheless skew things. Indeed, whatever notions we have in our heads are bound to fall short of what really is. As Rumi says, no words can describe someone we love.

If we forget the limits of words and concepts, they make fools of us and "tear us to pieces." Because we shape our lives with the stories we tell about reality, our language stories wield an invisible power over us, and if we're not wary, "the images we invent could change into wild beasts":

> Is it right to make images
> of how the Unseen world works?
>
> Only the One who knows such things can do that.
> How can our bald heads explain hair?
>
> Moses thought what he saw was a stick,
> but it had a dragon inside it.
>
> If such a spiritual King
> could not see inside a piece of wood,
> how can we possibly understand temptation and destiny,
> the grain thrown out and the Thrower's purposes?
>
> We're mice peeking around
> and meddling where we ought not.
>
> The images we invent
> could change into wild beasts
> and tear us to pieces![32]

We have a remedy in our Wise Fools. Our Wise Fools can use language and yet not be "caught in our own pretentious beard." First, our Wise Fools know that we don't know. Second, they're the scourge of pretentiousness—of pretending our words claim more than we're able to know. In the poem about "plucking out the feathers and becoming a fool," Rumi shows our Wise Fools stripping away pretenses, both about what we know and about who we are.

About what we know, our Wise Fools strip away the pretense that language can do anything more than help us explore reality. Absolute statements—especially those given with an aura of certainty—are counterfeits, appearing to be something they're not, which is why Socrates had such fun dismantling ancient versions of them. Working assumptions, yes; final, authoritative conclusions, no, or we're in wild beast territory.

As to who we are, our Wise Fools strip away the pretenses both that we're more than we are and that we're less. They don't say we're higher or better, smarter or richer, more spiritual or more enlightened than others. They do, however, say that we're "married to God" and that "pearls want to be like us":

> Rescue this man from his mustache,
> curling so proudly, while inside he tears
> his hair. Married to God, married
> to God, but pretending not! . . .
>
> Dive into the Ocean.
> You're caught in your own pretentious beard
> like something you didn't eat.
> You're not garbage! Pearls want to be
> like you. You should be with them
> where waves and fish and pearls and seaweed and wind
> are all one. No linking, no hierarchy,
> no distinctions, no perplexed wondering, no speech.
> Beyond describing.[33]

"Beyond describing"—that's our Wise Fools' sense of reality. All the words of Rumi's 25,632-verse *Mathnawi*, indeed, all the words of the Bible or the Qur'an are fingers pointing us to the invisible Presence. The more we connect with that Presence, the less the words and the particulars of the quest matter. How we describe reality, what steps brought us to the quest, what traumas we've suffered along the way—it all gets "drowned in the beauty," "in the true bewilderment of the soul":

> "Don't be a searcher wrapped in the importance of his quest.
> Repent of your repenting!" The old man's heart
> woke, no longer in love with treble
> and bass, without weeping
>
> or laughter. In the true bewilderment of the soul
> he went out beyond any seeking, beyond words
> and telling, drowned in the beauty,
> drowned beyond deliverance.[34]

Beyond Religious Forms

Going beyond words and doctrines—and using humor to do it—
doesn't endear Wise Fools to the religiously correct. Socrates was
charged, among other things, with heresy, that is, believing in gods
other than those recognized by the State. But that didn't stop him
from questioning forms, including religious ones. If our God-concepts
reflect our condition more than reality's, he reasoned, then we must
question them as much as anything else. Rumi agrees:

> A calf thinks God is a cow.
> A donkey's theology changes
> when someone new pets it
> and gives what it wants.[35]

Wise Fools and the religiously fervent are bound to differ, because
their methods are so different. Whereas religions teach formalized
ways of thinking, Wise Fools disrupt forms, so the formlessness beyond
them can slip through. That's irreverent only if we assume that the
form of God, our God-concept, supersedes God's beyond-concepts reality. Neither Wise Fools nor mystics assume this, so their reverence remains intact:

> There's no one more openly irreverent than a lover. He, or she,
>   jumps up on the scale opposite eternity
>   and claims to balance it.
>
> And no one more secretly reverent.[36]

Not bound to forms, Wise Fools aren't as interested in religions as in
the reality they point us toward. Wise Fools appreciate the different
ways of pointing, but they're inclined to think there's just one moon.
The sun's light looks different on different walls, Rumi says, "but it's
still one light":

> What is praised is One,
> so the praise is One, too,

many jugs being emptied
into a huge basin.

All religions,
all this singing,
is one song.

The differences are just
illusion and vanity.

The sun's light looks a little different
on this wall than it does on that wall,
and a lot different on this other one,
but it's still one light.[37]

For Wise Fools, what matters is our inner experience of the one light. Shams said, "God enters the love we have for each other, stays there, and will not leave to go to any so-called 'house of God,' kaaba, temple, church, or sacred grove."[38] He used the Muslim custom of praying facing the sacred black stone in Mecca, the Kaaba, to make his point: "The Kaaba is in the middle of the world. All faces turn toward it. But if you take it away, you'll see that each is worshipping the soul of each."[39] It's natural, then, for the mystic path to lead beyond religious forms. Mystics don't negate what religions say; they're simply "silent," assuming that the reality lies beyond language:

Human beings live in three spiritual states. In the first, we pay no attention to God. We notice only the stones and the dirt of the world, the wealth, the children, the men and the women. In the second, we do nothing but worship God. In the third, most advanced state, we become silent. We don't say, 'I serve God,' or 'I don't serve.' We know that God is beyond being present or absent. The creator of absence and presence! And other than both.[40]

Given that forms aren't ultimate, our Wise Fools tell us to live as we're inwardly moved, not as we think we should live to be "a better person." We search our inner presence and follow it. If that means confronting how "undisciplined and toxic" we are, then that's our prayer, the best mystical practice. The "full sentence" for the mystic "drunk,"

one who's surrendered to "the Friend," is to live and be the Friend and
not to second-guess what this means:

> I saw the Friend clearly, and I stopped reading
> books and memorizing poems.
> I quit going to church, and I quit fasting
> to be a better person.
> I quit worrying about when I should be praying.
> I saw how I was undisciplined and toxic.
> I saw how lovely and strong.
> No mercy for the drunk, a full sentence![41]

Doing what our Friend does, we go our own way, though the rightness of it may be "invisible" to others. The way of Wise Fools can seem
foolish and off-track, as if we're "losing faith," but our Wise Fools are
used to that:

> Those on the way are almost invisible
> to those who are not. A man or a woman
> recognizes God and starts out. The others
> say he, or she, is losing faith.[42]

Oneness-Freedom: Rolling Around Anywhere

By living the Friend, our Wise Fools claim a freedom that *is* freedom—
the freedom to live our souls and loves. But what does this freedom really mean, if our souls and loves are themselves expressions of
something higher? If we're moving at-one with the holomovement,
is there such a thing as freedom? Does the whole call all the shots, or
have we a say?

> Love, tell an incident now
> that will clarify this mystery
> of how we act freely, and are yet
> compelled. One hand shakes with palsy.
> Another shakes because you slapped it away.

Both tremblings come from God,
but you feel guilty for the one,
and what about the other?

These are intellectual questions.
The spirit approaches the matter
differently. Omar once had a friend, a scientist,
Bu'l-Hakam, who was flawless at solving
empirical problems, but he could not follow Omar
into the area of illumination and wonder.[43]

As Rumi suggests, "these are intellectual questions" and a case of language tying us in needless knots. To unravel this one, our Wise Fools look beyond language to our inner experience, so we're not misled by images:

> . . . Predestination
> and freewill: We can argue them,
> but they're only ideas. What's real
> is a presence, like Shams.[44]

Mystics do, of course, assume that everything is moved by the holo-movement. We're made up of its unfoldings and enfoldings, the ocean and its currents:

> *There Is No Reality But God,*
> says the completely-surrendered sheikh,
> who is an ocean for all beings.
>
> The levels of creation are straws in that ocean.
> The movement of the straws comes from an agitation
> in the water. When the ocean wants the straws calm,
> it sends them close to shore. When it wants them
> back in the deep surge, it does with them
> as the wind does with the grasses.
> This never ends.[45]

What mystics don't assume is that the holomovement ocean is out-side us—"other" than who we are. For us to be dominated, something has to be out there and alien to our nature to do the dominating. If the holomovement isn't outside us, if it's our core being, then how can we experience it as an external, pushing-us-around power? "Everyone here is a king. No servants":

> Those full of fear are not really on the way.
> Everyone here is a king. No servants.
>
> The wave can never be afraid of the ocean.
> Inside that motion, how can anything be "other?"[46]

We do, however, experience freedom as a two-sided affair. We feel something greater than us at work in our lives, yet we also feel we have a say, a choice along the way. Our inner experience of freedom has two faces.

Writer Arthur Koestler discussed this "Janus-faced" experience as the norm in holistic systems.[47] He coined the term *holarchy* for a whole system that includes many levels of sub-wholes, "holons." The body, for example, is a holarchy, composed of many subsystems that function as sub-wholes—the respiratory, digestive, circulatory, and immune systems. Within their own realms, sub-wholes assert autonomy; they run their own shows. But they're not isolated. Each sub-whole "looks up" to the greater whole of which it's a part. Holons integrate with the larger holarchy and are moved from that source. Whereas freedom versus determinism language makes a knot of the mystic's freedom, Koestler's language makes sense of it. We're both moved by the holo-movement *and* choosing our own course, "held in a hand, yet free":

> Whether I say *pen* or *flag*, it is with this wonderful
> conscious unconsciousness: the mind unable to include
> its own description, composing blindly.
> Held in a hand, yet free.[48]

Granted, our Wise Fools lean on the looking-up, held-in-a-hand side. They focus on integrating with the whole's unfoldings and en-

foldings, a choice that paradoxically expands our freedom. By looking
to the whole, we discover unimagined worlds. We're more free in an
open field of sunlight than we are down in a well—one of Rumi's many
variations on Plato's allegory of the cave. He also uses the image of
being in the womb versus life outside of it. Choosing self-assertively
within womb-well-cave realms—the ego's world—is too narrow a freedom, which is why our Wise Fools opt for a larger:

> Do you think I know what I'm doing?
> That for one breath or half-breath I belong to myself?
> As much as a pen knows what it's writing,
> or the ball can guess where it's going next.[49]

Wise Fools don't conceive of freedom, therefore, as a fight over who
calls the shots. Nor do they perceive it as a test to see if we can make all
the right choices. Oneness-freedom is the freedom to move with the
ocean unhindered, and anywhere we move is ocean too. Fish don't
think they're shoved around by the ocean; it's their element, giving
them not only life but a universe to explore. Our Wise Fools live that
kind of freedom. In "the meadow of union," we don't "have to decide
which of ten roads to take." With oneness-freedom, we "can just roll
around anywhere." It's all holomovement; it's all meaningful; therefore, it's all bound up with where our souls and loves want us to be:

> Freewill is the perplexity of being pulled
> in opposite directions, an ambush on the way.
> O Destination of both pullers, help us!
>
> This two-way way,
> duality, feels
> like a fight.
>
> This oneness path
> feels like a banquet.
>
> God explains in the *Qur'an*, *They shrank*
> *from bearing it*, meaning that,
> when God offered the trust of freewill

to the rest of the universe, they refused,
fearing it, but humanity accepted.

Now we are constantly questioning,
"Is this better, or that?
Will I fail, or succeed?"

The tide ebbs and flows,
else the ocean would be still.

Source that gave this perplexity,
unperplex me! I'm a skinny camel
with unbalanced baskets on my back.
The panniers slip from side to side.

Freewill scrapes a bad sore on me!
Let the baskets drop off.

When that happens, I'll look up,
and there will be the meadow of union,
where I won't have to decide
which of ten roads to take.

I can just roll around anywhere,
involuntarily, like a ball.[50]

Free to Have Fun

"Rolling around anywhere," we abandon expectations of where we
ought to be—of what societies, associates, religions, families, or even
we ourselves say we should be doing. With mystic freedom, we explore
what excites us, our loves being how the whole communicates with us.
For our inner mystics, nothing makes us happier than moving with a
deep inner love that's also born of something higher:

That I am part of the ploys
of this game makes me
amazingly happy.[51]

This mystic sense of life's meaning isn't heavy or ponderous but the opposite. We relax into who we are, whatever that is, and have fun doing it. Rumi tells a story about a wise person, a Sheikh, who spends his time playing with children and riding stick-horses around the town square. When a young man seeks his advice, he finds the Sheikh in the thick of play. The Sheikh barely has time for him, warning:

> "Speak quickly. I can't hold this one still for long.
> Whoops. Don't let him kick you.
> > This is a wild one!" . . .
>
> > "Now get out of here,
> before this horse kicks you in the head! Easy, now!" . . .
>
> > "Back away.
> > I'm going to turn this rascal around!"
>
> He gave a loud whoop and rode back,
> calling the children around him.[52]

The young man can't fathom what's going on—a wise man behaving like a fool?—so he presses the Sheikh:

> "One more question, Master!"
> > The Sheikh circled,
> "What is it? Quickly! That rider over there needs me.
> I think I'm in love."
> > "What is this playing that you do?
> Why do you hide your intelligence so?"
> > "The people here
> want to put me in charge. They want me to be
> Judge, Magistrate, and Interpreter of all the texts.
>
> The Knowing I have doesn't want that. It wants to enjoy itself.
> I am a plantation of sugarcane, and at the same time
> I'm eating the sweetness."
> > Knowledge that is acquired
> is not like this. Those who have it worry if

audiences like it or not.

It's a bait for popularity.
Disputational knowing wants customers.
It has no soul.

Robust and energetic
before a responsive crowd, it slumps when no one is there.
The only real customer is God.

Chew quietly
your sweet sugarcane God-Love, and stay
playfully childish.

Your face
will turn rosy with illumination
like the redbud flowers.[53]

The World Needs Us to Be Who We Are

What's the Sheikh doing? Jesus said we should become as little children, but isn't this a bit much? Rumi himself says in another poem that
we should take an active role in shaping society's course, otherwise we
leave "the caravan of civilization" vulnerable to ambush by Malvolio-
fools—or worse:

God called the Prophet Muhammed *Muzzammil*,
"The One Who Wraps Himself,"

and said,
"Come out from under your cloak, you so fond
of hiding and running away.

Don't cover your face.
The world is a reeling, drunken body, and You
are its intelligent head.

Don't hide the candle
of your clarity. Stand up and burn
through the night, my Prince.

Without your Light
a great Lion is held captive by a rabbit!

Be the Captain of the Ship,

Mustafa, my Chosen One,
my expert guide.
                  Look how the caravan of civilization
has been ambushed.
                Fools are everywhere in charge.
Do not practice solitude like Jesus. Be *in*
the assembly,
              and take charge of it.
                      As the bearded griffon,
the *Humay*, lives on Mt. Qaf because he's native to it,
so You
          should live most naturally out in public
and be a communal teacher of souls."[54]

Wise Fools don't shirk responsibilities; they simply believe that we each have our own ways of fulfilling them. How we "live most naturally out in public" is something we work out with our Friend, and that's unique to each of us. After all, isn't it worthy to play with children, to nurture coming generations? Is it less worthy than moving around masses of money for the sheer greed of it or commanding massive powers of destruction to use in power plays? Whose life is being spent more foolishly?

Whatever way is ours, whether playing with stick-horses or heading governments, our Wise Fools embrace it. By his playing, the Sheikh said more to the people of his town about what's important in life than if he stood all day in the square lecturing them.

The Sheikh lives who he is with such abandon because of an assumption deep in mystical thought: what moves the universe also moves us. The holomovement made us who we are because that's what the universe needs us to be at this point in time, space, and culture. When we're true to who we are, we are precisely what the world most needs. The two are secretly synchronized, united in purpose, though in unseen ways:

A secret turning in us
makes the universe turn.
Head unaware of feet,

and feet head. Neither cares.
They keep turning.[55]

This brings us full circle to the issue of soul bargaining that launched us on the mystic path. The prevailing paradigm—the one behind most of our social institutions—says we need to give up who we are and conform to social demands in order for social systems to work. Social order represents a contractual truce in the supposedly inevitable conflict between individuals and society: how much of ourselves do we have to give up to be accepted into social systems? Who we are is taken as a threat to social order, or at least as an annoying wrinkle to be ironed out by family, educational, psychiatric, economic, or penal systems.

Our Wise Fools assume the opposite. By following the "secret turning in us," we do what the holomovement wants us to do, and that's the best thing for society as well. Only from our essence can we fulfill what our families, communities, and nations truly need—the form busting that breaks unhealthy patterns and the creativity that evolves new forms. Whereas not being who we are diminishes society, being who we are enriches it. When we're true to our souls, "a star comes out":

As salt dissolves in ocean,
I was swallowed up in you,
beyond doubt or being sure.

Suddenly here in my chest a star
came out so clear, it drew
all stars into it.[56]

In other words, being who we are aligns us with whole-guided change. Operating from this mystic premise—that the same holomovement that moves us moves everyone else too and invisibly unites us in purpose—our "souls flow like clear water." Social order becomes effortless, coordinated as it is from unseen levels. Because of this invisible coordinating, whatever we do becomes maximally effective—"We can sail this boat lying down":

Some souls flow like clear water.
They pour into our veins
and feel like wine.

I give in to that. I fall flat.
We can sail this boat lying down![57]

Given that we've been socially coerced into ignoring who we are,
getting back to our souls is a process—the mystic journey, in fact. As we
develop on the mystic path, our relationship to society and to how we
can help each other changes. Down in the well of soul-rejecting systems, we can render each other only so much help. Paddling around in
black water, we can at best buoy each other up when we get so de-
moralized that we start to sink.

But as we move away from soul-rejecting models, we climb out of
the well—"forget the world"—and go into the open field of sunlight.
There we find a freedom greater than choosing which way to paddle
and so gain a capacity to help that's greater too. If the problems of society arise not from our souls but from soul loss, then the more we
come back to who we are, the more we give our social systems what
they need to heal. We do what's ours to do—the essence of justice according to Socrates and Plato—and our societies evolve naturally as a
result. From being "a source of pain" and "an unsafe house," we become "the delight," "the One who sees into the Invisible":

Forget the world, and so
command the world.

Be a lamp, or a lifeboat, or a ladder.
Help someone's soul heal.
Walk out of your house like a shepherd.

Stay in the spiritual fire.
Let it cook you.

Be a well-baked loaf
and lord of the table.

Come and be served
to your brothers.

You have been a source of pain.
Now you'll be the delight.

You have been an unsafe house.
Now you'll be the One
who sees into the Invisible.[58]

Free as Beings of Both Time and Eternity

Held in a hand yet free, living from our invisible souls but doing it in
visible ways, being both profound and goofy—our experience is two-
sided because we're two-sided. We're visible and invisible, because we
live in both time and eternity. That's just "how it is with a True Human
Being":

> This is how it is with a True Human Being:
> He or she is made of two figures.
>
> One is here explaining subtle points.
> The other is whispering with God.
>
> One listens to these words.
> The Other One's ears receive the Creation-Word, BE!
>
> One eye watches these forms moving about,
> while the Other takes in the dazzle
> inside the text that says,
>
> > *That Eye does not look away.*
>
> One set of feet stands even with the others
> in the line of worshipers at the mosque.
> The Other set ambles in the sky.
>
> To be clearer: Part of a True Person
> is inside Time, and part is beyond Time.

The Time-part dies. The Other
is the Good Friend of Forever.

For That One,
a forty-day fast is not necessary.
The cave of such seclusion
would begin to glow
like the sun lived in it.

Abstinence, disbelief, unfaithfulness,
these words do not apply.

A True Person is like the vertical stroke of the *alif*.
There's nothing else there, just a naked line of Being.[59]

It feels good to be "just a naked line of Being," our essence without anything else to worry about—no coverings, no images to keep up, no expectations, no social systems to step around. In fact, it feels so good we'd have half a mind to "trade in this overcoat made of leaves and dirt." But what would we gain? All that we'd want from such a trade, we have now. The unseen Presence is not other than where we are:

Drinking wine with you, getting warmer and warmer,
I think why not trade in this overcoat
made of leaves and dirt.
Then I look out the window.
For what? Both worlds are here.[60]

"Both worlds are here"—here in us and in the world too. The mystic path takes us to the heights of mystical experience where we find our souls, loves, and freedom united—"the naked line of Being"—but it doesn't leave us there in "ecstasy" and "excitement" ungrounded. As the unity of soul, love, and freedom emerges, we experience the inner joining of time and eternity, visible and invisible. Neither dominated by the visible nor escaping to the invisible, we find both worlds moving in balance—the grounded mysticism that's so essentially Rumi:

Walk into the river,
and then walk out.

How long do you plan to stay in your ecstasy,
where all you can say is, "I don't know *anything*?"

Let your *I don't see* become *I see*.
Move beyond the excitement,
and your *ideas* of surrendering.

There are hundreds of love-drunkards
walking the street. Wake into the sobriety
that says, "I am sustained from within."[61]

Notes

Introduction

1. Studs Terkel, *Coming of Age: The Story of Our Century by Those Who've Lived It* (New York: The New Press, 1995), 379.
2. Barks, *One-Handed Basket Weaving*, 87.
3. Moyne and Barks, *Unseen Rain*, 30.
4. Moyne and Barks, *Open Secret*, 13.
5. Moyne and Barks, *Open Secret*, 12.
6. Barks, *Feeling the Shoulder of the Lion*, 88–89.
7. Moyne and Barks, *Open Secret*, 75.
8. Lectures by Inayat Khan, translations by Coleman Barks, *The Hand of Poetry: Five Mystic Poets of Persia* (New Lebanon, N.Y.: Omega Publications, 1993), 100.
9. Barks, *We Are Three*, 82–83.
10. Moyne and Barks, *Open Secret*, 55.
11. These words are from the opening of Frank Capra's film *Lost Horizon*, with Ronald Colman.
12. Barks, *One-Handed Basket Weaving*, 109.
13. Barks, *We Are Three*, 46.
14. Barks and Moyne, *This Longing*, 29–30.
15. Barks, *Birdsong*, 36.
16. Paraphrased from Reynold A. Nicholson, translator, *The Mathnawi of Jalalu'ddin Rumi*, Book IV, v. 521 (Cambridge, England: E. J. W. Gibb Memorial Trust, 1926, reprint 1990), 301.
17. Moyne and Barks, *Unseen Rain*, 29.
18. Moyne and Barks, *Unseen Rain*, 40.
19. Moyne and Barks, *Say I Am You*, 113.
20. Moyne and Barks, *Open Secret*, 80.
21. Moyne and Barks, *These Branching Moments*, 22.
22. Barks, *One-Handed Basket Weaving*, 17.
23. Moyne and Barks, *Open Secret*, 8.
24. Moyne and Barks, *Unseen Rain*, 33.
25. Barks and Moyne, *This Longing*, 96.
26. Barks, *Like This*, 55
27. Although David Bohm's ideas are being discussed by many different writers, perhaps the clearest source is Michael Talbot's *The Holographic Universe* (New York: HarperCollins, 1991).
28. Moyne and Barks, *Open Secret*, 79.
29. Barks, *We Are Three*, 10.
30. Moyne and Barks, *Say I Am You*, 66.
31. Moyne and Barks, *Say I Am You*, 66–67.
32. Barks, *We Are Three*, 32.
33. Moyne and Barks, *Unseen Rain*, 37.
34. Barks, *Like This*, 58.
35. Barks, *Delicious Laughter*, 83.

Chapter 1

1. Barks, *Birdsong*, 38.
2. Moyne and Barks, *Open Secret*, 75.
3. Annemarie Schimmel, *Mystical Dimensions of Islam* (Chapel Hill, N.C.: University of North Carolina Press, 1975), 111.
4. Paraphrased from Nicholson's translation of the *Mathnawi*, Book I, v. 2632, 143.
5. Barks, *Feeling the Shoulder of the Lion*, 42.
6. Eva de Vitray-Meyerovitch, *Rûmî and Sufism* (Sausalito, Calif.: The Post-Apollo Press, 1977, English ed. 1987), 83.

7. Moyne and Barks, *Open Secret,* 15.
8. Moyne and Barks, *These Branching Moments,* 13.
9. Moyne and Barks, *Open Secret,* 69.
10. Moyne and Barks, *Open Secret,* 11.
11. Barks, *Birdsong,* 16.
12. Barks, *We Are Three,* 8.
13. Barks, *We Are Three,* 48.
14. Moyne and Barks, *Say I Am You,* 40.
15. Moyne and Barks, *Say I Am You,* 72.
16. Josef Schmidt, Introduction to *Johannes Tauler Sermons* (New York: Paulist Press, 1985), 7, and Steven E. Ozment, *The Age of Reform 1250–1550: An Intellectual and Religious History of Late Medieval and Reformation Europe* (New Haven and London: Yale University Press, 1980), 115.
17. Barks, *One-Handed Basket Weaving,* 35.
18. Barks, *Feeling the Shoulder of the Lion,* 1, 4–5.
19. Moyne and Barks, *Open Secret,* 37.
20. Barks, *Feeling the Shoulder of the Lion,* 53-54.
21. Moyne and Barks, *Open Secret,* 37.
22. Barks, *Birdsong,* 22.
23. Barks, *Delicious Laughter,* 11.
24. Barks, *One-Handed Basket Weaving,* 66.
25. Moyne and Barks, *Open Secret,* 27.
26. Paraphrased from Nicholson's *Mathnawi,* Book II, v. 2517, 351.
27. Moyne and Barks, *Open Secret,* 45.
28. Moyne and Barks, *Unseen Rain,* 11.
29. Moyne and Barks, *Open Secret,* 16.
30. Barks, *Birdsong,* 19.
31. Moyne and Barks, *Unseen Rain,* 3.
32. Barks, *Delicious Laughter,* 116.
33. Barks and Moyne, *This Longing,* 85.
34. Moyne and Barks, *Open Secret,* 22.
35. Helminski, *The Ruins of the Heart,* 26.
36. Moyne and Barks, *Say I Am You,* 105.

Chapter 2

1. Moyne and Barks, *Open Secret,* 66.
2. Moyne and Barks, *Unseen Rain,* 43.
3. Moyne and Barks, *Unseen Rain,* 52.
4. Moyne and Barks, *Open Secret,* 41.
5. Barks, *Feeling the Shoulder of the Lion,* 56.
6. Barks, *We Are Three,* 18.
7. Moyne and Barks, *Unseen Rain,* 76.
8. Moyne and Barks, *Open Secret,* 5.
9. Barks, *Like This,* 37.
10. Barks, *Feeling the Shoulder of the Lion,* 87.
11. Barks, *Birdsong,* 48.
12. Barks, *Feeling the Shoulder of the Lion,* 101.
13. Plato, *Symposium,* 204b, 202e–203a. From Edith Hamilton and Huntington Cairns, eds., *Plato: The Collected Dialogues* (Princeton, N.J.: Princeton University Press, 1961), 555–56.
14. Barks, *Delicious Laughter,* 9–10.
15. Moyne and Barks, *Unseen Rain,* 47.
16. See: James Hillman, *The Soul's Code: In Search of Character and Calling* (New York: Random House, 1996).
17. Barks, *Delicious Laughter,* 109.
18. Barks, *Birdsong,* 48.
19. Moyne and Barks, *Open Secret,* 7.
20. Barks, *One-Handed Basket Weaving,* 72.
21. Barks, *Delicious Laughter,* 25-26.
22. Moyne and Barks, *Open Secret,* 28.
23. Barks and Moyne, *This Longing,* 36.
24. Moyne and Barks, *Unseen Rain,* 75.
25. Barks, *Birdsong,* 24.
26. Khan and Barks, *The Hand of Poetry,* 95.
27. Robin Campbell, translator, *Letters from a Stoic* (New York: Penguin Books, 1969), 71.
28. Josef Pieper, *The Silence of Saint Thomas* (Chicago: Henry Regnery, 1957, 1965), 40.
29. Barks, *We Are Three,* 18.
30. Barks, *Like This,* 12.
31. Barks, *Delicious Laughter,* 55.
32. Barks, *Delicious Laughter,* 9.
33. Khan and Barks, *The Hand of Poetry,* 102.
34. Barks, *One-Handed Basket Weaving,* 44.
35. Barks, *Like This,* 18.

36. Barks and Moyne, *This Longing*, 104.
37. Barks, *Like This*, 31.
38. Barks, *Birdsong*, 20.
39. Moyne and Barks, *Unseen Rain*, 56.
40. Barks, *Birdsong*, 29.
41. Moyne and Barks, *Say I Am You*, 83.
42. Barks, *We Are Three*, 83.
43. Barks, *Birdsong*, 24.
44. Gilbert Murray, *Hibbert Journal* (1918).
45. Barks, *Birdsong*, 25.
46. Moyne and Barks, *Open Secret*, 17.
47. Barks, *One-Handed Basket Weaving*, 71.
48. Barks, *Feeling the Shoulder of the Lion*, 56–57.

Chapter 3

1. Barks and Moyne, *This Longing*, 26–27.
2. Barks and Moyne, *This Longing*, 6.
3. Barks, *One-Handed Basket Weaving*, 80.
4. Barks, *Like This*, 7.
5. Barks, *One-Handed Basket Weaving*, 80.
6. Barks, *One-Handed Basket Weaving*, 70.
7. Barks and Moyne, *This Longing*, 26.
8. Barks, *We Are Three*, 4; also Barks and Moyne, *This Longing*, 10.
9. Moyne and Barks, *Say I Am You*, 22.
10. Moyne and Barks, *Say I Am You*, 9–10.
11. Moyne and Barks, *Open Secret*, 62.
12. Barks, *Feeling the Shoulder of the Lion*, 24.
13. Moyne and Barks, *Unseen Rain*, 82.
14. Moyne and Barks, *Open Secret*, 68.
15. Barks, *One-Handed Basket Weaving*, 126.
16. Barks, *One-Handed Basket Weaving*, 79.
17. Barks and Moyne, *This Longing*, 18.
18. Barks, *Delicious Laughter*, 128.
19. Barks, *Delicious Laughter*, 50.
20. Barks, *One-Handed Basket Weaving*, 86.
21. Barks, *One-Handed Basket Weaving*, 119.
22. Barks, *Delicious Laughter*, 132.
23. Barks, *One-Handed Basket Weaving*, 54.
24. Barks, *Delicious Laughter*, 50.
25. Barks, *Like This*, 23.
26. Barks, *One-Handed Basket Weaving*, 37.

27. Moyne and Barks, *Unseen Rain*, 42.
28. Barks, *Delicious Laughter*, 45.
29. Barks, *Delicious Laughter*, 40.
30. Barks and Moyne, *This Longing*, 19–20.
31. Barks and Moyne, *This Longing*, 21–22.
32. Barks, *Delicious Laughter*, 129.
33. Barks and Moyne, *This Longing*, 48.
34. Barks, *Birdsong*, 30.
35. Barks and Moyne, *This Longing*, 6–9.
36. Barks, *One-Handed Basket Weaving*, 41.
37. Moyne and Barks, *These Branching Moments*, 25.
38. Moyne and Barks, *These Branching Moments*, 18.
39. Barks, *Like This*, 33.
40. Barks and Moyne, *This Longing*, 49.
41. Moyne and Barks, *Say I Am You*, 35.
42. Barks, *One-Handed Basket Weaving*, 97.
43. Barks, *Delicious Laughter*, 109.
44. Barks, *Delicious Laughter*, 108.

Chapter 4

1. Barks, *Feeling the Shoulder of the Lion*, 60.
2. Barks, *One-Handed Basket Weaving*, 112.
3. Barks, *Delicious Laughter*, 113.
4. Moyne and Barks, *Say I Am You*, 40.
5. Moyne and Barks, *These Branching Moments*, 36.
6. Moyne and Barks, *Open Secret*, 27.
7. Barks, *Birdsong*, 60.
8. Moyne and Barks, *Open Secret*, 19.
9. Moyne and Barks, *Open Secret*, 8.
10. Moyne and Barks, *Say I Am You*, 41.
11. Barks, *Delicious Laughter*, 32.
12. Moyne and Barks, *Say I Am You*, 112–13.
13. Barks, *Like This*, 52.
14. Moyne and Barks, *Say I Am You*, 54.
15. Barks, *Feeling the Shoulder of the Lion*, 67.
16. Moyne and Barks, *Unseen Rain*, 34.
17. Moyne and Barks, *Unseen Rain*, 24.
18. Barks and Moyne, *This Longing*, 73.

19. Moyne and Barks, *These Branching Moments*, 36.
20. Barks, *One-Handed Basket Weaving*, 29.
21. Moyne and Barks, *Unseen Rain*, 4.
22. Moyne and Barks, *Open Secret*, 18.
23. Barks, *Feeling the Shoulder of the Lion*, 21.
24. Barks, *We Are Three*, 39.
25. Khan and Barks, *The Hand of Poetry*, 79.
26. Barks and Moyne, *This Longing*, 71.
27. Barks, *One-Handed Basket Weaving*, 121.
28. Barks, *Delicious Laughter*, 61.
29. Barks, *One-Handed Basket Weaving*, 47–48.
30. Barks, *One-Handed Basket Weaving*, 47.
31. Barks, *Delicious Laughter*, 82.
32. Barks, *Delicious Laughter*, 82–83.
33. Barks, *Delicious Laughter*, 74.
34. Barks, *Feeling the Shoulder of the Lion*, 4.
35. Barks, *Delicious Laughter*, 75.
36. Barks, *One-Handed Basket Weaving*, 29.
37. Moyne and Barks, *These Branching Moments*, 33.
38. Barks, *Feeling the Shoulder of the Lion*, 66.
39. Barks, *Birdsong*, 39.
40. Moyne and Barks, *Open Secret*, 9.
41. Moyne and Barks, *These Branching Moments*, 36.
42. Moyne and Barks, *Unseen Rain*, 71.
43. Moyne and Barks, *Unseen Rain*, 27.
44. Moyne and Barks, *These Branching Moments*, 11.
45. Barks, *We Are Three*, 36.

Chapter 5

1. Moyne and Barks, *Open Secret*, 68.
2. Khan and Barks, *The Hand of Poetry*, 82.
3. Moyne and Barks, *Say I Am You*, 59.
4. Barks, *One-Handed Basket Weaving*, 115.
5. Barks and Moyne, *This Longing*, 45.
6. Barks and Moyne, *This Longing*, 43.
7. Barks, *Feeling the Shoulder of the Lion*, 8–9.

8. Idries Shah, *The Sufis* (New York: Doubleday, 1964), 134–35.
9. Barks, *One-Handed Basket Weaving*, 107.
10. Barks, *One-Handed Basket Weaving*, 107.
11. Moyne and Barks, *Unseen Rain*, 14.
12. Barks, *Feeling the Shoulder of the Lion*, 14.
13. Moyne and Barks, *Open Secret*, 71.
14. Moyne and Barks, *Open Secret*, 68.
15. Barks, *One-Handed Basket Weaving*, 47.
16. Khan and Barks, *The Hand of Poetry*, 91.
17. Barks, *Feeling the Shoulder of the Lion*, 14.
18. Barks, *Open Secret*, 57.
19. Barks, *Feeling the Shoulder of the Lion*, 85.
20. Moyne and Barks, *Unseen Rain*, 82.
21. Moyne and Barks, *Open Secret*, 76.
22. Barks, *One-Handed Basket Weaving*, 60–61.
23. Barks, *Delicious Laughter*, 80.
24. Barks, *Feeling the Shoulder of the Lion*, 84–85.
25. Moyne and Barks, *Say I Am You*, 27.
26. Barks, *Birdsong*, 23.
27. Barks, *Delicious Laughter*, 132.
28. Moyne and Barks, *Say I Am You*, 124.
29. Barks, *Delicious Laughter*, 59.
30. Moyne and Barks, *These Branching Moments*, 31.
31. Barks, *Birdsong*, 63.
32. Moyne and Barks, *Open Secret*, 36.
33. Barks, *Like This*, 44.
34. Moyne and Barks, *Say I Am You*, 52.
35. Khan and Barks, *The Hand of Poetry*, 82.
36. Barks, *One-Handed Basket Weaving*, 99.
37. Barks, *Delicious Laughter*, 119.
38. Barks, *Birdsong*, 13.
39. Moyne and Barks, *Say I Am You*, 16.
40. Barks, *Like This*, 26.
41. Moyne and Barks, *Unseen Rain*, 12.
42. Barks, *We Are Three*, 14.

Chapter 6

1. Barks, *Feeling the Shoulder of the Lion*, 43.
2. Barks, *Like This*, 26.

3. Moyne and Barks, *Say I Am You,* 51.
4. Barks, *Delicious Laughter,* 77.
5. Barks, *Delicious Laughter,* 103–4.
6. Moyne and Barks, *Say I Am You,* 62.
7. Moyne and Barks, *These Branching Moments,* 9.
8. Moyne and Barks, *Open Secret,* 57.
9. Moyne and Barks, *Unseen Rain,* 8.
10. Barks, *One-Handed Basket Weaving,* 57.
11. Barks, *One-Handed Basket Weaving,* 86.
12. Moyne and Barks, *Open Secret,* 5.
13. Moyne and Barks, *Unseen Rain,* 16.
14. Barks, *Like This,* 56.
15. Barks, *Like This,* 26.
16. Moyne and Barks, *Say I Am You,* 96.
17. Barks, *Delicious Laughter,* 46.
18. Barks, *Delicious Laughter,* 129.
19. Moyne and Barks, *Open Secret,* 25.
20. Moyne and Barks, *These Branching Moments,* 9.
21. Barks, *Like This,* 30.
22. Moyne and Barks, *Say I Am You,* 123.
23. Moyne and Barks, *Unseen Rain,* 63.
24. Moyne and Barks, *Say I Am You,* 94–95.
25. Moyne and Barks, *Say I Am You,* 98.
26. Barks, *One-Handed Basket Weaving,* 57–59.
27. Barks, *One-Handed Basket Weaving,* 92.
28. Moyne and Barks, *Say I Am You,* 101.
29. Moyne and Barks, *Open Secret,* 59.
30. Moyne and Barks, *Open Secret,* 16.
31. Barks, *Delicious Laughter,* 93.
32. Barks, *Feeling the Shoulder of the Lion,* 45.
33. Moyne and Barks, *Open Secret,* 18.
34. Barks, *One-Handed Basket Weaving,* 44.
35. Moyne and Barks, *These Branching Moments,* 36.
36. Barks, *One-Handed Basket Weaving,* 45.
37. Moyne and Barks, *Say I Am You,* 126.
38. Barks, *Birdsong,* 23.
39. Moyne and Barks, *Say I Am You,* 105–6.
40. Moyne and Barks, *Unseen Rain,* 22.
41. Barks, *Birdsong,* 57.
42. Barks, *We Are Three,* 2.
43. Moyne and Barks, *Say I Am You,* 116.
44. Barks, *Like This,* 21.

45. Barks, *One-Handed Basket Weaving,* 49.
46. Moyne and Barks, *Open Secret,* 48.
47. Barks and Moyne, *This Longing,* 82.
48. Barks, *Feeling the Shoulder of the Lion,* 29.
49. Moyne and Barks, *Open Secret,* 26.

Chapter 7

1. Barks, *Delicious Laughter,* 41.
2. Barks and Moyne, *This Longing,* 58.
3. Barks, *Like This,* 54.
4. Barks, *Like This,* 16.
5. Barks and Moyne, *This Longing,* 52.
6. Barks, *We Are Three,* 38.
7. Arthur Versluis, *The Mysteries of Love* (St. Paul, Minn.: Grail: Studies in Literature and Religion, 1996), 22–23.
8. Barks, *Feeling the Shoulder of the Lion,* 69.
9. Moyne and Barks, *Open Secret,* 19.
10. Barks, *Like This,* 28.
11. Barks, *Delicious Laughter,* 90.
12. Barks, *Delicious Laughter,* 125.
13. Moyne and Barks, *Say I Am You,* 77.
14. Barks, *One-Handed Basket Weaving,* 117.
15. Moyne and Barks, *These Branching Moments,* 6.
16. Barks, *Like This,* 48.
17. Moyne and Barks, *Open Secret,* 42.
18. Barks, *Delicious Laughter,* 13.
19. Barks, *Birdsong,* 22.
20. Barks, *Like This,* 14.
21. Moyne and Barks, *Open Secret,* 31.
22. Barks, *Like This,* 51.
23. Barks, *Feeling the Shoulder of the Lion,* 10.
24. Moyne and Barks, *Open Secret,* 31.
25. Act 1, Scene 1.
26. Moyne and Barks, *Open Secret,* 42.
27. Barks, *Birdsong,* 28.
28. Barks, *We Are Three,* 65.
29. Moyne and Barks, *Open Secret,* 58.
30. Khan and Barks, *The Hand of Poetry,* 78.
31. Barks, *One-Handed Basket Weaving,* 73–74.

32. Moyne and Barks, *Say I Am You*, 73.
33. Moyne and Barks, *Open Secret*, 61.
34. Barks, *Like This*, 47.
35. Moyne and Barks, *These Branching Moments*, 15.
36. Barks, *Like This*, 59–60.
37. Barks, *Feeling the Shoulder of the Lion*, 30–31.
38. Barks, *One-Handed Basket Weaving*, 102.
39. Moyne and Barks, *Say I Am You*, 82.
40. Moyne and Barks, *Unseen Rain*, 77.
41. Barks, *Delicious Laughter*, 101.
42. Barks and Moyne, *This Longing*, 47.
43. Barks, *We Are Three*, 15.
44. Moyne and Barks, *These Branching Moments*, 38.
45. Barks, *One-Handed Basket Weaving*, 92.
46. Barks, *One-Handed Basket Weaving*, 73.

Chapter 8

1. Barks, *Delicious Laughter*, 45–46.
2. Proverbs 29:18.
3. Barks, *One-Handed Basket Weaving*, 101.
4. Moyne and Barks, *Open Secret*, 67.
5. Barks, *Delicious Laughter*, 128.
6. Barks, *One-Handed Basket Weaving*, 79.
7. Moyne and Barks, *Say I Am You*, 78.
8. Barks, *Delicious Laughter*, 72–73.
9. Barks, *Like This*, 30.
10. Barks, *One-Handed Basket Weaving*, 88.
11. Barks and Moyne, *This Longing*, 46.
12. Barks and Moyne, *This Longing*, 64.
13. Barks and Moyne, *This Longing*, 95.
14. Moyne and Barks, *Say I Am You*, 115.
15. Moyne and Barks, *Say I Am You*, 27.
16. Barks, *Like This*, 62.
17. Barks, *Delicious Laughter*, 76.
18. Barks, *Birdsong*, 28.
19. Moyne and Barks, *Say I Am You*, 108.
20. Barks, *Birdsong*, 52.
21. Barks, *One-Handed Basket Weaving*, 95.
22. Moyne and Barks, *Unseen Rain*, 60.
23. Moyne and Barks, *Say I Am You*, 29.

24. Barks, *One-Handed Basket Weaving*, 29.
25. Barks, *Feeling the Shoulder of the Lion*, 59.
26. Barks, *One-Handed Basket Weaving*, 121.
27. Barks, *Birdsong*, 60.
28. Barks, *Like This*, 38.
29. Barks, *One-Handed Basket Weaving*, 93.
30. Barks, *Like This*, 38.
31. Barks, *Birdsong*, 45.
32. Barks, *One-Handed Basket Weaving*, 69.
33. Barks, *Birdsong*, 21.
34. Barks, *We Are Three*, 56.
35. Moyne and Barks, *Open Secret*, 64.
36. Barks, *One-Handed Basket Weaving*, 48.
37. Barks, *One-Handed Basket Weaving*, 78.
38. Barks, *Like This*, 42.
39. Barks, *Feeling the Shoulder of the Lion*, 62.
40. I Corinthians 15:31.
41. Barks, *Delicious Laughter*, 57.
42. Heinrich Harrer, *Seven Years in Tibet*, Richard Graves, translator (New York: E. P. Dutton, 1954), 184.
43. Barks, *We Are Three*, 79.
44. Moyne and Barks, *Say I Am You*, 92.
45. Barks, *Birdsong*, 42.
46. Moyne and Barks, *Open Secret*, 8.
47. Moyne and Barks, *Unseen Rain*, 50.
48. Moyne and Barks, *These Branching Moments*, 23.
49. Barks, *Feeling the Shoulder of the Lion*, 55.
50. Barks, *We Are Three*, 52.
51. Barks, *We Are Three*, 40–41.
52. Barks, *One-Handed Basket Weaving*, 48.
53. Barks, *Like This*, 35.

Chapter 9

1. Abu Bakr, mentioned in this story as an example of a True Person, was Muhammad's closest personal friend. When Muhammad died, Abu Bakr became the first Caliph of Islam and is referred to as "the faithful."
2. Barks, *Feeling the Shoulder of the Lion*, 1–2.

3. We first read about Mr. Athavale's work in *Hinduism Today* and then on the Internet: John Templeton Foundation, The Templeton Prize. It is no credit to the Western media that slight attention has been given to such a pioneering, poverty-healing, community-building model. Only since Athavale received the Templeton Prize in May 1997 has coverage increased somewhat, though the model has been working successfully since the 1950s.

4. Barks, *Feeling the Shoulder of the Lion*, 80.

5. Moyne and Barks, *Unseen Rain*, 14.

6. Moyne and Barks, *Unseen Rain*, 20.

7. Barks and Moyne, *This Longing*, 39–40.

8. Barks, *Like This*, 53.

9. Moyne and Barks, *These Branching Moments*, 10.

10. Barks, *Feeling the Shoulder of the Lion*, 81–82.

11. Moyne and Barks, *Say I Am You*, 108.

12. Barks, *Birdsong*, 45.

13. Barks, *Like This*, 38.

14. Barks, *Like This*, 11.

15. Barks, *Like This*, 25.

16. Barks, *We Are Three*, 16.

17. Barks, *Delicious Laughter*, 70.

18. Moyne and Barks, *Say I Am You*, 72.

19. Moyne and Barks, *These Branching Moments*, 33.

20. Barks, *We Are Three*, 52.

21. Barks, *Like This*, 34.

22. Barks, *Birdsong*, 61.

23. Moyne and Barks, *Say I Am You*, 70.

24. Barks, *We Are Three*, 69–70.

25. Barks, *Delicious Laughter*, 45.

26. Barks and Moyne, *This Longing*, 55.

27. Moyne and Barks, *Say I Am You*, 57.

28. Moyne and Barks, *Say I Am You*, 75.

29. Barks, *Birdsong*, 47.

30. Moyne and Barks, *Say I Am You*, 43.

31. Moyne and Barks, *Say I Am You*, 86–87.

32. Barks, *Delicious Laughter*, 28.

33. Khan and Barks, *The Hand of Poetry*, 106.

34. Hazrat Inayat Khan, *The Sufi Message of Hazrat Inayat Khan, Volume I: The Inner Life* (Geneva: International Headquarters of the Sufi Movement, 1960, re-edited 1979), 16.

35. Barks, *We Are Three*, 11.

36. Barks, *One-Handed Basket Weaving*, 56.

37. Barks, *We Are Three*, 85.

38. Barks, *One-Handed Basket Weaving*, 43.

39. Barks, *One-Handed Basket Weaving*, 43.

40. Seneca, *Letters from a Stoic*, Robin Campbell, translator (New York: Penguin Books, 1969), 72.

41. Barks, *Like This*, 57.

42. Barks, *Birdsong*, 49.

43. Barks, *One-Handed Basket Weaving*, 81.

44. Barks, *Like This*, 39.

45. Barks, *Delicious Laughter*, 11–12.

46. Moyne and Barks, *Say I Am You*, 15.

47. Barks, *Feeling the Shoulder of the Lion*, 72–73.

48. Barks and Moyne, *This Longing*, 48.

Chapter 10

1. Barks, *One-Handed Basket Weaving*, 38.

2. Moyne and Barks, *These Branching Moments*, 2.

3. Moyne and Barks, *Open Secret*, 72.

4. Barks, *Feeling the Shoulder of the Lion*, 40.

5. Barks, *Delicious Laughter*, 41.

6. Barks, *We Are Three*, 9.

7. Moyne and Barks, *Open Secret*, 30.

8. Barks and Moyne, *This Longing*, 15–16.

9. Moyne and Barks, *Say I Am You*, 34.

10. Moyne and Barks, *Say I Am You*, 100.

11. Moyne and Barks, *Open Secret*, 36.

12. Barbara Crossette, *So Close to Heaven: The Vanishing Buddhist Kingdoms of the Himalayas* (New York: Vintage, 1995), 187.

13. Barks, *Feeling the Shoulder of the Lion*, 16.

14. Barks and Moyne, *This Longing*, 32.

15. Moyne and Barks, *Unseen Rain*, 79.
16. Viktor E. Frankl, *Man's Search for Meaning* (New York: Simon and Schuster, 1959), 98.
17. Moyne and Barks, *Open Secret*, 78.
18. See: Idries Shah, *The Hundred Tales of Wisdom* (London: The Octagon Press, 1978), 27–28.
19. Barks, *One-Handed Basket Weaving*, 96.
20. Thomas à Kempis, *Imitation of Christ*, I.xix. Thomas à Kempis was a German monk and writer (c. 1380–1471).
21. Barks, *We Are Three*, 17.
22. Barks, *Delicious Laughter*, 12.
23. Khan and Barks, *The Hand of Poetry*, 83.
24. Khan and Barks, *The Hand of Poetry*, 82.
25. Barks, *Delicious Laughter*, 138–39.
26. Barks, *Delicious Laughter*, 100–1.
27. Barks and Moyne, *This Longing*, 48–49.
28. Barks, *We Are Three*, 29.
29. Barks and Moyne, *This Longing*, 71.
30. Frankl, *Man's Search for Meaning*, 97.
31. Barks, *One-Handed Basket Weaving*, 81.
32. Barks, *One-Handed Basket Weaving*, 117.
33. Sogyal Rinpoche, *The Tibetan Book of Living and Dying* (San Francisco: HarperSanFrancisco, 1992), 59.
34. Barks, *We Are Three*, 36.
35. Barks, *One-Handed Basket Weaving*, 116.
36. Moyne and Barks, *Unseen Rain*, 10.
37. Barks, *Like This*, 22.
38. Barks, *One-Handed Basket Weaving*, 34.
39. Barks, *Feeling the Shoulder of the Lion*, 81.
40. Barks and Moyne, *This Longing*, 49.
41. Barks, *Feeling the Shoulder of the Lion*, x–xii.
42. Moyne and Barks, *These Branching Moments*, 19.
43. Moyne and Barks, *Unseen Rain*, 11.
44. Khan and Barks, *The Hand of Poetry*, 95.
45. Mircea Eliade, *The Forge and the Crucible: The Origins and Structures of Alchemy* (New York: Harper Torchbooks, 1956), 225.
46. Barks, *Feeling the Shoulder of the Lion*, 40.
47. Barks, *We Are Three*, 24.
48. Khan and Barks, *The Hand of Poetry*, 80.
49. Barks, *One-Handed Basket Weaving*, 38–39.
50. Barks, *One-Handed Basket Weaving*, 68.

Chapter 11

1. Barks, *Birdsong*, 15.
2. Barks and Moyne, *This Longing*, 70.
3. Moyne and Barks, *Say I Am You*, 80.
4. Barks, *This Longing*, 70.
5. Barks, *One-Handed Basket Weaving*, 28.
6. Barks, *One-Handed Basket Weaving*, 27.
7. Barks, *One-Handed Basket Weaving*, 20.
8. See: Barks, *This Longing*, 81–107.
9. Moyne and Barks, *Say I Am You*, 96–97.
10. Barks, *We Are Three*, 44–45.
11. Moyne and Barks, *These Branching Moments*, 26.
12. Barks, *One-Handed Basket Weaving*, 30.
13. Moyne and Barks, *Say I Am You*, 48.
14. Khan and Barks, *The Hand of Poetry*, 74.
15. Moyne and Barks, *Say I Am You*, 110.
16. Moyne and Barks, *Say I Am You*, 38.
17. Barks, *We Are Three*, 6.
18. Moyne and Barks, *Say I Am You*, 123.
19. Barks, *We Are Three*, 25.
20. Barks, *Feeling the Shoulder of the Lion*, 61.
21. Barks, *Feeling the Shoulder of the Lion*, 58.
22. Barks, *Delicious Laughter*, 9.
23. Moyne and Barks, *Say I Am You*, 39.
24. Moyne and Barks, *Say I Am You*, 13.
25. Idries Shah, *The Hundred Tales of Wisdom* (London: The Octagon Press, 1978), 104.
26. Barks, *One-Handed Basket Weaving*, 95.
27. Barks, *Birdsong*, 27.
28. Barks, *One-Handed Basket Weaving*, 76–77.
29. Barks, *Delicious Laughter*, 106.
30. Barks, *Feeling the Shoulder of the Lion*, 12.
31. Barks, *Delicious Laughter*, 130.
32. Barks, *One-Handed Basket Weaving*, 84.

33. Barks, *One-Handed Basket Weaving,* 97–98.
34. Eliot Cowan, *Plant Spirit Medicine* (Newberg, Ore.: Swan Raven & Company, 1995), 29, 33.
35. Barks, *One-Handed Basket Weaving,* 69.
36. Barks, *One-Handed Basket Weaving,* 45–46.
37. Moyne and Barks, *Say I Am You,* 47.
38. Moyne and Barks, *Open Secret,* 10.
39. John Booty, editor, *John Donne: Selections from Divine Poems, Sermons, Devotions, and Prayers* (New York: Paulist Press, 1990), 272.
40. Barks and Moyne, *This Longing,* 49.
41. Moyne and Barks, *Say I Am You,* 98–99.
42. Moyne and Barks, *Say I Am You,* 81.

Chapter 12

1. Barks, *Like This,* 50.
2. Moyne and Barks, *Say I Am You,* 87.
3. Moyne and Barks, *Open Secret,* 31.
4. Moyne and Barks, *Open Secret,* 31.
5. Barks, *One-Handed Basket Weaving,* 62–63.
6. Barks, *One-Handed Basket Weaving,* 21.
7. Moyne and Barks, *These Branching Moments,* 7.
8. Shakespeare, *Twelfth Night, or What You Will,* Act 3, Scene 1.
9. I Corinthians 3:18–19.
10. Shakespeare, *Twelfth Night, or What You Will,* Act 5, Scene 1.
11. Barks and Moyne, *This Longing,* 22.
12. Barks, *Birdsong,* 19.
13. Moyne and Barks, *Say I Am You,* 16.
14. Barks, *We Are Three,* 69.
15. Barks, *We Are Three,* 13.
16. Moyne and Barks, *Say I Am You,* 14.
17. Moyne and Barks, *Unseen Rain,* 13.
18. Barks, *Feeling the Shoulder of the Lion,* 69.
19. Moyne and Barks, *Say I Am You,* 76.
20. Barks, *Like This,* 20–21.
21. Barks and Moyne, *This Longing,* 22.
22. Moyne and Barks, *Say I Am You,* 57.
23. Barks, *Delicious Laughter,* 94.
24. Barks, *Feeling the Shoulder of the Lion,* 52.
25. Seneca, *Letters from a Stoic,* Robin Campbell, translator (New York: Penguin Books, 1969), 72–73.
26. Barks, *Feeling the Shoulder of the Lion,* 64.
27. Barks, *Delicious Laughter,* 96.
28. Barks, *Delicious Laughter,* 94.
29. Moyne and Barks, *Say I Am You,* 71.
30. Barks, *One-Handed Basket Weaving,* 15.
31. Moyne and Barks, *Say I Am You,* 112.
32. Barks, *Delicious Laughter,* 6.
33. Barks and Moyne, *This Longing,* 59.
34. Moyne and Barks, *Say I Am You,* 90.
35. Moyne and Barks, *Say I Am You,* 58.
36. Barks, *We Are Three,* 30.
37. Barks, *One-Handed Basket Weaving,* 30.
38. Moyne and Barks, *Say I Am You,* 114.
39. Moyne and Barks, *Say I Am You,* 114.
40. Moyne and Barks, *Say I Am You,* 86.
41. Moyne and Barks, *Open Secret,* 60.
42. Moyne and Barks, *Unseen Rain,* 44.
43. Barks, *One-Handed Basket Weaving,* 88–89.
44. Moyne and Barks, *Open Secret,* 72.
45. Barks, *Feeling the Shoulder of the Lion,* 18–19.
46. Moyne and Barks, *Say I Am You,* 30.
47. See: Arthur Koestler, *Janus: A Summing Up* (New York: Random House, 1978).
48. Moyne and Barks, *These Branching Moments,* 6.
49. Moyne and Barks, *Open Secret,* 21.
50. Barks, *Feeling the Shoulder of the Lion,* 78–79.
51. Barks, *Like This,* 21.
52. Barks and Moyne, *This Longing,* 3–4.
53. Barks and Moyne, *This Longing,* 4–5.
54. Barks and Moyne, *This Longing,* 54.
55. Moyne and Barks, *Unseen Rain,* 29.
56. Moyne and Barks, *Say I Am You,* 17.
57. Moyne and Barks, *Say I Am You,* 75.
58. Barks, *Like This,* 13.
59. Barks, *Delicious Laughter,* 130–31.
60. Moyne and Barks, *Open Secret,* 18.
61. Barks, *Feeling the Shoulder of the Lion,* 85.

About the Authors

DENISE BRETON and CHRISTOPHER LARGENT, a wife-husband writing and teaching team, have done freelance teaching in colleges and universities for more than twenty years, focusing on philosophy and comparative religion. They also conducted seminars on philosophy and religion throughout the United States, Canada, and England. Their other titles include *The Soul of Economies* and *The Paradigm Conspiracy*.